Bridging Knowledge, Data, and AI

Joseph Hilger
Lulit Tesfaye · Zachary Wahl

Bridging Knowledge, Data, and AI

Harnessing the Semantic Layer Framework to Drive Intelligence

 Springer

Joseph Hilger
Suite 500
Enterprise Knowledge LLC
Arlington, VA, USA

Lulit Tesfaye
Suite 500
Enterprise Knowledge LLC
Arlington, VA, USA

Zachary Wahl
Suite 500
Enterprise Knowledge, LLC
Arlington, VA, USA

ISBN 978-3-032-17177-1   ISBN 978-3-032-17178-8   (eBook)
https://doi.org/10.1007/978-3-032-17178-8

This Springer imprint is published by the registered company Springer Nature Switzerland AG
The registered company address is: Gewerbestrasse 11, 6330 Cham, Switzerland

If disposing of this product, please recycle the paper.

Foreword

The word "semantics" is one you've probably used often enough in conversation. If you work in any field that touches enterprise data and analytics, you've undoubtedly heard the phrase "semantic layer" as well—probably quite often over the past few years. Like most others, you probably wish there was a clear, concise definition. This is the challenge that this book embraces, and we'll explore further in just a bit.

But first, let's take a step back. What you may not have encountered quite directly is the notion of computable semantics. In other words, how can machines make sense of the definitions used by people?

This is a problem because, within any large organization, definitions used by people in one business unit tend to differ from definitions used by people in other business units. For example, the word "consideration" means one thing for Marketing, but something entirely different for Legal, and you don't want to get these definitions confused in front of a customer. Recognize that understanding does not translate well across domains: people who fix compressors in a manufacturing plant make notes that can have consequences measured in the billions, and their colleagues in sales make consequential notes, too. These two groups probably could not understand each other's notes, and it's even less likely executives would understand either.

Understanding across domains is an intensely difficult problem, leading to costly mistakes and sorely missed opportunities. Don't hold your breath for automation to solve these issues, given how inference by large language models (LLMs) has been shown to fall apart specifically when faced with reconciling cross-domain semantics. Language is a living thing; every product release or feature update changes the semantics of your business. Instead of deferring crucial knowledge outside your organization, your organization should own the process of defining and understanding.

Since the 1990s, a deeply entrenched view of the world in enterprise IT is that all of an organization's data must be collected into a data warehouse—or "data lake" in more contemporary tech-speak. Intense pressures regarding digital transformations as well as increasing globalization drove enterprise firms to adopt practices that centralized their data internally. In this view, there is schema, which defines the semantics for data in the warehouse. IT manages the data, IT controls these semantics, and everyone else simply consumes. That's how the fairy tale story goes. Large vendors sell platforms which deliver exactly this. Done and done.

The IT-centric world view is a conceit and a deeply problematic one in several ways. First off, IT simply does not own all the details. The real knowledge about your business isn't in your data; only traces of it exist there. Crucial knowledge is instead in content, which gets scattered across the relatively unstructured documents used by Legal, HR, Marketing, Sales, Procurement, and so on. Typically, there is a 3:1 ratio in enterprise where the content is much larger than the data. This content may be managed within enterprise content management (ECM) frameworks or handled by dedicated knowledge management teams though generally not by IT. This means that 75% of the problem—content—lives outside the scope of the assumed solution.

Moreover, meaning doesn't translate across domains. When you pull datasets from across an organization and pile them all into a data warehouse, their semantics get mangled. For example, imagine having three tables for "sales," "returns," and "support," each of which has a column named "date." Then someone new to the firm runs a query that joins these tables. In practice, your data warehouse probably has 30 or even 300 tables with similar information, but let's keep this example simple. Does "date" refer to when a product was invoiced, when the invoice was paid, when the items were returned, or when a customer called for help? How can these be aligned into a broader report? Good luck finding out; it may take a while. Some large firms have hired linguists to resolve conflicting cross-domain definitions, while many organizations pull people out of retirement to help translate the semantics of crucial data, long warehoused but no longer quite understood.

Back in the 1990s, right about when data warehouses first began catching traction, it was also the early days of the World Wide Web, as a means of sharing content widely. Technology leaders who'd pioneered WWW recognized the need for having "agents" read the semantics of any web page and be able to interpret these definitions across many domains. Ora Lassila et al. drafted specs for the Resource Description Framework (RDF) in the mid-1990s, which became adopted as a global standard a decade later. Today, many web pages include RDF—to repeat, most web page content includes computable semantics—because businesses care about search engine optimization (SEO).

Later, the economics of the Internet led to large, centralized search engines. These became authorities which businesses focused on as the external arbiters of knowledge. "Just do a Google search" became a catch phrase, and businesses learned to care deeply about SEO. Vast realms of technology emerged to support this global ecosystem of knowledge. The content being indexed and becoming searchable crossed through different modalities: far beyond using keywords to search text and extending into searches of images and video, maps, music, and so on. Now, we see a range of AI assistants become available for nearly every search engine.

Imagine that, instead of outsourcing to some behemoth tech giant, we appeal to the internal arbiters of knowledge as authorities that we talk about enterprise knowledge optimization instead of SEO.

This is the practice of the semantic layer, which provides a much more holistic view of handling content, managing metadata about an organization's domains, and enabling AI capabilities downstream.

But let's step back once more to consider an enduring problem in semantics: what is the definition of artificial intelligence (AI) from a business perspective? Definitions seem slippery.

Despite all the noise flooding out from Silicon Valley, I have been working in this field of AI for decades and insist on using a long-standing definition, one which has rung true since the Macy conferences in the 1950s:

> AI is defined as teams of people and machines collaborating to realize capabilities beyond any individual.

In other words, AI is a practice, not a thing, and never has any pronouns in correct usage. It's about bringing complex problems back to human scale, getting teams of people and machines to work together more effectively for business outcomes that would've seemed unimaginable just a few years prior.

I'll speculate that if the tech industry hadn't taken such a sharp left-turn away from agents in the 1990s, veering on the one hand publicly toward massive search engines as our ubiquitous "source of knowledge" and on the other hand privately toward amassing internal data warehouses, we might not have the perilous disconnects we face in enterprise today. We might have reached more robust AI capabilities earlier, albeit the necessary hardware wasn't quite ready. It is what it is. Even so, recall the words of George Santayana from more than a century ago: "Those who cannot remember the past are condemned to repeat it."

Circa 2025 we've come full circle: agents are being presented as a future we want, probably in lieu of ubiquitous search engines. For example, the larger AI services are taking away market share—and initial customer contact—from search engines. With Santayana in mind, this begs an important question in business: do you defer "knowledge" and "intelligence" to some (costly) external source? Or do you leverage the assets you have internally? This could quickly become an existential choice for many organizations.

I'm going to take a wild guess that many business leaders prefer a definition of "AI" in which their people and their machines leverage their own knowledge assets over "AI" as the product of some external authority that overtakes mission-critical tasks, along with the margins implied.

If you have an ear to the ground today in communities based around data engineering, machine learning operations, etc., you'll know that semantics is having a moment. The tech leaders upon whom business leaders rely have noticed an uptick in the use of "semantics" and they are trying to understand: Is this real? What is a business glossary? What is a knowledge graph? How could we use this?

Looking at the game-changing technologies which have emerged over the past 15 years or so, I have a hunch that over the next few years, your organization will become more and more engaged with semantic layer practices and "enterprise knowledge optimization" than with managing SEO or deploying data warehouses.

The Rubicon many organizations must now cross is whether their business leaders and their tech leaders are on the same page regarding how to make this happen.

This book provides a vital guide for crossing that Rubicon. In a nutshell, the purpose of a semantic layer is to connect knowledge assets, allowing your teams of people and machines to interpret shared meaning across your domains. Good luck developing an agentic workflow for mission-critical tasks when the machines involved cannot understand the data and content they're being provided. Or worse yet, both the people and machines *misunderstand* and charge ahead doing the wrong thing.

Semantic layer practices, instead, enable your organization to optimize your enterprise knowledge. I'm grateful to get to work alongside the authors—my friends Joe Hilger, Lulit Tesfaye, and Zach Wahl—and watch their team in action working with large customers on complex problems. They're brilliant. They've evolved the process and practice of implementing and leveraging the semantic layer, and it shows especially when engaged in the most difficult customer problems.

Use this book as both the start of an important journey and as a reference to which you return—particularly for the many outstanding diagrams and accompanying explanations, which are gold. Harness a living network of your organization's collective intelligence, aligning what your organization has learned with how your people actually think and how your machines must make inference. Become the future we hope to find.

Senzing, Inc.   Paco Nathan
Sebastopol, CA, USA

Preface

In the early 2000s, the authors discerned a trend: technology was no longer the limiting factor in delivering the right information to the right people. Early iterations of enterprise portals and search tools sought to unite organizational knowledge and data, but these technologies were unable to deliver on their promise. The state of these organizations' information was too disorganized, and their semantic designs were misaligned. At that time, many organizations lacked any set semantic standards, with words like "taxonomy" and "ontology" wholly foreign to even the most mature, global organizations. And those that did possess some level of semantic foundation found that they lacked the ability to align these principles across their organization.

Over the last 20 years, the authors of this book have individually, and then, collectively sought to solve this problem. They did this by helping the world's largest and most complex organizations design and apply taxonomies, metadata, ontologies, and business glossaries to their information, working to improve the quality and consistency of that information. And, they did this by designing and building semantic applications and connecting those applications to content and data repositories, working to improve the findability and discoverability of organizational information. In the last decade, these efforts have utilized knowledge graphs and ontologies to not only deliver information, but to unite it with context, implementing new ways to explore, combine, and understand it. All of these efforts have yielded value for countless organizations and have comprised the authors' careers, a collective 70+ years of consulting. But it wasn't until recently that these efforts began to solidify into a collective solution, one that unites previously discrete fields and solutions.

The combined fields of data management, information management, and knowledge management are at a remarkable point of inflection. Generative AI and the broader "Artificial Intelligence Revolution" have created a focus on the collective knowledge assets of an organization, leading key leaders and stakeholders to seek the ability to connect all of these assets in context, reliably delivering the collective knowledge of an organization in an automated manner.

This goal is far from new, dating back well before the dawn of computing and spawning myriad methodologies and approaches. Indeed, the unique fields of data, information, and knowledge management were all born out of this goal for an organization's reliable use and reuse of its assets. So, what's different about this time?

The answer, put simply, is the semantic layer. The semantic layer framework is not a singular technology, nor is it a discrete methodology or design concept. Rather, it is the methodical combination of core technologies and best-in-practice design principles that deliver a framework uniting all of an organization's knowledge assets in context and with the greatest accuracy.

The semantic layer can be harnessed for a number of uses, many of which drive an organization's ability to deliver real AI for their organization. Intelligent chatbots, recommendation engines, content assembly tools, and predictive knowledge capture and delivery systems are all solutions that the semantic layer framework can support.

This book is intended for practitioners seeking to implement the semantic layer within their own organization, for those interested in learning how to do so, as well as for executives or business stakeholders that may find themselves overseeing such a program. The reader should be proficient in the core disciplines of data, information, and knowledge management, but need not be an expert in any, as this book is intended to deliver the expertise necessary to understand and implement the semantic layer. Additionally, the reader may read the book from cover to cover or choose to use it as a lookup-style reference, depending on their needs. Even for organizations and individuals not yet ready to implement a complete semantic layer, this book can be approached as an advance planning guide, helping the reader to conceptualize and begin laying the foundation for a future initiative.

In this book, we'll navigate the reader through every element of the semantic layer, from its core definition and business value, associated components and design requirements, methodological keys to success, real-world success stories and applications, and finally, through its relationship with AI. The book is divided into five parts. "Chapter 1: Understanding the Semantic Layer" defines the semantic layer, explains its value, and details business outcomes and potential areas of return on investment. "Chapter 2: Semantic Layer Component Design and Implementation" breaks the semantic layer down into its core components (knowledge assets, business glossary, metadata, taxonomy, and knowledge graph) defining each, explaining their role in the semantic layer, discussing associated technologies, and delving into the modeling of these components. "Chapter 3: Methodologies for Designing and Integrating the Semantic Layer" delivers a step-by-step guide to the design and implementation of a semantic layer, covering a range of best practices to ensure the success of an initiative. "Chapter 4: Real-World Success Stories" expands on various real-world examples, presenting case studies from a range of organizations that have successfully implemented a semantic layer and detailing the use cases, approaches, and outcomes. Finally, "Chap. 5: Powering Artificial Intelligence and Beyond" covers the interrelationship between the semantic layer framework and AI, elaborating on the ways in which these two fields can mutually benefit one another and how they can be combined within an enterprise architecture.

Everything herein is based on our collective experience. None of it is theoretical; all of it is proven. This book will arm any organization with the ability to unite all of its knowledge assets to deliver true, actionable intelligence in the ways they've always sought, but seldom achieved.

Arlington, VA, USA   Joseph Hilger
Arlington, VA, USA   Lulit Tesfaye
Arlington, VA, USA   Zachary Wahl

Contents

About the Authors

Joseph Hilger is a graduate of Boston College and has over 30 years of experience leading and implementing cutting-edge, enterprise-scale IT projects. He was an early pioneer in the use of Agile techniques for knowledge management systems design, implementation, and integrations projects. Joe is an expert in implementing enterprise-scale graph, search, and data analytics solutions. In addition to his role as COO of Enterprise Knowledge, he is a speaker and instructor on topics including enterprise search, graphs, and AI. Joe is the coauthor of *Making Knowledge Management Clickable*, published by Springer in 2022.

Lulit Tesfaye brings close to 20 years of experience leading strategy and delivery for enterprise knowledge and data programs across diverse sectors. She holds an LL.B from Jimma University and an MBA from Keller Graduate School of Management. At Enterprise Knowledge, she founded the Semantic Data and AI Engineering Practices, spearheading the adoption of semantic standards, knowledge graphs, and AI integration in organizational information strategies. Lulit is a published expert, keynote speaker, and educator, serving on advisory boards for industry organizations and iSchool/data management programs at various universities.

Zachary Wahl is a graduate of Dickinson College and has over 25 years of experience leading programs in the knowledge and information management space. Early in his career, he defined the business taxonomy concept to address the need for human-centered taxonomy designs, a formative element of today's advanced semantic solutions. He has worked with hundreds of public and private organizations in over 40 countries to successfully strategize, design, and implement advanced KM and semantic solutions. In addition to his role as CEO of Enterprise Knowledge, he is a frequent speaker and facilitator on the combination of KM, semantics, and AI. Zach is the coauthor of *Making Knowledge Management Clickable*, one of the leading books on knowledge management strategy and design.

Understanding the Semantic Layer

1

We open this book by laying the foundation for understanding the semantic layer and answering the questions: What is it? Why does it matter? And why is it rapidly becoming a strategic priority for organizations? We begin with a broad view of industry trends across sectors, showing how the growing complexity and fragmentation of organizational information and data combined with the increasing demands of artificial intelligence and analytics have made meaning, context, and shared understanding essential. This discussion is grounded in our collective experience across knowledge and information management, data management, software engineering, and artificial intelligence, providing a multidisciplinary lens on why the semantic layer is not just timely, but critical.

To ground this discussion, we explore the historical roots of semantics in computer science, artificial intelligence, and enterprise information systems, giving readers the background needed to appreciate the evolution and urgency of semantic thinking. We define the semantic layer and introduce its core components (knowledge assets, metadata, taxonomies, business glossaries, ontologies, and knowledge graphs) alongside key business applications, expected outcomes, and real-world use cases and case studies.

We also explore how the semantic layer serves as a convergence point for the previously siloed disciplines of knowledge management, data management, information management, and artificial intelligence. By examining each field's contributions and showing how they intersect within the semantic layer framework, we offer a practical and strategic lens for enterprise leaders, data teams, and AI practitioners alike. This part of the book is especially valuable for those looking to "articulate" the semantic layer to their internal stakeholders and executives, as it equips readers with the vocabulary, business rationale, and compelling examples needed to gain buy-in. Our intent is not only to provide a definition of the semantic layer, but also to make a case for its essentiality to the future of your organization's knowledge, data, and AI initiatives.

© The Author(s), under exclusive license to Springer Nature Switzerland AG 2026
J. Hilger et al., *Bridging Knowledge, Data, and AI*,
https://doi.org/10.1007/978-3-032-17178-8_1

Why the Semantic Layer? Why Now?

Traditionally, semantic components and models such as taxonomies, ontologies, business glossaries, and information architecture were considered niche tools, primarily used by library scientists to impose order on content-heavy systems or to add structure to unstructured information. Their role was largely limited to creating shared vocabularies and hierarchies for organizing content within repositories like document management systems (DMS), content management systems (CMS), or digital asset libraries. These structures helped support search, navigation, and basic file management through faceting and filtering.

But this view has radically changed. As organizations increasingly come face-to-face with the complex reality of data diversity, rampant silos, inconsistent definitions, and the limited impact and adoption of analytics and opaque AI outputs, the role of semantic models has evolved from peripheral to priority. Today, these semantic models are being woven into shared, enterprise semantic layers, a foundational, machine-readable framework that provides the organizational context for knowledge, data, engineering, AI, and analytics practices and intelligent information retrieval. This semantic layer connects organizational business logic and data by defining rich relationships across structured data, unstructured content, and processes alike (Tesfaye 2024b). Most importantly, the semantic layer is on the rise today because it transcends the boundaries of traditional systems to enable a shared understanding of information across the enterprise, irrespective of organizational informational types and formats.

Especially over the last decade, we have seen a powerful trend taking root within large and complex industries such as finance, pharmaceutical, retail, manufacturing, and engineering. Organizations are realizing that the path to effective intelligence—and ultimately to unlocking real, AI-driven value—doesn't lie in simply scaling platforms, expanding data lakes, or deploying more advanced algorithms. Instead, it lies in the growing recognition that without a common understanding of enterprise data, even the most sophisticated AI and analytics efforts will fail. In other words, the answer is semantics. This is a markedly different approach from traditional, application-centric strategies that see new, trendy technology as a quick fix to what is, as we argue, a methodological problem with the way that we think about data. This fracture is illustrated by the fact that, according to a 2025 MIT report titled "The GenAI Divide," global institutions continue to struggle with AI pilots with a 95% failure rate (Challapally et al. 2025). These pilots and new technologies do not work without attention to the data and semantics that underpin them.

For those firms in the financial sector, how will their AI pilots interpret metrics for "active customer," "net exposure," or "risk event," without understanding the definitions of these terms to differing divisions? Without this context and semantic clarity, how can users trust these results, especially when insights are conflicting, actions are delayed, and controls and compliance cannot be ensured? In pharma, organizations are finding that the integration of research and development (R&D) data, clinical trial results, real-world evidence, and commercial datasets can only be effective if those data are linked through a common set of definitions and relationships. And, in retail, a global chain that connected shared performance data from over 40,000 stores via a semantic layer reported a threefold increase in the accuracy of performance metrics and major time and cost reductions in data aggregation, reporting, and executive dashboard delivery (EK Team 2025). Throughout this book, we present a selection of real-world case studies that illustrate this transformation in action.

As the consumers of enterprise information shift from exclusively human to increasingly machine-based (think AI models, bots, and soon, AI agents), the semantic layer will be essential ad it enforces a consistent business vocabulary, governs definitions, connects structured and unstructured data, and provides the context needed for both humans and machines to operate with the same understanding. For AI, the semantic layer is the lens through which it sees your world. The more tuned this lens is into your organization, the more effective your AI will be. The semantic layer framework is a priority today because it enables knowledge to be delivered intuitively for humans, while offering the granularity and contextual richness machines and algorithms require. As one of the organizations we worked with once put it, the semantic layer is "the brain" of an organization, determining how to connect and interpret data to make decisions.

Revolutionizing Knowledge Management, Data Management, and Information Management with the Semantic Layer

To understand the impact of this increasing, industry-agnostic demand for a semantic framework that can deliver artificial intelligence within the context of increasingly complex data environments and the existence of silos, we must first contextualize the historically discrete fields that the semantic layer seeks to merge: knowledge management, data management, and information management. In the enterprise "data" environment of today, we must think differently about what constitutes an organization's knowledge and information, being careful not to trap ourselves in reductive boxes that actually, as we wish to highlight, are harmful to the efficiency and productivity of the organizations that we, as data/information/knowledge/content management professions, wish to help.

Thus, throughout the book, we use the term **knowledge assets** to define and encompass both traditional concepts of knowledge such as content, data, information, and documents, as well as an organization's people, processes, products, places, and even equipment. The term "knowledge assets" is one we coined, born from our thinking on the semantic layer, and it begins to break down these artificial barriers that plague our industry. From this perspective, all of the assets that comprise an organization can and do become linkable, traversable, and understood through the semantic layer framework, proving how revolutionary the semantic layer, and the thinking behind it, truly are.

- **Knowledge Management**—Typically, **knowledge management (KM)** practitioners will offer the simple definition of KM as getting the right knowledge to the right people at the right time. Some KM professionals focus primarily on the idea of **tacit knowledge**, or the experiential information individuals possess in their heads, and the practice of converting that tacit knowledge into **explicit knowledge**, which can be retained by an organization, but we find this definition alone to be overly limiting. Our one-sentence definition of KM is designed to encompass all elements crucial for an organization's success: "Knowledge management involves the people, process, content, culture, and enabling technologies necessary to capture, manage, share, and find information" (Hilger and Wahl 2022).

In recent years, as **artificial intelligence (AI)** and semantics have crystalized, we've added a new sentence to this definition of KM: "The new mission of KM is to link all of an organization's knowledge, in all of its forms, together, making it not just findable, but understandable, actionable, and machine computable." This definition puts the field of KM squarely in the center of advanced semantics and AI, purposefully and importantly. Perhaps some of the traditionalists in the field will dispute this idea, but in our experience, the *right* KM professionals are well-equipped to play this increasingly important role within an organization. We discuss AI throughout the book and define it here as a technology that simulates human comprehension, creativity, problem-solving, and decision-making. In the enterprise context, AI involves leveraging advanced machine and cognitive capabilities to discover organizational knowledge in a way that closely aligns with how humans look for and process information.

- **Data Management—Data management** is the development, execution, and supervision of plans, policies, programs, and practices that deliver, control, protect, and enhance the value of data and information assets throughout their lifecycles. **Data** consists of collected, unsynthesized facts, values, or statistics stored in a **structured** format such as a table, hierarchy, or key-value pair. Data management encompasses a range of disciplines and processes that collectively enable organizations to derive meaningful insights, make informed decisions, and maintain compliance with regulatory standards. The goal of data management is to ensure that data is accurate, consistent, and available to aid in business decision-making. Many organizations deal with multiple stores of data that use different measures, values, and definitions. Picture, for instance, a global organization that keeps revenue numbers in multiple currencies with fluctuating values as a simple example. Data management professionals often spend much of their time ensuring the quality and consistency of the data so that it can be extracted and acted upon.
- **Information Management—Information management** encompasses the planning, strategy, and implementation of systems and practices for handling an organization's collective data and information assets, meaning both structured and unstructured assets. But, in many organizations, information management focuses more on **unstructured content** (files, documents, multi-media, etc.). This makes it a bit of a catch-all term in many organizations, rather than indicating a specific function like data management tends to do. Therefore, the field can include design of information architecture and **governance** (the process of set-

ting standards, defining rules, establishing policies, and implementing oversight to ensure the quality and usability of an organization's assets) for quality, accessibility, security, and compliance. Effective information management can yield operational efficiency, informed decision-making, and delivery of the appropriate learning and guidance to individuals within an organization.

- **Content Management**—Content management is the process of creating, editing, organizing, and publishing content. **Content** as a term can refer to data or documents, but in the field of content management, it often refers to "blocks" of text or images that can be assembled in different ways. While the goal is to make it easy to find and use content, the biggest challenge is that most content is unstructured and created by many different people within an organization. Modern content management goals for an organization commonly focus on customizing and personalizing content for specific groups or individuals, making it an important topic for marketing, sales, and other client-facing functions, which explains recent interest in generative AI within the content management field. We define **generative AI (GenAI)** as a type of artificial intelligence that uses deep-learning models to create new content like text, images, and videos, based on patterns learned from training data and natural language prompts. Content management efforts are also often focused on content assembly and delivery.

- **Document Management**—Document management is the process of organizing, storing, and managing documents and other files. The goal of document management professionals is to make it easy to find and use documents, apply security and accessibility measures, and govern documents to ensure their quality and reliability. In many ways, document management relates to unstructured content in the same way that data management relates to structured content.

Putting it all together, data management and document management both focus on the organization and delivery of information (structured data in the case of data management), and unstructured content for document management. Content management, meanwhile, is concerned with assembling and delivering information that often becomes documents or digital assets. Information management serves as a broader umbrella, encompassing all of these forms. Knowledge management stands somewhat apart; traditionally aimed at converting tacit knowledge into explicit information, and its real value lies in connecting all the pieces across systems and stakeholders.

The most significant shift today is the need to reconcile this long-standing divide between data teams or IT's ownership of structured data, typically housed in data warehouses or data lakes, and the decentralized ownership of content by functions like marketing, HR, legal, and customer support. As AI applications increasingly rely on both structured and unstructured data to deliver value, the content owned by these siloed departments is becoming just as critical as traditional enterprise data, making integration, semantics, and cross-functional collaboration more important than ever.

If your head is spinning, you're not alone. What you may now realize is that, by dividing these types of content into different and disparate fields, the ability of organizations to actually manage their information is wrought with inefficiencies. We use the term **silo** throughout the book to describe the way in which information, data, content, and knowledge are treated as independent rather than interconnected aspects of an organization. There are separate governance plans, separate policies and procedures, and separate administrators, all based on whether something is (often loosely) defined as data, content, a document, or information. This way of thinking is, at best, antiquated, and at its worst, the source of internal confusion, conflict, and error. This is the type of thinking that the methodology of the semantic layer disparages.

History of Semantics in Computer Science, Artificial Intelligence, and the Enterprise

Semantics, in the briefest of definitions, is the study of how language makes meaning. It is all about context. A word can mean one thing to one person and still something different to another. If you're new to the field, you've most likely heard the word in the dismissive phrase, "it's just semantics," but we can assure you that there is nothing dismissible about the word or the field. Semantics, and the need for context to completely define a word, has fascinated philosophers, philologists, and linguists for centuries. And, in relation to the subject matter of this book, it has also infiltrated the interconnected fields of programming language theory, AI knowledge representation, and the development of the Semantic Web.

In the 1960 and 1970s, early computer science borrowed the concept of semantics from the field of linguistics to define the meaning of programming languages mathematically. Semantics came out of an emerging need to formalize meaning in programming as a framework for ensuring that computers had reasoning, i.e., to ensure machine comprehension of human language and data (Hutton 2023). When we consider computer programming, we understand code as a language that instructs a computer to execute specific actions: inputs resulting in outputs. These instructions are "understood" semantically as operational, denotational, or axiomatic, which define logical assertions about the program's state using a system of rules and axioms.

In the following years, AI researchers sought to give machines knowledge of the real world, not just formal instructions. In the 1980s and 1990s, the term "ontology" was adopted from philosophy to describe systems for organizing knowledge. Tom Gruber, a pioneer in the field, defined an ontology in 1993 as an "explicit specification of a conceptualization," providing a technical perspective distinct from its philosophical roots (Roe 2012). This drive to enable machine understanding of language fueled early work in **natural language processing (NLP)**, a field of AI focused on enabling computers to understand and generate human language. NLP has evolved from rule-based systems to today's advanced statistical and neural network-based approaches.

Over time, these different strands of semantic research converged in modern enterprise technology stacks, architectures, and knowledge and data organization frameworks. This evolution led to the development of today's semantic layer framework, progressing through several key phases, which we outline next.

From IT-Centric Complexity to Business Abstraction (1990s–2000s)

Early efforts in semantics focused on abstracting complex database structures for business intelligence and analytics. **Business intelligence (BI)** is the process of collecting, analyzing, and presenting organizational data to yield insights that help organizations make informed business decisions. In the early 1990s, the term "semantic layer" was popularized by the BI tool Business Objects, which pioneered the idea of hiding complex database joins and schema details from end users. This layer aimed to translate technical data fields into business-friendly terms like "Customer," "Product," and "Revenue," allowing non-technical users to build their own reports using spreadsheets or legacy/custom-built interfaces. A **legacy system** is an outdated software application that is still in use within an organization but is no longer actively supported by its vendor (applicable to a vendor product) or enhanced by its development team (applicable to a custom product).

Despite these tools, organizations grew more complex, accumulating content and data in disconnected silos across different departments and applications. The semantic definitions were often locked inside specific BI tools, leading to inconsistent access and thus differing definitions across the organization. This was further exacerbated by the historical separation of organizational knowledge assets. Data was structured and owned by IT, whereas content was unstructured and handled by departments focused on enterprise content management (ECM) or dedicated knowledge management teams. These ECM and KM teams and systems operated almost completely independently from data management initiatives.

From Centralized Data Warehouses to the Semantic Web (2000s–2010s)

As the volume and variety of data grew, the centralized data warehouse and BI models proved insufficient. Semantic technology, initially developed for the World Wide Web, provided a new path for enterprise data. The invention of the Internet and, later, the World Wide Web was facilitated by the creation of languages that could connect previously disparate networks, allowing them to communicate with one another. The World Wide Web specifically added languages HTTP and HTML to the Internet's TCP/IP, which enabled the creation of web pages containing information that could be searched and accessed by human users. Both the information contained on the World Wide Web and the language supporting this information were intended to be user-friendly, using the natural language that humans use to communicate. Without translating natural language into some machine-readable format, computers were exempt from interactions on the World Wide Web. In 2001, Berners-Lee made the World Wide Web machine-readable through new languages. This new "web" was coined the Semantic Web, and, instead of linking documents, it links data within the documents as real-world entities or objects, evolving the web from a collection of documents into a global database using standard frameworks (Foote 2023).

In conjunction, this new era also led to the rise of the Chief Data Officer (CDO), who was tasked with establishing control and governance over corporate data assets. This new role exacerbated the traditional silos between content/KM teams and data management. These two enterprise functions (content/knowledge management and data management) were not only governed by different sets of rules, they also resided in disparate systems, and were managed by disparate teams. As such, departmental and information silos became more entrenched, with each function solidifying its own set of practices.

From Physical Migration to Data Virtualization (2010s)

Because moving data into a single, centralized location continued to be slow and expensive, data virtualization emerged as a solution. Data virtualization uses a layer to integrate data without physically moving it. Emerging tools aimed to allow organizations to create a unified, logical view of their data though a metadata layer. The metadata layer allowed organizations to leave their data where it was. This virtualized approach connected structured data based on database IDs/keys and provided a "map" that tells systems how to access and combine data on-the-fly, giving users a single, consistent entry point. This metadata layer is the first attempt at an enterprise semantic layer because it was focused on enabling centralized analytics within a company. Because of its conflation with the concept of metrics, we now refer to this metadata layer as a "metrics layer." The **metrics layer** is an evolution of the original use of the term "semantic layer" and was first coined by Business Objects in the 1990s to describe a product that enabled end users to query databases without knowing **structured query language (SQL)** or the underlying structure of databases (Horwitz 2024). A **query**, we should add, is a request or command that retrieves, inserts, updates, or deletes data from a system/database. It serves as a way through which users or applications can interact with a database by specifying the required data and any conditions for filtering, sorting, or aggregating that data.

Despite these advancements, this version of the "semantic layer," or, as we call it, the metrics layer, did not include the core components of standard semantic or meaning-focused frameworks for machine understanding and often failed to deliver organization-wide results due to issues with lack of focus in context or meaning, system access and performance issues, and, most critically, the lack of a holistic approach to content. Most importantly, the metrics layer largely overlooked unstructured knowledge and content, which account for over 80% of organizational assets (Rizkallah 2017). This gap hindered, and continues to hinder, a comprehensive, enterprise understanding of an organization's knowledge, limiting the ability to leverage this knowledge to make informed, strategic decisions.

At the same time, this timeframe also saw some enterprise architects (early adopters), beginning to experiment with Tim Berners-Lee's Semantic Web standards such as the Resource Description Framework (RDF) and Web Ontology Language (OWL) to formalize business knowledge beyond structured data. These standards define entities, their properties, and their relationships in a machine-readable way and can be used across systems and diverse content types. This innovation was a major step beyond simple data abstraction, and it created a powerful way of representing knowledge, ultimately leading to the development of enterprise knowledge graphs. Knowledge graphs store data as interconnected entities (nodes) and explicit relationships (edges), which allow computers to reason through these connections. Knowledge graphs became the core of a new approach to building a semantic layer, providing a flexible and scalable way to integrate data from many disparate sources and store it with meaning and context.

From Data Fabric and Data Mesh to the Semantic Layer Framework (2020s–Present)

In the early 2020s, data fabric and data mesh emerged as architectural responses to the limitations of traditional, monolithic **data warehouses** and **data lakes**, which are scalable, centralized data repositories. A **data fabric** is a top-down, technology-centric, logical architecture that serves as a knowledge layer, enabling the application of semantic labels and rules (e.g., taxonomies, business glossaries, ontologies, etc.) to automate data management tasks like integration, governance, and discovery. The fabric is intended to weave together data from different systems, including data lakes and data warehouses (Jonker and Krantz 2025). This ability to access disparate data sources and manipulate assets virtually, without physically moving the data to a central location is called **data federation**. A key component is its focus on connectivity and creating reusable data pipelines (the "plumbing") needed to solve the technical challenges of moving and managing data in hybrid and multi-cloud environments.

The **data mesh**, on the other hand, is more of an organizational and cultural approach that treats data as a product. It advocates for decentralized ownership, shifting the responsibility for data management from a central team to the business domains that own and understand the data. This is achieved by employing tools or solutions that are based on a microservice architecture as well as open source linked data sources and software applications that decentralize data ownership and management (Tesfaye 2022). **Open source** refers to software that has a codebase that is freely available for anyone to view, use, modify, and distribute under a specific license, and **linked data** is a method of structuring data so that it can be connected with data from different sources, for instance, to create a machine-readable, interconnected knowledge graph.

While data fabric and data mesh addressed critical technical and organizational problems related to data access and integration, they had inherent gaps in meeting the demand of users and the organization as a whole. Data fabric aimed for technical unification and data mesh for decentralized ownership; however, both struggled to provide a unified, business-friendly view of diverse data across the organization.

These approaches resulted in expensive migrations and created bottlenecks that struggled to handle the explosion and variety of enterprise data.

The reality of this decade is that content and data for the average enterprise are housed in at least five or more distinct systems or within a data lake or warehouse, with diverse but interrelated information spread throughout the organization in various forms. Whether it is finance, marketing, engineering, sales, or customer service, each department handles its data differently, using unique terminology, processes, and methods for data creation and curation. For AI models to address complex organizational problems effectively, they need access to a significant amount of this disparate data.

This is where the semantic layer framework, the basis for this book, has evolved to play a central role in modern data, content, and knowledge architectures. GenAI and the missing context behind unstructured data further exacerbated the weaknesses of traditional, relational database solutions and operating models, cementing the need for a programmatic framework to link and contextualize organizational knowledge, content, and data, regardless of their format or location.

As enterprises realize the value of this converged approach, the mandate for IT and data teams has begun to broaden. Their role has evolved from simply ensuring data quality to driving business value from all knowledge assets, including unstructured content. As a result, in modern architectures like the data fabric and data mesh, the semantic layer is a critical component and sits on top of these architectures, adding a layer of standardized business meaning and context for AI that is currently missing. It consumes semantic data like business glossaries, taxonomy, ontology, and metadata and provides a business-friendly, logical architecture that makes decentralized data consistent and usable.

Over the last decade, enterprise semantic layers have been rising to the challenge, playing a transformational role in providing enterprise 360 views, content, and product personalizations, improving data quality and governance, and providing organizational knowledge in a machine-readable format. Knowledge graphs, a core component of the semantic layer, offer a more intuitive, connected view of organizational data entities as they shift the focus from the physical data itself to the context, meaning, and relationships between data, providing a connected representation of an organization's knowledge and data domains, without the need to make copies or incur expensive migrations, and most importantly, today, delivering connected data and knowledge to enterprise AI.

The Semantic Layer Defined

A **semantic layer** is a standardized framework that organizes and abstracts organizational knowledge assets through semantics (context and meaning) to connect business users and machines to an organization's information (Tesfaye 2024a). Put more simply, a semantic layer is a middle layer between your various sources of information and the humans and machines that will consume that information. In this way, the semantic layer serves to translate, define, and contextualize your organization's underlying information, ensuring that it can be understood and connected by both humans and applications in consistent and actionable ways. This can be as simple as aligning different words that mean the same thing across the enterprise or setting a definition for a term that is used loosely. In more complex examples, however, the semantic layer may capture business systems, processes, and enterprise operations in a web that relates these concepts to each other.

> ❝ A **semantic layer** is a standardized framework that organizes and links organizational knowledge assets (structured, unstructured, semi-structured knowledge, content, and data) to connect business users and machines with their organization's information.

Throughout the book, we use the term **business users**, or end users, to refer to consumers of the semantic layer, someone who is impacted indirectly by the implementation of a system or process, like data analysts and human resources professionals. The word "framework" is also purposeful, as it demonstrates that the semantic layer is more than just a technology or even a collection of technologies. A complete semantic layer framework will be the combination of, yes, appropriate technologies, but also design elements, supporting methodologies, specifications, standards, and governance to monitor and iteratively improve the solution(s). A semantic layer framework cannot be delivered as a single point solution or one-stop-shop technology purchase. On the contrary, it is its complexity that grounds its success. This explains the semantic layer's elusiveness to so many organizations.

As discussed in the history above, it's important to note that this definition of a semantic layer, and the framework that supports it, is different from what you may have previously encountered. Early semantic layers were considered data-centric constructs, focused primarily on metadata mapping, database keys, and metrics definitions. Their purpose was to virtualize structured data for centralized analytics and reporting, creating a single source of truth for business intelligence. This is still the case for some solutions that are still on the market.

Here, we are focusing on the evolved and most practical concept of semantics and the semantic layer framework. Today, a semantic layer is not limited to data virtualization or metrics management. It extends into knowledge representation, ontologies, taxonomies, and graph structures that capture the meaning and relationships behind business concepts. Rather than simply telling people and systems *where* to find content, data, and other knowledge assets, this expanded framework helps both machines and humans understand *what those assets mean* in its context, enabling more intelligent applications, interoperability, and AI-driven reasoning across an enterprise.

Larger and more comprehensive than a data fabric, which is typically focused only on structured data, a semantic layer connects all organizational knowledge assets, including content items, files, videos, media, etc. via a well-defined and standardized semantic framework (Fig. 1.1). It allows organizations to represent organizational knowledge and domain meaning to systems and applications, establishing

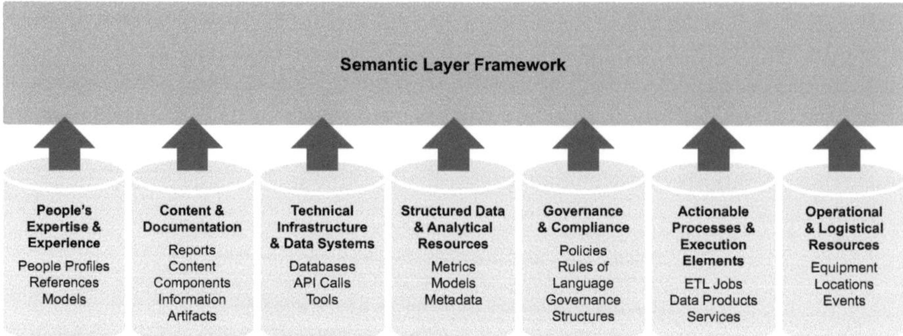

Fig. 1.1 Knowledge assets connected by a semantic layer framework

the relationship between data (unsynthesized numbers and facts) and content (synthesized data). Specifically, a semantic layer:

- Makes data accessible to both humans and machines
- Captures and connects content and data based on business meaning and value
- Aggregates and unifies unstructured and structured data to connect data of all formats
- Enables data federation and virtualization.

Semantic layers are the product of a noticeable shift in business focus and the consequent realization that business insights are not gained from having data physically co-located in one place, such as a data lake, but from assigning context-driven and relational meaning to an organization's data (Fig. 1.2).

Components of the Semantic Layer

As stated, a semantic layer is not a single platform or application; rather, it is an optimized standard that, when implemented correctly, manages a collection of data or knowledge assets with applied organizational meaning and context and is uniquely designed for users to answer organization-specific questions and solve business problems. A successful implementation requires a collection of the following components, which we detail and visualize in "Chap. 2: Semantic Layer Component Design and Implementation." It is important to note two key points before we list these components. First, not all components are required to form a semantic layer in every case. Second, many organizations already possess at least some form of these components within their enterprise. In other words, one size does not fit all, and, typically, a successful semantic layer initiative begins with an organization's understanding of its existing building blocks rather than a series of brand-new procurements and "from-scratch" design efforts.

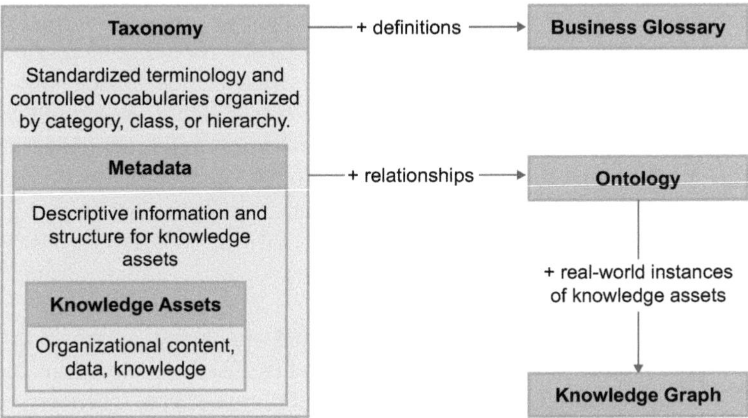

Fig. 1.2 Semantic layer components

- **Knowledge Assets**—Knowledge assets are the data and information, in all of its forms, that can be integrated via a semantic layer. These knowledge assets can be structured (like tabular data) or unstructured (like documents and presentations) but can also be virtually any other item that contains information, including people, places, and products. Knowledge assets are housed throughout most organizations, with repositories including any content, document, or records management system, file shares, databases, or other applications. Most organizations have an excess of knowledge assets, rife with legacy material that is duplicate, near duplicate, obsolete, or incorrect. Therefore, the successful harnessing of knowledge assets for a semantic layer typically has a great deal to do with governance and cleanup of these assets, which we cover in detail in Chap. 3.
- **Business Glossary**—Business glossaries pool the definition of terms used within an organization's taxonomies, ontologies, metadata, and knowledge assets to ensure mutual understanding of these terms across an organization and create consistency within the semantic layer. Business glossaries serve as one of the most common components of a semantic layer because they facilitate effective communication across an organization and its systems, aligning business users with technical understanding.
- **Metadata**—Put simply, **metadata** is data or information that describes existing knowledge assets: it is data about data. Metadata makes an organization's knowledge assets easier to organize, understand, and manage. In the semantic layer, metadata establishes a shared approach to provide the organization with information about data sources, standardized data, relationships between data elements, security and access controls, versioning, lineage, data quality and governance measures, and other relevant details to drive efficient labeling and categorization. In most instances, taxonomy and metadata are highly interrelated, as specific taxonomy values are applied as metadata on individual knowledge assets to deliver findability, consistency, and **interoperability**, which is the ability of systems to exchange and use information.

- **Taxonomy**—A **taxonomy** is a structure that classifies business or other industry terms as concepts according to their characteristics, revealing hierarchical, parent–child relationships. Business taxonomies (as well as broader concepts of information architecture) allow an organization to describe, align, and represent organizational vocabulary in a structured format through hierarchies, lists, and other forms of **controlled vocabulary**. Controlled vocabularies are standardized lists of terms that are used to organize and index information, ensuring consistency, accuracy, and improved information retrieval. For the purposes of this book, the term "taxonomy" is used broadly to encompass both controlled vocabularies and thesauri. Together, these structures extend and formalize business glossaries by standardizing terminology and managing synonyms, thereby reducing ambiguity and enhancing searchability. Taxonomies, at the enterprise level, deliver interoperability, ultimately facilitating data discovery and the exploration of shared data through **faceting** or filtering and by serving as reference data for analysis. By leveraging these shared taxonomies in multiple systems across the enterprise, organizations can achieve greater consistency and connectivity, merging and relating disparate sources. As such, taxonomies and information architecture promote a standardized approach to information and data management as well as governance practices, providing a structured business context that allows the semantic layer to adapt to evolving business environments, processes, and terminologies.
- **Ontology**—An **ontology** is a standard data model that organizes structured and unstructured information through entities, their properties, and their relationships. Like taxonomy, an ontology is a visual and machine-readable representation of business or other industry concepts and functions, capturing not only hierarchical but *all* existing relationships between entities. Much like how a blueprint defines the structure, relationships, and purpose of each room in a building, an ontology provides the logical schema that defines the structure, relationships, and meaning of data within a system and across the organization, enabling a clear and organized understanding of this data in an organization-specific context. Ontology acts as a layer of translation between business users and data, providing language to describe disparate data in a way that business users understand and allowing users to visualize the relationships between different data or knowledge assets. Ontologies are also machine-readable and can power recommendation functions because of their manifestation of the relationships within an organization.
- **Knowledge Graph**—**Knowledge graphs** leverage ontologies and other semantic components to represent knowledge assets and the information they contain as interconnected entities and relationships, providing a structured and graph-based approach to knowledge representation. A knowledge graph can be created using an ontology or other semantic model as its schema or from identifying and linking concepts, entities, and relationships directly from existing knowledge assets. Specifically, when a business ontology is permeated with real-world instances of organization's knowledge assets, the resulting structure is a knowledge graph. A knowledge graph allows organizations to connect heterogeneous

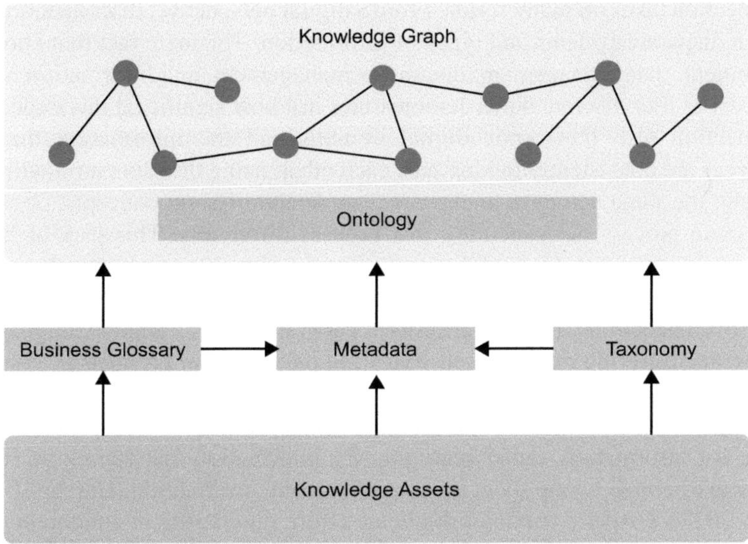

Fig. 1.3 Component interactions within the semantic layer

data sources across different datasets, to store business rules and logic with data, and to transform raw data into meaningful information.

It is helpful to think of organizing your closet as a simple analogy: taxonomy defines how items are grouped (shirts, pants, shoes or based on color, use, etc.), whereas ontology defines relationships (e.g., "these shoes go with that outfit"). Here, the knowledge graph is the actual closet, filled with real items, arranged and connected, so you can quickly find what you need (Fig. 1.3).

Of course, simply implementing these components in isolation is not enough to build a semantic layer. In fact, doing so can compound your organization's existing silo issues. Many organizations likely have some permutation of these components already. A semantic layer framework is realized only when at least two or more of these various components are aligned and integrated, working together to provide the contextualized and connected knowledge assets in an understandable and actionable manner. Chapter 2 of this book will detail how these components can be implemented independently, while Chap. 3 details the associated design and implementation methodologies necessary to translate these components into a true semantic layer within the enterprise.

Value of the Semantic Layer

Before diving too deeply into the value of the semantic layer, we must first understand the core problem that organizations have faced throughout their digital history. Organizations, both large and small, suffer from disconnection. This disconnection takes on many forms. From a digital perspective, disconnections exist between disparate systems and types of information. The mere fact that knowledge management, data management, document management, and information management exist as four discrete fields demonstrates just how significant this issue is. This disconnection also transcends digital systems and the information they hold. Employees are consistently talking past each other, using the same term with different intent, the same acronym to express completely different concepts, or referring to the same process but executing that process differently. This lack of business alignment is a common form of disconnection faced by organizations. As organizations grow and become more global, they also become more heterogeneous, proliferating disconnections. Individual offices, geographic areas, unique languages and cultures, and differing management styles and purview over products or systems all feed into this disconnect.

As a result of this disconnect, organizations are far less efficient. Time is wasted looking for information, either searching for information that cannot be found or being overwhelmed by the sheer amount of existing information (Harvard Business Review 2023). Larger companies duplicate effort, purchasing or conducting redundant research, data products, and redoing work that has already been done. Organizations suffer from misalignment and confusion, as disparate groups are working off of varying policies or methodologies, often using old or outdated versions of the same material. The cost of this disconnect goes far beyond efficiency, as individuals delivering the wrong or outdated information can expose the organization to regulatory penalties or lawsuits. In the very worst cases, an organization and its employees acting on old or outdated information can cause accidents, injuries, or even death.

The semantic layer alone cannot "fix" this disconnect, but it can play a massive role in addressing one of disconnection's most pervasive symptoms. With all of the aforementioned disconnections, organizations generate artificial barriers in how they think about, manage, and interact with information. Data goes into a database, content goes into a content management system, files go on a file drive, knowledge goes into a knowledge base, and so on and so forth, creating more and more disconnections between different types of information solely because of the information's form. Worse yet, these divisions are compounded further by the intended use or function of that information: training content goes into a learning management system (LMS), while product content goes into a product information management (PIM) system; financial data goes into a financial management database, while people data goes into an HR database, whereas pharmaceutical research data and content are stored in electric lab notebooks (ELNs), and customer information goes into a customer relationship management system (CRM) (Fig. 1.4).

This is not to suggest that all systems should be merged into one. Many organizations have tried and failed at massive migrations and consolidations of systems. Though there are likely some redundancies and thus opportunities for consolidation, these different systems have different purposes and features and are designed for different types of users and use cases. Consolidating them would only strip away these features and accommodations, resulting in a mangled mess of content, data,

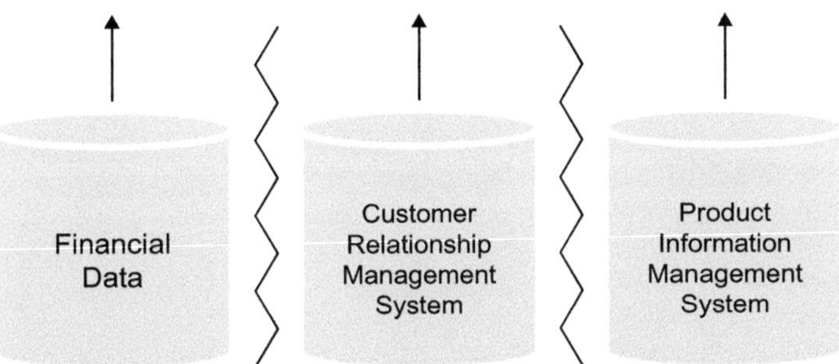

Fig. 1.4 Disconnected systems

and many disgruntled end users and data engineers. However, just because valid reasons exist for different types of information being housed in different locations, these various repositories should still be connected.

Past decades have already attempted to solve the problem we are describing here. Enterprise search systems attempted to connect unstructured content (i.e., files, documents, presentations, etc.), just as data warehouses and **master data management (MDM)** systems attempted to standardize and connect structured data (i.e., databases, tables, etc.). With the dawn of graph databases and then knowledge graphs, a single solution could connect structured *and* unstructured content, creating traversable links between different forms of content. For many organizations, this remains the goal ("Knowledge Graphs" 2025).

This is where the power of the semantic layer is realized. As we previously defined, a semantic layer is a standardized framework that organizes and abstracts organizational data or knowledge assets (structured, unstructured, or semi-structured) and serves as a connector. Consider the semantic layer not as a single solution, nor as a user-facing experience or application, but rather as a middle layer that serves to connect, align, and merge the disparate types, forms, and states of information into a shared layer (Fig. 1.5). We implement, and, in fact, originate the term "knowledge asset" to describe all of the places where information can exist within an organization. Yes, much, if not most, of this information will still be classifiable as either structured or unstructured content, data, or files, but with a semantic layer, organizations can and should think more broadly. A complete semantic layer can connect organizational information, in all of its forms. Breaking out of this notion that content or information must exist as a digital file or a collection of 1s and 0s, a knowledge asset can be a place, a building, a product, a person, a piece of machinery, or a client.

By considering all of the different parts of an organization's business as knowledge assets, we're able to better envision the complete potential of a semantic layer. Now, rather than simply finding, combining, or contextualizing pieces of information, we are traversing the organization based on what it does, who knows what, how it operates, how it learns, and what it produces. For instance, we can combine these different knowledge assets to answer complex questions such as, "What employees have the most experience addressing component X of product Y, for a

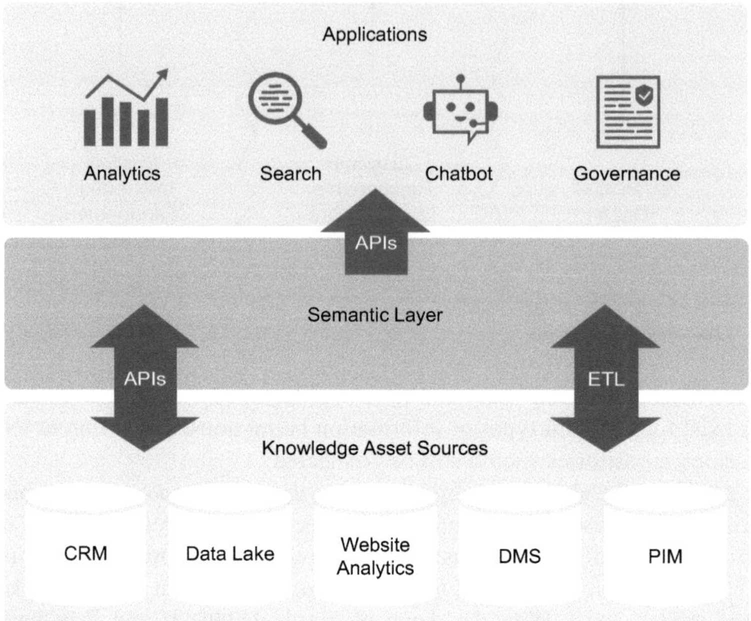

Fig. 1.5 The semantic layer

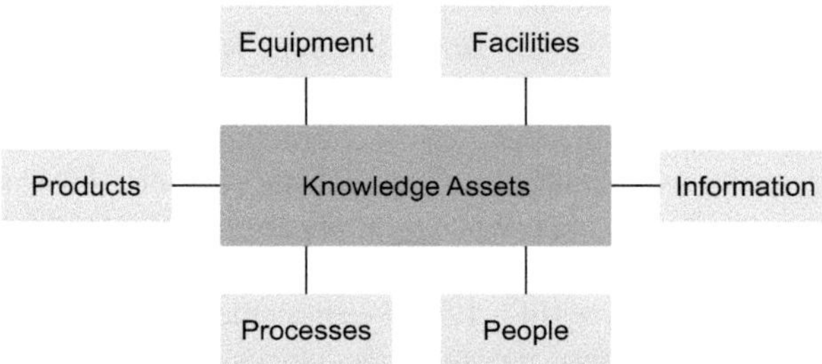

Fig. 1.6 Knowledge assets

particular industry?" And we can refine those answers to identify which of those employees has the most availability and is closest to the location where the need exists. Accomplishing this type of advanced questioning or query requires, first, the wiring together of different types of knowledge assets from different repositories; then, the business logic and consistent semantic design to "understand" and answer this query; and finally, the appropriate governance and quality assurance to deliver high-accuracy answers that can be trusted without a rampant fear of errors or **hallucinations** (query results with fabricated conclusions or misinformation that are presented as fact) (Fig. 1.6).

Diving more deeply into the value of a semantic layer, each of the following are key points of value, use case dependent, that a semantic layer may offer for an organization:

Connection with Context

Semantic layers can provide the connective tissue between an organization's knowledge assets, relating these various types and sources of information into a cohesive, metaphorical unit. These assets remain physically disparate but are united in meaning. Moreover, a semantic layer provides a common understanding of these assets, making it easier to prepare, query, and analyze the collective set. This means that each asset can be related to each other asset, making them all relatable and traversable. The existence of enterprise search tools, MDM solutions, and enterprise portals makes evident the long-time goal of connecting disparate sources of information. What a semantic layer offers beyond these tools is two-fold. First, the semantic layer is type-agnostic, meaning it isn't just for data or files, but for all knowledge assets. Secondly, the semantic layer adds consistent meaning and understanding, resulting in the ability to not just return results, but to return them in context, related to one another in a way that powers greater **findability**, **discoverability**, and understanding. The difference between findability and discoverability is intent. Information that is findable has been explicitly asked for, while information that is discoverable may be totally unknown to the seeker, but it is made visible by the system because of its relevance and connection to the queried item, functioning like a recommended asset, or supporting exploratory analysis.

Understanding of Intent

Intent requires an understanding of the individual end user, the queries that they are making, and their past user behavior to infer meaning and anticipate what each unique user is seeking. Does the word "Eagle" refer to the bird, the national symbol, the golf score, or the struggling professional American football team? Does "Mercury" refer to the chemical element, the space program, or the planet? Without intent, a search tool or other systems would rely solely on whether the word "Eagle" or "Mercury" appeared in a text or, perhaps, the metadata of an asset. With intent, however, humans and applications alike get contextualized results with maximized intelligence, inferring what the consumer likely intended. With all knowledge assets linked with context, a semantic layer can deliver this **inference** with high degrees of accuracy.

Creation of New Knowledge Assets

Beyond findability, discoverability, and a shared understanding of data, the semantic layer can also formulate answers and construct new material by merging existing assets. This concept has recently become popular with the quick advances in generative AI. Unlike standard generative AI tools, which are prone to hallucinations and require untoward computing power and massive training sets, the semantic layer can deliver similar and far more reliable results that are specific to an organization's own vocabulary and processes ("Graphwise – Unlocking Enterprise Potential" 2025). The key concept here is that new assets can be created, combined from disparate existing assets and sources to deliver something more valuable or actionable to the organization.

Improvement of Accuracy and Quality of Assets

For as long as organizations have been recording information, they've been struggling with issues of maintenance, reliability, and accuracy (Data Accuracy vs. Data Integrity 2023). The semantic layer is not a panacea for this, but it can play a strong role in improving the accuracy and quality of knowledge assets. Because the semantic layer is a framework and not a tool or repository, it should include integrated quality controls, or governance, to ensure the quality, reliability, and value of the knowledge assets it incorporates. By strategically managing these knowledge assets through linking, organizations can identify assets, recognize innovation, and avoid duplication (UK Government 2024). Importantly, it also becomes easier to identify gaps in knowledge assets, thereby enabling an organization to proactively fill those gaps and deliver a more complete body of knowledge over time. Moreover, the semantic layer can incorporate its own framework for governance, enforcing security and compliance policies.

Business Alignment

As discussed above, organizations naturally fall out of alignment as they grow, expand, and evolve. A semantic layer can help to counteract this trend, building alignment through shared vocabulary, meaning, and knowledge assets. This is not to say that all groups or people within an organization will suddenly use the same words, definitions, processes, and content, but rather that the semantic layer will serve as a layer of translation throughout the organization. This allows for enterprise-wide alignment without forcing everyone to change the way they talk, think, and act, which is an initiative that would surely fail. As an added point of value, the semantic layer is highly flexible, so as new repositories, groups, or even companies, through an acquisition, for instance, are added to the framework, it can grow and adapt to ensure smoother alignment throughout.

Flexibility of Uses

Remember that the semantic layer as a framework is not necessarily a user-facing front end, but rather a middle layer. Organizations often ask us what a semantic layer will look like to an end user, and the reality is that the semantic layer itself is not typically visible to the average user. This feature, however, is part of its value. A well-designed semantic layer can be applied to numerous different use cases and **front-end solutions**, including advanced searches, chatbots, recommendation engines, content assembly tools, data dashboards, or customized content delivery systems. Each of these solutions, independently, could cost multiple millions of dollars to deliver, but when leveraging a shared semantic layer and its components to power them, there is minimal to no need for point-to-point system integration and the per solution cost drastically decreases. This flexibility enlarges the scope of service, as a single enterprise semantic layer can power a myriad of applications, audiences, and business areas. As you consider business cases and potential return on investment for a semantic layer framework, this ability to reuse the semantic layer with frequency should be factored into these equations.

Linked Data Discovery

Because the primary role and purpose of the semantic layer is unifying siloed data, the connections and structure created by the underlying semantic models provide immense value by overcoming the challenges of integrating heterogeneous data sources through a common framework for representing data and its relationships. This ultimately supports linked data discovery by creating a layer of meaning and context over raw data, transforming disconnected data points into an interconnected network of knowledge. This application of the semantic layer is especially crucial for both investigative and exploratory use cases (such as fraud detection, drug discovery, uncovering criminal network analysis, etc.), as it facilitates the uncovering of hidden relationships that would be difficult to detect with traditional, structural-only data models and analysis techniques.

Gateway to Enterprise AI

At its core, the semantic layer is about consistent, reliable, machine understanding of knowledge assets such that they may be leveraged in different ways. Semantic layers provide consistent definitions, context, quality assurances, and more, such that "questions" or **queries** to AI, when used in tandem with a semantic layer, are properly understood in context and that the right documents and data are consulted, resulting in accurate, complete, and consistent answers. Moreover, by abstracting complex data and content structures through metadata, a semantic layer provides an AI framework that delivers a consistent representation of data and its business meaning, without having to physically relocate assets. Organizations are spending billions on internal AI initiatives, many rife with errors and overall failure (Challapally et al. 2025). The semantic layer is a foundational piece of the puzzle to deliver high-accuracy AI capabilities for an organization (Keydunov 2024a, b).

Business Outcomes and Return on Investment

Each of the previous points communicate what the semantic layer framework can do for your organization. Depending on the use case, scope, and knowledge assets incorporated, implementing a semantic layer can improve findability and discoverability of knowledge assets, increase interoperability of those knowledge assets, and support analysis and innovation (Diamantini et al. 2013). It can also enhance asset management and quality and improves consistency and accuracy of data products (Tesfaye 2024a). Though these are all positive outcomes that any organization would be pleased to realize, they don't offer hard returns on investment that can be easily quantified in dollars, euros, or yen.

Next, we will address the real return on investment (ROI) and other measurable business outcomes associated with semantic layer implementation. **Return on Investment (ROI)** is a financial metric used to measure the profitability or efficiency of an investment, or set of investments, relative to its cost. It is calculated by dividing the net profit or gain from the investment by the initial cost of the investment, typically expressed as a percentage. Organizations will need these outcomes and an understanding of the ROI to justify the organizational expense of designing, implementing, and supporting a semantic layer. We have found that the ROI for a semantic layer is similar to many other knowledge management, information management, or data management initiatives, but unlike these initiatives, the semantic layer is reusable, potentially magnifying the ROI.

Taken as a whole, these aforementioned, qualitative outcomes can directly impact key performance metrics, yielding measurable hard and soft ROI for an organization (Fig. 1.7):

Employee Productivity—A semantic layer can vastly improve employee productivity by providing them with the ability to swiftly access and explore data (Jain 2023). For a large enterprise, employees may spend up to 40% of their time looking for information, waiting for answers from others, or recreating information that already exists but of which they were unaware. A fractional improvement in this percentage could save thousands of hours, allowing employees more time for customer service, innovation, and collaboration, resulting in far more productive undertakings than searching for uncatalogued data. Despite the immense potential value, we typically don't recommend leveraging productivity as a measure for hard ROI. Though alluring to multiply potential savings by the number of employees and their salary/cost, such a calculation proves artificial unless it is accompanied by a reduction in force commensurate with the amount of time saved. This is an unlikely and inadvisable business maneuver. For that reason, it is best to consider employee productivity to be a measure of soft ROI, rather than hard.

Organizational Transparency and Risk Mitigation—A business with a semantic layer will be better aligned, equipped with a shared set of definitions and a unified, comprehensive view of the organization's operations. Regardless of the industry, this means that key decision-makers will have the ability to understand bottlenecks, spot inefficiencies, and even predict areas of savings. For many organizations today, the inability to keep pace with evolving regulations (such as GDPR, HIPAA, or financial reporting standards) and the risks of misreporting, data misuse, or noncompliance rank among their top concerns. To address these challenges, many are turning to the semantic layer to standardize terminology and embed business rules directly into data structures. This approach enables

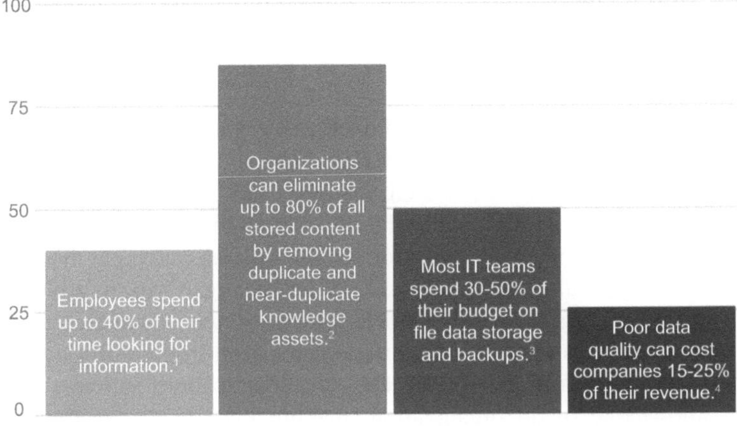

Citations

1. Hilger, Joseph and Zachary Wahl. Making Knowledge Management Clickable: Knowledge Management Systems, Strategy, Design, and Implementation." Springer, 2022: 7.
2. Hilger, Joseph and Zachary Wahl. Making Knowledge Management Clickable: Knowledge Management Systems, Strategy, Design, and Implementation." Springer, 2022: 93.
3. Cunningham, Darren. "The True Cost of Traditional File Storage," Microsoft. April 27, 2023.
https://techcommunity.microsoft.com/blog/azurestorageblog/the-true-cost-of-traditional-file-storage/3797945
4. Redman, Thomas C. "Seizing Opportunity in Data Quality," MIT Sloan Management Review. November 27, 2017.
https://sloanreview.mit.edu/article/seizing-opportunity-in-data-quality/

Fig. 1.7 Current state of content and data

traceability, data lineage, provenance, and auditability, allowing organizations to demonstrate compliance and respond to regulatory inquiries with confidence. The ROI of this application extends beyond reduced compliance costs and fewer penalties; it is also delivering stronger governance and enhanced trust in enterprise data. Ultimately, this foundation leads to better decision-making and, with the right use cases, measurable, hard ROI in savings.

Consolidation of Licenses and Reduction of Administrative Burden/Storage— Though one of the benefits of a semantic layer is the fact that it can connect to knowledge assets in their native repositories rather than requiring relocation and consolidation, semantic layer initiatives nonetheless surface redundant systems, thereby creating an opportunity to remove recurring software license costs and the accompanying administrative and staffing burden to maintain these systems. Over several years, this alone can pay for the cost of a semantic layer. Even if an organization does not identify opportunities to cut out redundant software, significant savings can be realized by identifying duplicate or near-duplicate knowledge assets. Many large organizations can eliminate 70–80% of all stored content, and the storage costs of these assets are significant. This is especially significant considering that the amount of new data created annually is growing at a compound annual growth rate of about 26% (Seagate 2020). As an added benefit, these storage savings also have a direct impact on environmental, social, and corporate-governance (ESG) goals. Reducing storage consumption conserves energy and thereby lowers an organization's carbon emissions (Adamson 2017).

Management of Data and Content Purchases—Similar to the idea of system redundancy and consolidation, many organizations, depending on the industry, require external sources of research, datasets, and other third-party, purchased content. As an unfortunate result of the silos that exist within these organizations, different divisions of an organization may unintentionally purchase the same data or content, resulting in duplicate costs for the organization. With a semantic layer uniting an organization's knowledge assets, the occurrence of duplicate purchases can be avoided, shielding the organization from unnecessary costs.

Employee Learning and Performance—A semantic layer delivers the institutional knowledge of an organization, making knowledge assets available to employees. This allows employees to upskill faster and more effectively through linked learning materials, how-to guides, lessons learned, and the ability to connect with actual experts within their organization who can be leveraged as a resource when needed, all of which ensure an employee's success on the job. From an ROI perspective, this can directly lower training costs and shorten the **performance cycle**, the amount of time it takes for an employee to become competent in their new position. More broadly, employees that feel they are valued in their role and are being given the resources to succeed are more likely to stay and grow within an organization (Harris Interactive 2012). Given this potential, another source of ROI for the semantic layer is higher retention rates and thus lower recruiting costs.

Achieving and Scaling Explainable AI—The rapidly evolving AI landscape is considered one of the top concerns and/or opportunities for most organizations ("AI Adoption in 2024" 2024). But, a recent MIT report titled "The GenAI Divide" reveals a concerning truth: despite significant investments in AI, 95% of organizations are not seeing any benefits from these investments (Challapally et al. 2025). Though extremely promising, many AI solutions don't deliver the accuracy and reliability necessary to be trusted for use by organizations. Imagine a situation where the AI of a medical supply company recommends the wrong product, where an airline offers a steeply discounted ticket, or where a leading services firm's chatbot insults a potential customer. The risk for error is steep, and with errors comes potential impact on revenue, regulatory fines and other legal complications, tarnished brand reputation, or even physical harm. The semantic layer can yield hard ROI in avoidance of these risks.

Semantic Layer Capabilities

The primary role of a semantic layer is to simplify the interaction between its consumers and disparate sources of information. Similar to how an index aggregates and streamlines the search for relevant content in a book, a semantic layer abstracts the underlying complexity of enterprise data and content without the need to move or migrate physical data from its source. Here we document some of the most impactful applications and enterprise capabilities enabled by the semantic layer.

Customer 360/Enterprise 360

The semantic layer employs a knowledge graph to map knowledge assets to the people, places, and things (entities) that organizations interact with. This map allows organizations to show a connected picture or 360-degree view of their organization and its interactions. One investment banking organization, through a semantic layer, was able to view data and content from close to 20 different systems through a single web portal. On one screen, every aspect of an investment was visible through the semantic layer's knowledge graph. The organization could access data about each bank that they had done business with, viewing specific investments and their outcomes, deals and their staffing, and even information about the company's CEO. The impact of this tool was immense, as every layer of management could and did use the semantic layer to make faster, better informed, and more reliable investment decisions, grounded in real knowledge.

This same solution can be used within other industries. A manufacturing company can use the semantic layer to examine products, customers, factories, and partners. A professional services firm can apply a semantic layer to examine consultants, clients, projects, and service offerings. The semantic layer graph is reusable in nearly every industry and allows organizations to make better decisions based on a more complete picture of their organization (Fig. 1.8).

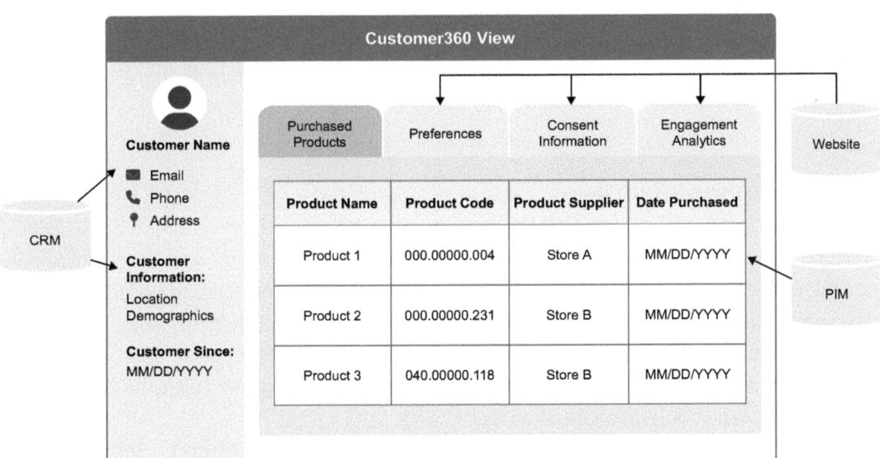

Product Name	Product Code	Product Supplier	Date Purchased
Product 1	000.00000.004	Store A	MM/DD/YYYY
Product 2	000.00000.231	Store B	MM/DD/YYYY
Product 3	040.00000.118	Store B	MM/DD/YYYY

Fig. 1.8 Customer 360

Context and Reasoning for AI and Machine Learning

AI enterprise use has taken off due to increased accessibility, and Gartner predicts that its usage will continue to grow at an annual rate of 19.1%, which is likely a conservative estimate (Gartner 2023). The more we learn about AI, the more we realize the importance of context and the quality of information being supplied to AI engines. Over 60% of current AI projects are failing to meet expectations (Bell 2024). They are failing specifically because they lack reliable foundations of information. AI engines rely on information to provide answers to queries. If the engine does not have access to information on the subject of the query, incorrect or incomplete responses will result. It is not enough to point the AI engine at all of your Microsoft SharePoint documents. Even if they are current, and they are often not, the information remains siloed and disconnected.

A compelling example here comes from a supply chain consultancy we've partnered with, which aims to help clients reduce their carbon footprints. Their out-of-the-box supply chain AI optimization system was designed to recommend the most cost-effective transportation options. However, the system kept prioritizing the cheapest routes, which often resulted in significantly higher emissions. This misalignment occurred because the out-of-the-box AI model was trained to optimize solely for cost, without taking into account the environmental impact, a key priority for the organization. While the system achieved financial efficiency, it failed to align with the clients' sustainability goals, highlighting the importance of planning for a more holistic, organizational context-aware framework (through semantic enrichment) when designing AI solutions.

Thus, the most successful AI implementations use metadata and knowledge graphs to provide this context to the information that the AI engine is ingesting. The additional context allows the AI engine to make representative decisions when responding to organization-specific questions. This also provides an audit trail, explaining how an answer was derived by AI solutions so that problems can be resolved more quickly in the future.

Content Personalization

Content personalization is an important marketing strategy, and it is becoming increasingly important to the way people look for information. Researchers, analysts, and managers are overwhelmed with the amount of information available to them. Personalized information in marketing initiatives, enterprise search, or information portals allows people to get to the right information without being overwhelmed by what is irrelevant.

For a long time, personalization was driven by metadata about the individual and the content. The more metadata that was collected and associated with people and products, the more accurate the personalization could be. The problem with personalization prior to semantic layers was that the gathering and maintenance of this metadata was too burdensome. A semantic layer adds a new dimension to personalization. While metadata is still important, graphs allow for personalization, making metadata driven by relationships *between* information. Information assets can be personalized based on their relationship to other information sources. For example, if a customer bought a product in the last year, the semantic graph might recognize that the company sells another product that is complementary to the product the customer just bought. The marketing department can send targeted recommendations based not only on metadata about products but also based on the relationship between those products. Relationships are typically more accurate ways to determine "like" things. They also are easier to manage. Thus, the semantic layer allows for personalization through relationships in a way that older technologies did not support.

Data Quality and Governance

Data continues to grow at an amazing rate, which can be alarming if not properly managed. Leaders want their organizations to be data-driven, but this requires that their direct reports know and are confident in the organization's data. A semantic layer helps with both of these necessities by using metadata from your master data, controlled vocabularies as reference data, or ontology as a schema to offer standardized, consistent, and quality data. This standardized approach simplifies the way in which data is brought together so that it can be reviewed more holistically. As a result, data analysts and data scientists can quickly see data that does not align with the expected results and make corrections. For example, a knowledge graph provides human and machine-readable rules for how data is brought together across silos. The data loaded into the graphs is standardized based on the controlled vocabularies of the semantic layer. With the data silos removed, data analysts can quickly see anomalies in the data and potentially spot issues or patterns that require new governance processes to ensure consistent and accurate analysis. In addition, the business glossary ensures that there is alignment on what data elements/terms mean. A large retailer we worked with used their business glossary to get agreement on what an average sale transaction is. This retailer had multiple point of sale systems, each of which had a different way of recording sales transactions. The glossary provided a definition as to what a sales transaction was, and this logic was implemented in ETL processes that aggregated sales transactions across each of the different point of sale systems. The glossary serves as the North Star to ensure that the information is aggregated the right way every time. Organizations that focus on semantics take a metadata first approach and are able to spot problems and identify solutions that were not possible when the focus was on fixing data in the application silos.

Semantic Search

Search is one of the most popular knowledge and information management solutions. It seems that no one is happy with their search function, and that's mostly because it's not Google. One of the biggest differences between most organizations' search technology and Google is the type of returned results. The top Google search results aggregate information from multiple sources to answer a question. Although it's evolving at a fast pace, most corporate searches still return a list of documents containing the word or phrase from the search query in the document's text. When users search for answers to help them do their job, a list of documents just means more work; next they'll need to find the right document and then read it to get the answer to their question. This is where the semantic layer can help. A semantic layer adds metadata to your content and identifies relationships between the things your searchers care about and the content the company retains using a knowledge graph. Instead of a list of documents, a semantic search generates answers by contextualizing data through a graph and metadata services. These answers are typically more helpful and more closely resemble the search function we are accustomed to through Google (Fig. 1.9).

Sometimes, searchers are looking for a specific document and not an answer to a question. The document could be a contract that needs review or a presentation that contains useful slides. To make things more difficult, they typically do not know the title or location of the document. The Google-esque, answer-centric search does not work for these types of requests. Searchers need a way to get a list of documents and filter them based on attributes such as type of document, document format, topic, author, or department. This is where taxonomies shine. Taxonomies provide a list of terms that can be used to filter search results. These taxonomies allow searchers to narrow down results to a shortlist of relevant documents so that they can quickly peruse and find the one that they are looking for.

Internal organization search tools remain one of the most frustrating KM and data services for employees to use. The semantic layer streamlines the user experience by providing necessary context about the organization's content, ultimately supplying correct and easy results for employees to more effectively execute their jobs, while eliminating frustration within the search process.

Mergers and Acquisitions

A huge expense for any merger or acquisition is the cost of aligning data across the two merging companies, as each company has its own reporting metrics, technology, processes, and data repositories, which, too, must be aligned. Traditionally, organizations have handled this through complex data consolidation efforts and rigid reporting dashboards designed to give leaders a unified view. However, this approach often comes with major challenges:

Dracula
Novel by Bram Stoker

Where to Read
Google Books, Internet Archive, Kindle Store...

Rating
4/5
Goodreads

Author
Bram Stoker

Summary
Dracula is an 1897 Gothic horror novel by Irish author Bram Stoker. The narrative is related through letters, diary entries, and newspaper articles. It has no single protagonist and opens with solicitor Jonathan Harker taking a business trip to stay at the castle of a Transylvanian nobleman, Count Dracula. *Wikipedia >*

Genres: Novel, Horror Fiction, Gothic Fiction, Fantasy Fiction, Epistolary Novel, Invasion Literature, Fantastique

Characters: Count Dracula, Abraham Van Helsing · *See More >*

Copyright Date: 1897, 1999, 2010, 2017, 2019, 2022, 2023

Original Language: English

People Also Search For

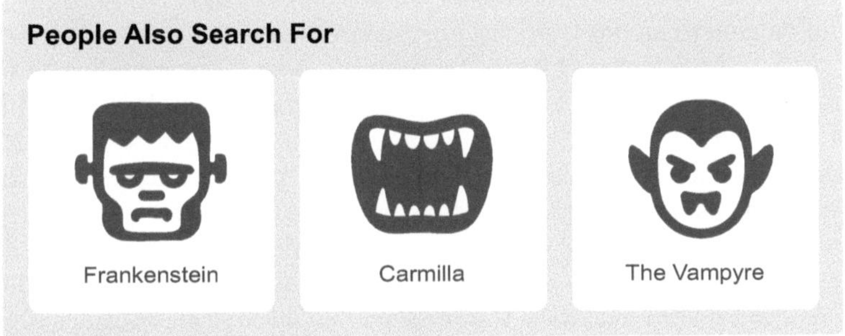

Fig. 1.9 Google-like knowledge panel

- The process of gathering and reconciling data from different systems is slow and error-prone, which can undermine confidence in the result.
- Teams become overly dependent on technical experts to interpret and organize information.
- The resulting data structures are inflexible, making it difficult to adapt as the business evolves.

The semantic layer uses a combination of semantic components (metadata, taxonomies, ontologies, and knowledge graphs) to map data and related data tools to the entities that business users care about. This approach creates a flexible and more reliable way to manage data across previously unrelated organizations, giving employees greater access to the information that they need in a format that makes sense.

Reporting on amalgamated metrics will always be a challenge and significant cost to merged or acquired companies, but implementing a semantic layer can alleviate key issues inherent to merging information. Executed as metadata in the data catalogs so that business users and data owners can quickly find and align information across their current sources, taxonomies are a great way to categorize data across problematic domains. A **data catalog** is a centralized, searchable inventory that collects and organizes metadata from an organization's data assets. In addition to taxonomies, the knowledge graph can map datasets and data elements to business objects. These maps can be used to pull information back dynamically without the need for complex and custom ETL processes. When an ETL process is required for performance purposes, the knowledge graph, rather than a data developer, can define how data is related. ETL routines can be developed against the knowledge graph rather than in code, so that, as the data changes, the map and corresponding processes can be updated to immediately reflect new changes.

Data as a Product

In 2019, Zhamak Dehghani introduced the concept of "data products" within the context of data mesh architecture, urging organizations to treat their data as a product with the same attention to quality, usability, and discoverability as physical products (Dehghani 2019). The idea of treating data as a product gained traction because it offered a practical solution to common challenges like siloed systems and inconsistent data, while also aligning with Agile and product management thinking. We define **Agile** as a value-based, iterative project management approach, methodology, and mindset. Common Agile attributes include a focus on iterative delivery, teams over individuals, and complex problem solving. However, organizations quickly realized that to treat data as a product, they needed a consistent framework to connect and standardize information: this is where the semantic layer becomes essential.

Because data is often trapped in siloed tools and legacy or fit-for-purpose systems, organizations looking to treat data as a product quickly recognize the need for a consistent framework to connect and standardize related information. Without this foundation, data products risk becoming fragmented, redundant, or misaligned. By defining business meaning, logic, relationships, and structure, the semantic layer acts as an operating layer, or, more simply, the "brain" of the data ecosystem. It gives consistent meaning to data, enabling it to be reliably understood, accessed, and used across different systems, teams, and use cases.

Simply defined, **data products** are curated, reusable datasets or knowledge assets that are designed to answer or serve specific business needs or use cases. Specifically, one organization in the financial services industry defines their data products as: "... live, refined, governed and ready-to-use data assets that answer specific business problems."

Data products need to be self-contained and understandable. They must be easily findable by data scientists, analysts, and other users within the organization. This is achieved by defining relationships between data elements through metadata, taxonomies, and knowledge graphs. These semantic models enable not only human searchability but also machine-readability, allowing for automatic integration of datasets for organizational use cases. In addition, the metadata embedded in the semantic layer ensures data quality and governance, providing context for data elements and ensuring they meet enterprise standards (e.g., enforcing access controls to protect sensitive information). As organizations scale their use of data products, the semantic layer becomes indispensable in creating a portable, functional product that serves various business needs, ensuring consistency, standards, and clarity across diverse use cases.

Risk and Compliance

The speed with which businesses operate and the amount of information created for their business operations make tracking risk and compliance issues more difficult. Moreover, organizations now work with more suppliers from a more diverse set of locations, increasing the quantity of applicable regulations. The result of this development is that organizations have hundreds of thousands of written agreements with their suppliers, partners, and clients, all defining their interactions through differing rules.

Managing the activity of your organization and, in some cases, the activities of the organizations that you work with, require automation. A semantic layer can facilitate this automation, evaluating complex business documents in the thousands. A combination of taxonomy and taxonomy management tools allows organizations to categorize content within a topic and specific risk profile. The taxonomy includes language that identifies the type of document and categorizes its liability and risk. Once these tags are in place, an organization can filter documents based on risk and type, easing manual evaluation of highest risk documents.

In addition to taxonomies, the process can be further refined through the use of knowledge graphs. Knowledge graphs can store a more complex set of rules defining the regulations and commitments of an organization. They can then be used to create a recommendation engine that can evaluate each document, and risks identified by taxonomy can be realized with more specificity. The semantic layer enables this level of dynamic automation to allow even the largest, most complex organizations to manage their compliance across a wide range of topics and industries.

In the remainder of the book, we'll share more use cases and detailed case studies. Put simply, with the right semantic layer framework, the use case possibilities are myriad.

References

Adamson, Justin. "Carbon and the Cloud," *Stanford Magazine*. May 1, 2017. https://stanfordmag. org/contents/carbon-and-the-cloud.

"AI Adoption in 2024: 74% of Companies Struggle to Achieve and Scale Value", *Boston Consulting Group*. October 24, 2024. https://www.bcg.com/press/24october2024-ai-adoption-in-2024-74-of-companies-struggle-to-achieve-and-scale-value.

Bell, Christen. 2024 "Between 70-85% of GenAI deployment efforts are failing to meet their desired ROI," NTT Data. https://www.nttdata.com/global/en/insights/focus/2024/between-70-85p-of-genai-deployment-efforts-are-failing.

Challapally, Aditya, Chris Pease, Ramesh Raskar, and Pradyumna Chari. "GenAI Divide: State of AI in Business 2025," Massachusetts Institute of Technology, 2025.

"Data Accuracy vs. Data Integrity: Similarities and Differences | IBM". August 30, 2023. https:// www.ibm.com/think/topics/data-accuracy-vs-data-integrity.

Dehghani, Zhamak. "How to Move Beyond a Monolithic Data Lake to a Distributed Data Mesh," *MartinFowler.com*. May 20, 2019. https://martinfowler.com/articles/data-monolith-to-mesh.html.

Diamantini, Claudia, Domenico Potena, Maurizio Proietti, Fabrizio Smith, Emanuele Storti, and Francesco Taglino. "A Semantic Framework for Knowledge Management in Virtual Innovation Factories," *International Journal of Information System Modeling and Design* 4(4) (2013): 70–92. https://doi.org/10.4018/ijismd.2013100104.

EK Team. "Enhancing Retail Performance with Semantic Layer As an Enabler for Data and Analytics Teams," *Enterprise Knowledge*. January 6, 2025. https://enterprise-knowledge. com/enhancing-retail-performance-with-semantic-layer-as-an-enabler-for-data-and-analytics-teams/.

Foote, Keith D. "A Brief History of Semantics." *Dataversity*. February 22, 2023. https://www. dataversity.net/brief-history-semantics/.

Gartner. "Invest Implications: Forecast Analysis: Artificial Intelligence Software, 2023-2027, Worldwide." November, 2023.

"Graphwise – Unlocking Enterprise Potential: The Strategic Power of a Semantic Layer", *Graphwise*. April 2, 2025. https://graphwise.ai/blog/graphwise-unlocking-enterprise-potential-the-strategic-power-of-a-semantic-layer/.

Harris Interactive, "The Stress in the Workplace Survey," American Psychology Association. 2012. https://www.apa.org/news/press/releases/2012/03/well-being.

Harvard Business Review. "Reducing Information Overload in Your Organization." May 1, 2023. https://hbr.org/2023/05/reducing-information-overload-in-your-organization.

Hilger, Joseph and Zachary Wahl. Making Knowledge Management Clickable: Knowledge Management Systems, Strategy, Design, and Implementation." Springer, 2022: 1, 7, 93.

Horwitz, Helyx. "A Tale of Two Semantic Layers," *Enterprise Knowledge*. June 26, 2024. https:// enterprise-knowledge.com/a-tale-of-two-semantic-layers/.

Hutton, G. "Programming Language Semantics: As Easy as 1,2,3," *Cambridge University Press & Assessment*. 2023. https://www.cambridge.org/core/journals/journal-of-functional-programming/article/programming-language-semantics-its-easy-as-123/EC2C046CF94382B 3B408036B84475DC7

Jain, Pratik. "Expert Reveals Semantic Layer Advantages in Modern Data Stack," *Solutions Review*, December 18, 2023. https://solutionsreview.com/business-intelligence/expert-reveals-semantic-layer-advantages-in-modern-data-stack/.

Jonker, Alexander and Tom Krantz. "What is a data fabric?" *IBM*. August 5, 2025. https://www. ibm.com/think/topics/data-fabric.

Keydunov, Artyom. "How A Universal Semantic Layer Helps AI Understand Data," *Forbes*. August 9, 2024a. https://www.forbes.com/councils/forbestechcouncil/2024/08/09/how-a-universal-semantic-layer-helps-ai-understand-data/.

Keydunov, Artyom. "How A Universal Semantic Layer Helps AI Understand Data," *Forbes*. August 9, 2024b. https://www.forbes.com/councils/forbestechcouncil/2024/08/09/how-a-universal-semantic-layer-helps-ai-understand-data/.

"Knowledge Graphs". 2025. https://www.turing.ac.uk/research/interest-groups/knowledge-graphs.

Rizkallah, Juliette. "The Big (Unstructured) Data Problem," *Forbes*. June 5, 2017. https://www.forbes.com/sites/forbestechcouncil/2017/06/05/the-big-unstructured-data-problem/.

Roe, Charles. "A Short History of Ontology: It's not just a Matter of Philosophy Anymore." *Dataversity*. June 7, 2012. https://www.dataversity.net/a-short-history-of-ontology-its-not-just-a-matter-of-philosophy-anymore/

Seagate. "Rethink Data: Put More of Your Business Data to Work—From Edge to Cloud," *Seagate Technology Report*. 2020.

Tesfaye, Lulit. "Data Management Trends in 2022: Data Fabric v. Data Mesh v. DataOps? What is Right for Your Organization?" *Enterprise Knowledge*. January 11, 2022. https://enterprise-knowledge.com/data-management-trends-in-2022-data-fabric-v-data-mesh-v-dataops-what-is-right-for-your-organization/.

Tesfaye, Lulit. "What Is a Semantic Layer? (Components and Enterprise Applications)." *Enterprise Knowledge*, February 1, 2024a. https://enterprise-knowledge.com/what-is-a-semantic-layer-components-and-enterprise-applications/.

Tesfaye, Lulit. "The Top 3 Ways to Implement a Semantic Layer." *Enterprise Knowledge*, March 12, 2024b. https://enterprise-knowledge.com/the-top-3-ways-to-implement-a-semantic-layer/.

UK Government. "The Rose Book: Guidance on Knowledge Asset Management in Government." *The National Archives*. March 27, 2024. https://www.gov.uk/government/publications/knowledge-asset-management-in-government/knowledge-asset-management-strategies-what-to-include-and-where-to-start.

Semantic Layer Component Design and Implementation

2

In this chapter, we deconstruct the semantic layer into each of its component parts and detail best practices for modeling and implementing these components. Each of the following sections (knowledge assets, business glossary, metadata, taxonomy, ontology, and knowledge graph) follows a similar format. The subsections in each of these sections first introduce the component, defining related terminology and providing historical background. Next, for each component, we explain its uses and the value it presents to an organization, independent of the semantic layer. This is a key point: that an individual component of the semantic layer offers efficacy irrespective of the completion status of the full framework means that an organization need not wait for its completion to realize value from their investment. Indeed, in Chap. 3, we detail the iterative and incremental approaches to building a semantic layer and stress the fact that value can be realized along the entire timeframe. For each of the sections in this chapter, we then describe the related technologies that aid in powering the component, explain the role that the component plays in a complete semantic layer, and, finally, provide a detailed, step-by-step guide to realizing each component as a data model.

By the end of this chapter, you should have a clear understanding of each of the components of the semantic layer, what they do independently and collectively, the supporting technologies that make them work, and how best to implement them within your organization. This understanding will enable you to identify and evaluate those components that already exist within your organization and allow you to create a plan to implement those missing or ineffective.

Understanding the Components of the Semantic Layer

As established in Chap. 1, the semantic layer should be considered as a framework rather than as a specific tool or software package. To comprise the semantic layer, there are certain key components that must be designed and integrated

J. Hilger et al., *Bridging Knowledge, Data, and AI*, https://doi.org/10.1007/978-3-032-17178-8_2

appropriately. The components necessary to architect a semantic layer depend on an organization's requirements, data governance maturity, and technologies in use. Together, these components represent the solutions to manage semantics and context within an organization's data ecosystem. Increasingly, vendors are marketing themselves as a one-stop-shop to deliver a complete semantic layer, though we have yet to see this come to fruition. While the market is continuously evolving, the following components remain the actual building blocks of a successful and scalable semantic architecture. By implementing these components individually, you can tailor a semantic layer solution to your organization's specific business needs rather than implementing some generic solution. And, in most cases, we find that these components already exist in some capacity within many organizations, lacking only the right design, architecture, integration, or data model to function as part of a semantic layer.

The six core components of a semantic layer are knowledge assets, business glossary, taxonomy, ontology, metadata, and knowledge graph. Each of these components plays a key role within the semantic layer (Fig. 2.1):

- **Knowledge Assets**, the reason for the semantic layer itself, will be of greatest value when properly governed, enhanced, and maintained.

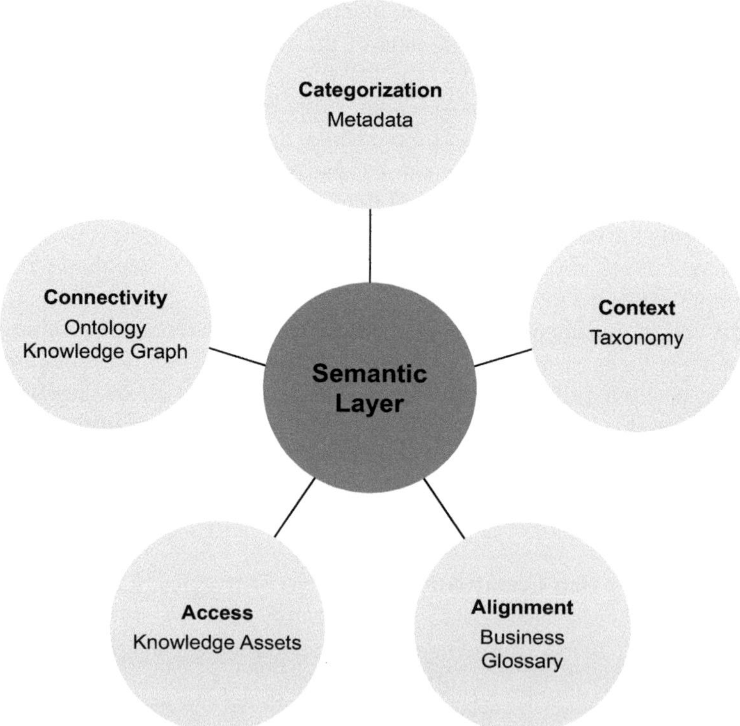

Fig. 2.1 Purpose of the semantic layer components

- **Business Glossaries** define and contextualize business terms, providing business alignment, clarity, and consistency.
- **Metadata**, when applied across all knowledge assets, delivers consistency and alignment.
- **Taxonomies** categorize, classify, and create hierarchy, delivering context and controlled vocabularies, including a thesaurus of synonyms and related terms that support business alignment and shared meaning.
- **Ontologies** further deliver context and alignment by adding connectivity, defining relationships between repositories and different types of knowledge assets.
- **Knowledge Graphs** connect disparate systems and sources of knowledge assets without requiring their relocation.

Collectively, these components make up the semantic layer. Readers should note overlapping uses and functions between the components, however, and the fact that it is only when these components are united that the full potential of the semantic layer is realized.

Each of the subsequent sections explains in greater detail the component, its supporting technologies, its role within the semantic layer, and how organizations should go about modeling and implementing these individual components. In Chap. 3, we will discuss enterprise design and integration practices in the context of the full design and implementation process, delving into best practices and business-aware methodologies.

Knowledge Assets

Knowledge assets are the first core component of a semantic layer. The knowledge assets are the raison d'être of the semantic layer. The entire purpose of the semantic layer is to find, connect, and merge knowledge assets.

We coined the term knowledge assets to express all of the information, in all of its forms, that exists within an organization. The term is purposefully broad because the most effective semantic layers will connect the breadth of information spanning all potential forms of knowledge, information, data, and content, as well as other elements including people, products, equipment, and offices. Knowledge assets are the fiber of our work, and we use them every day to make decisions, do our job "correctly," learn, and perform virtually every work task. And, we also generate new knowledge assets, meaning that an organization's complete collection of knowledge assets is always in flux and constantly growing.

By far, the three most common types of knowledge assets are data, content, and people, with content constituting the vast majority of semantic layer use cases. For the purposes of the semantic layer, virtually any explicit knowledge within an organization can be considered data or content. We typically restrict this scope to that which is in a digital format as few organizations are interested in going back through dusty file cabinets and launching scanning projects at scale, but there are use cases for that as well. Though we take a broad definition of content as the major category of knowledge assets, we can further refine this definition in a couple of key ways (Fig. 2.2):

- **Structured and Unstructured**—One of the great values of a semantic layer is that it integrates and even merges structured data and unstructured content. **Structured data**, like you would find in a database or application, such as a customer relationship management (CRM) or data stored in relational databases and spreadsheets or financial management system, is information that is organized in a predefined format, organized in a way that makes it easy for systems and machines to read and process (i.e., rows and columns). While ideal for automation, reporting, and integration across digital systems, it is more challenging for humans to interpret directly without the aid of a user interface, dashboard, or visualization tool as it often lacks context or narrative meaning to make sense of it and take meaningful action. In essence, structured data excels in precision and consistency but depends heavily on tools and interpretation to translate its rigid organization into human understanding. Unstructured content is the opposite. It is typically designed with the context necessary for human consumption, so it is much easier for humans to understand. Historically, machines struggled to understand unstructured content in a way that made it relatable or findable. The semantic layer addresses this problem by making both structured and unstructured content human and machine understandable.
- **Tacit and Explicit**—**Tacit** knowledge is that which is held in the human mind, rather than in a shareable or repeatable form. **Explicit** knowledge is that which has been captured in an independent form, typically as a digital file or data entry. Semantic layers, like organizations in general, depend heavily on explicit content to help people make decisions, learn, and perform, but tacit knowledge should play a role in this process and technology as well.
- **Knowledge and Information**—Knowledge and information are not the same thing, but both can be tacit or explicit. **Knowledge** is the expertise, experience, and "know-how" that people acquire through work and life. It is based on and created by an individual's learning and experience, making it extremely valuable but also difficult to translate into a digital and repeatable format. **Information**, on the other hand, is simply facts. It lacks the context of the aforementioned expertise and the benefit of any expert analysis. Said differently, every organization possesses content that is knowledge as well as content that is information, and to make things even more complex, most files or documents are a mix of knowledge and information.
- **Internal and External**—An internal asset is that which is intended for an organization's employees, and an external asset is that which is intended for an organization's customers, partners, or the public. The tone and style of these two types of assets are markedly different, and the rigor that goes into external data or content is often much greater. Overall, internal and external assets should align but be regarded differently. It is important to note that a semantic layer may leverage both internal and external knowledge assets to form a comprehensive collection. In organizations where internal and external assets are closely aligned

and consistent, this is not a problem, but in organizations that don't possess this alignment, the semantic layer may cause risks and issues that will have to be confronted during its implementation.

- **Original and Generated**—Original knowledge assets are those that already exist as discrete items within an organization's repository. Explicit assets, for example, are original because they have been created by a human, identified as unique, and are managed. Any file or dataset that you've created falls into this category. Given the increasing prevalence of generative AI, however, generated knowledge assets, those which are derived by AI, must be acknowledged. These generated assets are automatically created based on an organization's existing and original knowledge assets, forming new knowledge assets that may not possess the same level of rigor or governance.

As an added note, there are some in the field that spend an undue amount of time trying to draw clean lines between these differing types of assets, especially between knowledge and information. Don't fall into this trap; rather, spend this time merging all forms of assets within your organization. The semantic layer, once implemented, blurs the lines between an asset and its type. That is, in fact, part of its purpose and can be of extreme value when implemented properly.

As we move into the third type of knowledge asset (people) we must also revisit this idea of knowledge, specifically tacit knowledge. The field of KM is filled with experts, and it is also filled with efforts to capture tacit knowledge from these experts. Some studies estimate that tacit knowledge makes up as high as 80% of an organization's information (Serrat 2017). At the same time, organizations are faced with experts who are often resistant or too busy to document their knowledge and make it explicit. Too many programs with this intent are "clunky," breaking the natural flow of work by forcing someone to write down how they made a decision or came to a conclusion. In short, it is inherently difficult to consistently and completely capture tacit knowledge, especially within a large enterprise. A complete semantic layer can help to address this challenge in several ways.

By conceptualizing people as a knowledge asset, new avenues to capture tacit knowledge and transfer knowledge from person to person unfurl. This knowledge asset can map expertise, competencies, experiences, and relationships, creating

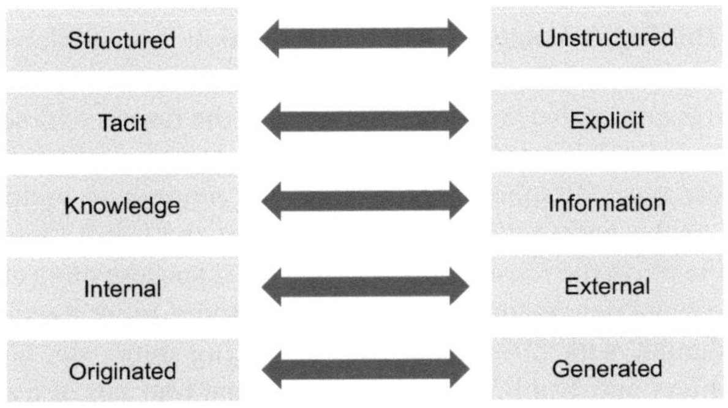

Fig. 2.2 Spectrum of knowledge assets

mechanisms to, in the most simple of use cases, find people from whom to learn or get answers, but also, through the development of more complex systems, to identify gaps in expertise, to staff projects, and to create new data and content through interactions.

When people are considered a knowledge asset, the potential for users to traverse from content to people, from explicit information to tacit knowledge, is unlocked via the semantic layer. For instance, an end user may search for information on a particular piece of company information (how to operate a piece of equipment, for example) and find various pieces of data and content on the topic, but still not understand how to execute the task. With a semantic layer that incorporates people as knowledge assets, employees within an organization could be analyzed and tagged if they have spent over a certain number of hours operating a piece of equipment or if they have a certification in its operation, creating an actionable option for the end user to connect with a person who can help. This interaction could then be captured as a new piece of knowledge asset to be included in future results.

Moving beyond data, content, and people, virtually any other entity or object within an organization can be considered a knowledge asset. Anything that can hold metadata and be connected to other knowledge assets can be an asset itself. A company product, office location, and a piece of machinery are all common examples of knowledge assets. Each use case reveals other potential organizational entities that may be incorporated into a semantic layer as knowledge assets.

Its Role in the Semantic Layer

The entire purpose of a semantic layer is to connect and expose knowledge assets. In short, the core function of knowledge assets in the semantic layer is to be used, whether that means made findable, connected, reassembled, or incorporated into a consuming application such as a chatbot or generative AI capability, among other possibilities. These functions power the front-end experience that the semantic layer supports, exposing knowledge assets in the form of results, answers, or newly generated assets.

There are several more detailed ways to understand the role of knowledge assets in the semantic layer:

- **Returning the Right Assets**—Finding information is a simple yet elusive goal. It's the reason why enterprise applications such as search, chatbots, and data dashboards remain such a hot topic, and it's also the reason why so few organizations have actually delivered an enterprise-scale experience that satisfies diverse users. In these types of solutions, organizations continue to jump from one new technology to the next, failing to recognize that the "stuff" they are trying to make findable plays the most important role in the success of an end-user experience. Most organizations maintain at least five times more the content and data than they should, with 80% of these assets being duplicate, old, obsolete, or incorrect (Hilger and Wahl 2022). This means that four out of five returns on an average search action are, for lack of a better word, bad. This detritus bogs down returned results, forcing users to wade past bad information to get to the good, which in turn arouses skepticism. Second, if knowledge assets don't possess complete and consistent metadata, end-user applications struggle to rank it properly, again producing bad or irrelevant results. Third, enterprise tools are often not connected to a complete set of repositories, meaning that the system is not ingesting the asset that can deliver all of the potential results to a query. Fourth, and finally, organizations forget to address the security, access, and entitlements of their assets: a search or analytics tool may not even "see" the appropriate content or data to be returned, may return a link to which a user does not have access, or, worst of all, may return a document or a summary to a user who *should not* have access. In short, all of these are knowledge asset-specific reasons why enterprise solutions fail to return the right information and satisfy users. A successful semantic layer depends on planning for each of these potential impediments.

- **Enabling Trustworthy Intelligence**—Beyond findability and discoverability, the quality and accuracy of knowledge assets are the core factor in enabling AI. To that end, the critical role of the knowledge asset within the semantic layer is to be "correct." While more advanced AI solutions can identify conflicts within the data, the most trusted, hallucination-free, and accurate experiences will be derived from systems where the sourced knowledge assets possess the same quality of trustworthiness and accuracy. This may seem obvious but recall that 80% of an organization's assets are dubious. Organizations cannot expect internal AI projects to work flawlessly if work has not been done first to clean up this asset quality issue. Semantic layers, too, depend on clean knowledge assets in order to deliver reliable, accurate, and efficient results.

- **Delivering Complete Answers**—Another aspect of trustworthiness, beyond accuracy, is completeness. Yet another critical role of knowledge assets within the semantic layer is to facilitate the full coverage of a topic in any given query. In our experience, this diligence tends to be a major blind spot for many organizations, often revealed during enterprise taxonomy design efforts. In a top-down taxonomy design effort, experts and stakeholders will identify all of the topics they consider critical to their business. We then test this taxonomy design by labeling data or tagging content, and, after further iteration, will leverage auto-tagging technologies to apply the taxonomy across enterprise assets. Our research finds that nearly 15% of topics identified by organizational subject matter experts (SMEs) and business stakeholders tend to be under-represented, meaning there is little to no data or content found in repositories with those identified taxonomy concepts. Many organizations simply do not possess sufficient explicit data to represent a meaningful percentage of their core business. A semantic layer will only be capable of delivering value when it has the appropriate depth and breadth of knowledge assets from which to draw. Said simply, a semantic layer, like any information solution, is only as smart as what you "teach" it.

- **Creating Diverse Experiences and Options**—The semantic layers capable of delivering the richest and most rounded experiments, like those able to help users accomplish their missions most efficiently and completely, will also include a robust diversity of knowledge assets. As previously defined, anything that can hold metadata and be connected to other knowledge assets can be an asset itself. Though data, content and people are the three most common types of knowledge assets, there are many potential types, and those semantic layers that introduce a variety of assets will deliver the richest experiences. Even within content, a great diversity exists. Within structured and semi-structured content, there exists learning content, video content, interactive content, and other expressly purpose-based content. A semantic layer connecting a diverse set of knowledge assets will provide more complete and flexible options, resulting in an experience where a user can choose their own path, traversing different types of assets and deciding how they want to complete their mission, so to speak. One user may find a simple answer and move on, while another user may go beyond the simple answer to explore the topic more deeply through a learning module, a video, or white paper. Another user may choose to go even further by interacting with experts in a community of practice or signing up to attend a lunch-and-learn session. To provide a unique range of knowledge experiences for users, organizations should think about all types and forms of their knowledge assets.

In Chap. 3, we discuss the ways in which knowledge assets can be organized and cleaned up so that the aforementioned quality issues are resolved prior to semantic layer implementation and do not impact the successfulness of your organization's initiative. For this discussion, see the subsection in Chap. 3 titled "Knowledge Asset Readiness."

Supporting Technologies

When you consider all of the systems that hold knowledge assets or hold the metadata about knowledge assets, the list is long. On the unstructured content side, this would include content management, document management, records management, and digital asset management systems. The structured data side includes databases, data warehouses, and data lakes, as well as more specialized systems such as product information management (PIM), customer relationship management (CRM), Enterprise Resource Planning (ERP) systems, and HR or financial data management solutions.

While the list continues, there are several common factors of the semantic layer that determine the ease or complexity of connecting knowledge assets from these various repositories to users:

- **Semantic Web Standards**—The key set of Semantic Web standards includes Simple Knowledge Organization System (SKOS), Resource Description Framework (RDF), Web Ontology Language (OWL), Shapes Constraint Language (SHACL), and SPARQL, which we will define and expand on in the "Taxonomy" and "Ontology" sections of this part. **Standards** are formalized, widely recognized frameworks or guidelines for structuring and defining terms within a domain. Data informed by standards is more easily integrated into a semantic layer. Systems that are based on standards are easier and less costly to integrate because they provide a common framework (predefined protocols and specifications) for different systems to communicate and interact through. Without standards, it would be difficult to ensure that different software components are compatible and can exchange data and services seamlessly, posing a challenge to the potential implementation of a semantic layer. To summarize, organizations that employ semantic standards will find the migration to a semantic layer to be much easier than those that do not (Fig. 2.3).

- **Homegrown vs. Off-the-Shelf**—Related to the existence of interoperability standards, systems that are purpose-built by an organization tend to be much more difficult to integrate into a semantic layer. Not only do "homegrown" systems often lack semantic standards that enable interoperability, but they tend to be built-in ways that actually confound this integration. To migrate to a semantic layer, these systems often rely upon custom application programming interfaces (APIs) that may or may not provide the access or format necessary to integrate information. An **API** is a set of rules and protocols that allow different systems to communicate with one another. The creation of the new APIs has to be done by the application owners who may not have the same priorities for their applications. The result is a semantic layer that uses the standard-built systems first and has gaps until the custom-developed applications can be integrated into the semantic layer.
- **Governance**—Systems with tighter and more centralized governance typically yield higher quality assets with more complete and reliable metadata, where looser governance systems often suffer from knowledge asset quality issues that will require more cleanup.
- **Security and Access**—Security and access tend to be major challenges to integration, presenting potential risks to the execution of a semantic layer. For years, organizations have accumulated and separated assets of various types into different systems, many of which have aged, are no longer actively managed, or are full of largely old, obsolete, and incorrect information. Moreover, these assets may not be properly secured. When a semantic layer is adopted to better surface old data or content, organizations may realize their poor security management. Assets that should have been archived or secured suddenly become visible. We address this issue more in Chap. 3.

Business Glossary

A **business glossary** is a collection of business terms and their definitions. The purpose of this glossary is to standardize key words and thus ensure that all business users within an enterprise have the same interpretation, understanding, and meaning when approaching a common business term. Business glossaries typically include the business term, its definition and description, its relationship to other relevant

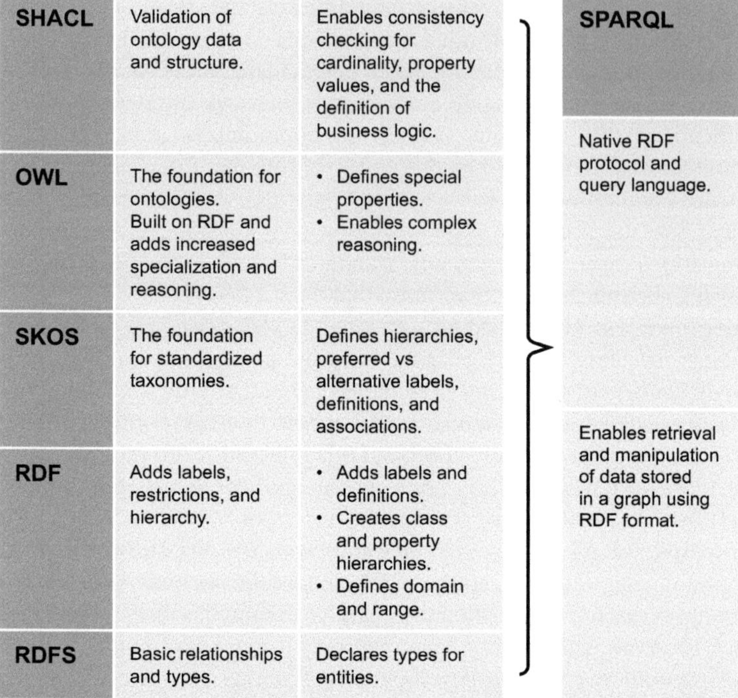

Fig. 2.3 Types of semantic web standards

terms, and any acronyms used for the term by an organization. This information is most often stored in a semantic model or information management system and data catalog, but we have also seen glossaries in spreadsheets, custom applications, or a wiki. Regardless of its location, the most important part is that the glossary is easily accessible to the organization's business users and consuming applications (Fig. 2.4).

Business glossaries are sometimes confused with data dictionaries. While they look similar, these two products have very different purposes (Fig. 2.5). Business glossaries reflect a business-centric view of terminology used by an organization, providing definitions of terms to ensure that *business* users are aligned. The audience for data dictionaries is, on the other hand, technical users. As a result, the definitions found in data dictionaries are typically about data assets and include information such as the field name, data types, and constraints. To specify, a **data dictionary** is a centralized repository of metadata that provides a standardized reference for data elements like names, definitions, types, formats, and rules.

The Value of Business Glossaries

Business glossaries offer value beyond their role within a semantic layer. Agreeing on the importance, use, and meaning of business terms to be included in the glossary

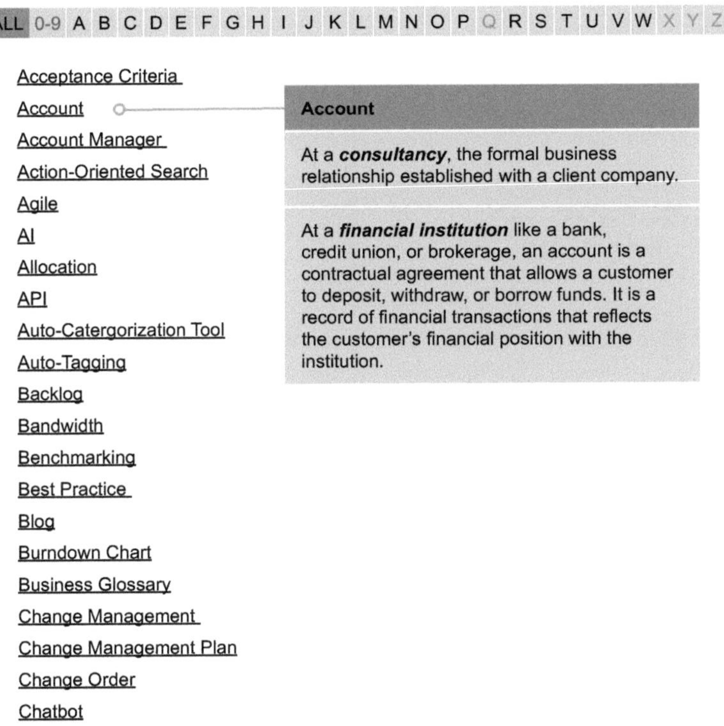

Fig. 2.4 Business glossary

Business Glossary	Data Dictionary
Business Glossaries define business concepts that are used daily within an organization, supporting both business users and technical teams.	Data Dictionaries describe the technical nature of data such as documentation of physical columns, integration requirements, etc. Its primary users are technical teams.

Fig. 2.5 Business glossary vs. data dictionary

requires a great deal of work for an organization. And the value of this work is not limited to your business intelligence or data teams. It is important that all users see consistent nomenclature across all areas in which they work and within all systems with which they interact. Creating and implementing a business glossary should ensure consistent understanding of terms used across applications, documentation, and formal business presentations, as well as functions handled by employees in all business units within an organization.

- **Communication**—The business glossary ensures that different business units can communicate using the same language in written reports, presentations, and verbal exchanges, simplifying business writing and minimizing confusion. For example, when the marketing department discusses increased average sales transactions, it is critical that there is common agreement as to what a sales transaction is. Is the transaction a single item or all of the items rung up at the register. Does this include sales tax? How are discounts factored into the result? The business glossary helps ensure that all of these questions are answered and that communication between executives or business units is consistent, reliable, and machine readable. Additionally, policies and procedures that are written using standard business terms from the glossary are easier to understand and more likely followed. We have, for example, seen policies that identify a specific action result in other, erroneous actions simply because business users misunderstand the language used to describe the intended action or do not know the definitions of key terms referenced in the policy. Business glossaries help close the semantic gap between an organization and its employees by offering a common vocabulary, minimizing errors and increasing the enforceability of these policies.

- **Governance**—User experience teams can manipulate business glossaries as governance tools for the development and configuration of and updates to applications. In this way, the terms as defined in the business glossary should appear and function in the same manner across all user applications.

- **Adoptability**—New technical systems can be easily and efficiently adopted, as users are already familiar with their terms and information per the business glossary and because these terms are standardized and used consistently and everywhere in the organization. Users can focus on learning the features of the tool and not worry about understanding what the terms are and how they relate to business processes.

Its Role in the Semantic Layer

The business glossary informs all of the semantic layers' components: controlled vocabularies found within the semantic layer's taxonomies are usually aggregated from terms defined in the business glossary; ontologies use the business glossary's definitions and relationships as rules for defining the data model; the definitions of metadata elements are also stored in the business glossary; finally, the business glossary contains the defined terms that function as the entities of the knowledge graph.

Because of this, creating a business glossary is a great first step in implementing a semantic layer. The work to define the business glossary forces an organization to align on key terminology describing all of those things that are shared and important to its business and its users.

The function of the business glossary within the semantic layer is concentrated in three areas:

- **Usability**—If the glossary is made available through a shared application or API, each term and its definition can be linked into and viewed in the applications that people use to access data, making this data easier to understand and use.

Definitions in the business glossary also compel employees to use these shared terms no matter their position within the organization. Communication is therefore easier, and business users and data or AI engineers spend less time agreeing on what it is that they are retrieving and more time actually getting and analyzing the data that they need.

- **Quality**—Data quality issues are often created when different groups have differing understandings of what terms like "transaction" or "purchase" actually are and thus how they should be represented in presentations, reports, AI algorithms, and other documentation. In some cases, multiple sources are merged, but each source has differing data. Business users then attempt to query the combined data source and receive inconsistent or incorrect results, causing a huge data quality breach. The cause of this is not poor controls or laziness; instead, the problem is one of misunderstanding. A well-defined glossary can solve this problem, providing data developers and data scientists with definitions as to what each dataset should represent. The result is that a number of common data quality issues can be caught upfront while data is still being captured and consolidated, rather than when frustrated business users are creating reports with inaccuracies.
- **Governance**—When business users are aligned on the definitions and expected value of data, governance activities and rules can be implemented to verify that the data is and works the way that it should.

Supporting Technologies

The most relevant supporting technology of the business glossary is the location in which it is stored and made available for consumption. Business glossaries are stored in three main locations:

- **Data Management Platforms**—Business glossaries do not require complex tools for implementation. Many large organizations typically maintain their business glossary integrated in data management tools with data catalog capabilities that provides a searchable inventory of all data assets. Because a data catalog can automatically connect glossary terms to the underlying technical metadata in databases, tables, and columns, it provides the capability to enrich technical assets with essential business context. Additionally, data catalogs typically include built-in governance features that help ensure the glossary remains accurate, consistent, and well-maintained over time.
- **Homegrown Applications**—Business glossaries can also be stored in a database behind a simple application. Organizations that are willing to invest IT resources in creating a glossary application can build a simple glossary that is accessible across the enterprise. This approach is most often used by organizations that believe in custom development of applications as a way to differentiate their tools from their competitors. A custom application makes it easier to enforce consistent terminology across all applications because the glossary terms can be retrieved by these existing applications. And, when a term changes in the busi-

ness glossary, it is automatically changed across applications. While creating a custom application is an expensive approach, it can be very successful for those organizations looking for greater flexibility and willing to spend the time and money to build and maintain it.

- **Document-Based Storage**—Spreadsheets or wiki-style pages are the most common place that we see business glossaries stored. This is a very simple, easy, and low-cost way to capture and share terms and definitions throughout an organization. Most employees are already familiar with these platforms, and most businesses already own the application. We have found this to be a workable solution for smaller organizations. This approach has also functioned as a great way to express the value of the business glossary to an organization that is not yet sold on its full implementation. It is not a great solution for medium to large businesses, though. The business glossary must be a single source of truth for the definitions of shared terms across and within an organization. When a new term is added or changed in the glossary, it is difficult to ensure that everyone has the same version of the wiki page or spreadsheet. Even if this storage is shared online, it is too easy for people to download copies and use them remotely or even accidentally edit or delete a term. Thus, the long-term maintenance of this approach makes them problematic for large-scale use.

For our recommendation as to where to store your organization's business glossary to support its function within a semantic layer, please see the next subsection, "Business Glossary Implementation within a Semantic Layer."

Business Glossary Implementation within a Semantic Layer

Too many data initiatives fail because they lack a business glossary. Take this scenario:

> The data and analytics team at a global retailer, with nearly 40,000 store locations worldwide, began working with us after migrating their data to a data lake to enhance their reporting and analytics capabilities. However, whenever leadership requested a new metric report, such as store performance, it triggered a lengthy project, often taking 5–6 months for a data analyst to understand the relevant data (spanning petabytes) and develop the necessary data pipelines. This process cost them nearly $900,000 per dashboard. Even after the report was delivered, the analysts frequently discovered inaccuracies, as metrics like "revenue," "headcount," and "store performance" were defined and applied differently depending on who worked on the report.

As stated earlier in this section, a business glossary, as part of a semantic layer, serves as the "translation bridge" between technical data and business users and is a key feature enabling data governance. Without a business glossary, data can be misinterpreted, leading to incorrect conclusions and business risk. When all business users, regardless of their technical background, understand and work with data in the same way, errors and risk are reduced, and overall data governance and quality are enhanced. The importance of the business glossary cannot be understated. This clarity not only improves internal processes but also strengthens an organization's ability to report and act on business insights across its global operations.

Identifying and Defining Glossary Terms

For organizations that have identified a use case (see "Use Cases" in Chap. 3) with data discovery, data quality, and governance priorities, a business glossary is a foundational starting place. Business glossaries often already exist in many organizations in the form of a spreadsheet with lists of terms and definitions, but these documents are rarely recognized as real business glossaries and are usually inaccessible or go unused. In theory, the business glossary should, like in the example above, define the term "revenue" with specific rules on what it includes and excludes (e.g., gross vs net revenue) and how it should be calculated. This standardized definition should be accessible in various systems and across all stores, regardless of geographic location.

To design a business glossary, stakeholders and the semantic layer task force will need to decide, based on the initial use case, which business areas and processes are relevant to its inevitable users. A hybrid top-down and bottom-up approach, as defined in Chap. 3, ensures that the glossary will reflect organizational priorities while also incorporating insights from the teams who directly interact with the data. The purpose of the top-down approach in this hybrid is to align leadership on the application of the business glossary, defining their strategic goals and driving buy-in. This process also clearly establishes the scope of the glossary, or the business areas, departments, or data domains that it will cover. If an organization chooses to begin with a top-down approach, subsequent activities will include engaging with business users and subject matter experts (SMEs) to identify commonly used terms and concepts that should be standardized within the glossary. Here, organizations can leverage interviews, focus groups, or other use case extraction methods discussed in Chap. 3. We find that creating working groups or communities of practice made up of business users, data analysts, and SMEs to collaborate on defining and refining terms ensures that the glossary is both comprehensive and aligned with real-world applications.

For example, at a large financial institution we work with, the executive team drove the overall vision for the business glossary, with terms that align with corporate goals and compliance requirements. However, the real value emerged when this team collaborated with data analysts and SMEs from various departments, such as risk management and operations, to define terms accurately and contextually with granular, department-specific knowledge. This blend of top-down direction and bottom-up input ensures that the glossary is not only strategic but also practical and relevant for everyday use, ultimately improving the likelihood of enterprise adoption of the glossary and its continued success.

In the parallel, bottom-up approach, the task force would also consult documentation, reports, and data dictionaries that contain relevant terminology to the use case's domains. This approach ensures that the glossary is built on existing knowledge and avoids "reinventing the wheel." Methods such as keyword extraction, data mining, and expert interviews help identify and collect relevant terms with efficiency. For example, we partnered with a global consultancy that advises logistics companies on reducing their carbon footprint. Using internal documents like shipment tracking reports and customer service manuals, while also mining data from their operational systems, we identified key terms like "green delivery routing" and "carbon neutral packaging" to align existing terminology with an ESG business glossary. Because over 70% of their domain concepts existed as unstructured content like PDFs, documents, emails, and PowerPoint presentations, we employed NLP and named entity recognition (NER) to automate keyword extraction from large text datasets, allowing us to quickly surface terms for further discussion. **Named entity recognition (NER)** is a component of NLP that identifies and categorizes key entities within text, such as people, organizations, and locations, based on a predefined list of entity names. By involving stakeholders who work closest with the data, the bottom-up approach ensures that the glossary is both accurate and deeply rooted in the business applications and context of each term, once again resulting in successful adoption and user consistency.

One of our recommended best practices is to use existing resources. For many organizations, the business glossary's ideal birthplace is some sort of spreadsheet that already exists, containing domain definitions. These spreadsheets may be owned by data architecture teams or embedded into data governance functions.

Organizing Your Business Glossary

The next step in developing a business glossary is structuring the terms and definitions in a way that is clear, consistent, and easily accessible. The purpose of this step is to categorize definitions, identify synonyms and acronyms, and align terms with business processes and data domains to reduce redundancy in the glossary.

For large organizations that plan on implementing an enterprise-wide semantic layer, defining and organizing a glossary may require segmenting terms by department (e.g., finance, marketing, operations) or by functional areas like customer data, product data, and performance metrics to make the glossary easier to navigate. One thing to note is that organizations should avoid creating terms for factors or business processes external to their own business operations, as this can ultimately confuse users and compromise data quality. By segmenting the business glossary by business area, teams can save time and energy by simply accessing the section relevant to their work. This structured thinking will be especially important as your organization implements iterative semantic layer use cases, as these use cases will each require additional terms and involve additional departments. As your semantic layer grows, your business glossary will grow as well, and it is imperative that this growth is accounted for in the structure of the first implemented version.

Methodologies like the conceptual model approach (Chap. 3) help to group terms by their relationships and context, while components of the semantic layer such as taxonomy can help organize terms hierarchically, with broader categories as the top and more specific terms beneath them. Additionally, using consistent terminology, style, language, and formatting to standardize definition entries is paramount to ensuring that terms have a precise and unambiguous meaning. For example, in the retail company scenario, terms like "revenue" and "sales" were both defined in the business glossary and categorized under a broader "Financial Metrics" taxonomy that contained subcategories like "Gross Revenue" and "Net Sales."

We have witnessed many organizations, when organizing their business glossary, fall into the trap of structuring it alphabetically or in some other way that seems convenient at the time, but ultimately lacks usability. Organizing terms alphabetically may seem like an easy solution, but it overlooks the true purpose of the glossary, which is to make terms easily searchable and understandable in the context of your business. Much akin to organizing a closet by color rather than by use, this kind of organization may look visually appealing, but it makes it more challenging to find specific items when you need them. What is more effective is to classify terms according to their business context, grouping terms by relevant categories like "financial metrics," "customer data," or "operations" so that users have a logical starting point for their search. It's okay to have more than one definition for a given term within one organization (think "credit" for your customers versus for your bank) so long as these separate concepts are well-defined and categorized, with their own respective, unique IDs.

Establishing a standardized intake template, in our experience, significantly optimizes this process. Early on, organizations should develop a template that includes essential fields such as term definitions, synonyms, related terms, business context, and ownership. By creating a format for glossary entries, organizations ensure clarity and alignment from the start. Additionally, establishing a hierarchical structure for the glossary, leveraging taxonomies on business logic and relevant categories, helps facilitate easier navigation and organization, making it simpler for users to find and apply terms effectively and efficiently. This structured approach lays a solid foundation for a comprehensive, user-friendly business glossary that supports consistency and collaboration across an enterprise.

Connecting the Glossary

To connect your business glossary to your organization's existing systems and data, the business glossary must first be structured within a supporting technology. Like previously mentioned, spreadsheets or wiki-style pages are a common host for simple glossaries, but this solution will require tedious, manual handling. While spreadsheets minimize complexity, they also limit the ability of your team to scale the application of the business glossary across an entire enterprise. To expand the glossary to multiple sources and large datasets, a more flexible, programmatic solution is required. A content or data management solutions with integrated data or semantic model catalogs, repositories often associated with metadata, and standard relationship modeling frameworks such as ontologies and knowledge graphs allow the definitions in the business glossary to be linked into relevant locations where users interact with business vocabulary, ensuring that terms defined in the glossary are not just relevant, but are tied to the real data they are supposed to represent. This "linking" is usually facilitated by APIs or other pipelines between the glossary's repository and consuming applications (Fig. 2.6).

As discussed above, all types of knowledge assets that can leverage metadata should be linked to the business glossary. For structured data, such as data that is stored in relational databases or data warehouses, this process involves linking glossary terms to data fields, tables, or views. For example, the term "customer lifetime value" should be mapped to corresponding fields in the customer database, ensuring that when users refer to this term, they can view, through an information icon or some other pop up, exactly what data is being used in its calculation. For unstructured content, like documents, emails, or social media content, the glossary must be linked through metadata tagging or text mining techniques, where entity extraction tools (NER/NLP) scan and tag content. Organizations should consider developing an auto-tagging and content classification framework that automates the application of business glossary terms to unstructured assets. Moreover, data quality rules and standards, such as "every product should have a price" or "every employee should have a first and last name," should be applied at this stage. By connecting the glossary to data and applying standards, organizations ensure that their glossary doesn't just reflect business terminology, but serves as a trusted, actionable resource that drives consistent data governance.

Plan for Errors

From our experience, connecting a business glossary to applicable content and data, especially when using the glossary to enforce data standards and business rules or when using tools like catalogs to automate the associated process, usually surfaces

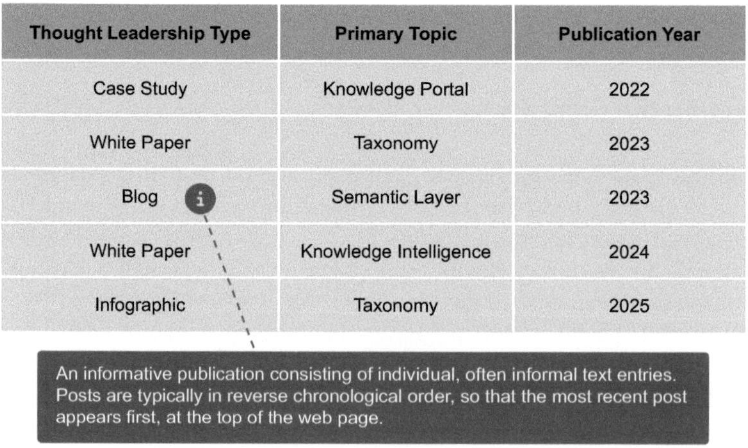

Thought Leadership Type	Primary Topic	Publication Year
Case Study	Knowledge Portal	2022
White Paper	Taxonomy	2023
Blog	Semantic Layer	2023
White Paper	Knowledge Intelligence	2024
Infographic	Taxonomy	2025

An informative publication consisting of individual, often informal text entries. Posts are typically in reverse chronological order, so that the most recent post appears first, at the top of the web page.

Fig. 2.6 Business glossary icon linked in dataset

errors or gaps within an organization's data. Thus, connecting the glossary will require human review, manual validation, and some protocol for flagging missing data and correcting errors. This protocol should consider the inconsistent application of terminology, misaligned definitions, challenges with data integration, and semantic drift because of a stale glossary. **Semantic drift** is the process by which the definition of a term or the relationships between business concepts and processes changes over time. The processes for managing such errors include:

- **Automated Validation**—Automated tools can validate business glossary terms and their application, especially when auto-tagging or integrating data. These tools flag inconsistencies or errors early in the process.
- **Feedback Loops**—Organizations should embed a framework that enables end users to report errors or suggest improvements, helping to ensure that the glossary remains relevant, useful, and doesn't go stale.
- **Semantic or Metadata-Driven Data Quality Checks**—Metadata can validate the quality of source data based on its meaning and relationships within a domain, facilitating a more nuanced and context-aware assessment. This approach goes beyond a basic data type or format validation and typically requires the availability of "domain knowledge" and "context" in a machine-readable format, provided by taxonomy, knowledge graphs, and other components of the semantic layer.

Make the Glossary Accessible and Collaborative

At the end of the day, an inaccessible business glossary is an ineffective business glossary. We recommend that the glossary be embedded into all of the workflows where users naturally interact with data for a given use case, as this will best support decision-making and data governance efforts. Additionally, we see better success in the adoption and scalability of the glossary when it is hosted on a platform that is easy to navigate, such as a data catalog tool with a user-friendly interface. Solutions that facilitate easy consumption such as APIs, search, navigation, and browsing of the glossary allow users to quickly find the definitions they need without disrupting their work, ultimately driving adoption and alignment for the organization.

Additionally, the business glossary should be a collaborative environment that does not silo the curation and editing of terms and instead supports workflows that allow users from all areas of the organization to recommend edits or suggest new terms. This way, the glossary will be a living, evolving resource that reflects the dynamic needs of business users. Collaborative enterprise platforms such as SharePoint, glossary management software, internal wikis, and data cataloging tools all allow users to propose, discuss, and vote on definitions in real time. It's important that these tools also help track version history so that updates to the glossary can be viewed.

Embed Ownership and Governance

Ownership and governance are foundational to maintaining the glossary's accuracy and relevance over time. As the glossary is developed use case by use case, business area by business area, we recommend that each specific domain be assigned to a respective, single owner. We find that the glossary initiative is most successful when owners are specific individuals and not groups of people. Governance councils and working groups often struggle to review terms collectively because of scheduling issues, ultimately resulting in semantic drift. Instead, the individual owners should be members of the business area that they oversee within the glossary, and their role is to continuously ensure that terms stay up to date. While we recommend, too, that terms are hosted on a collaborative platform where business users can recommend edits and updates to the glossary, this single owner should be responsible for reviewing and approving these suggestions based on their expertise. This expertise is why owners should be real business users. Clear ownership will also prevent ambiguity as new data enters the organization. For instance, when a new product line is introduced, a product manager should take ownership of terms related to those products.

The business glossary, once connected to underlying data and content, is a core component of semantic alignment, acting as a common language for enterprise users. To leverage the full power of data, the glossary will need structure (a taxonomy) and relational mapping (an ontology). Taxonomy and ontology will help to organize and connect data in even more meaningful ways. While the glossary defines terms, taxonomies organize these terms as concepts in a hierarchy, and ontologies explicitly illustrate how these concepts relate to one another. Together, these elements form a cohesive semantic layer that ensures that everyone, whether they are business users, analysts, programmers, or data scientists, can access data with a shared understanding of its meaning and context.

Metadata

Metadata is the descriptive information that describes or provides additional insight about knowledge assets of all types. Metadata is often likened to a card catalog in a library. Each physical card corresponds to a book or other document in a library. The card is, of course, not the book itself, but rather holds information about the book, such as its title, author, location, and genre. Metadata, then, has existed for as long as libraries. Today, digital metadata can be applied to any knowledge asset. Though many people think of metadata as applying to files and documents, any knowledge asset can assume metadata, including, but not limited to, products, buildings, people, or experts. This is a particularly important point as we consider how a semantic layer leverages metadata: consistent metadata across different types and locations of knowledge assets plays a major role in enterprise-level interoperability.

Metadata tags, terms, phrases, or other values are placed within a metadata field of a knowledge asset. Each "piece" of metadata may be fed from a taxonomy, may be original text, also known as "free-text entry," or may be automatically created or extracted by an application:

- **Taxonomy-Driven Metadata**—Some metadata employs terms derived from controlled vocabularies within taxonomies to populate metadata fields. This process of tagging the field can be done by hand or can leverage other automated systems. Taxonomy-driven metadata maximizes consistency and interoperability, especially when driven by consistent application of auto-tagging.
- **Free-Text Metadata**—Free-text metadata is that which is "typed" in by hand. This happens most commonly with "Title" fields, which can't be driven by a controlled vocabulary. Though necessary in certain cases, free-text metadata should be minimized due to its administrative burden and potential to create inconsistencies and semantic drift.
- **Automatic Metadata**—Automatic metadata can be derived from the bottom up, either from the content of the asset or the operations of the system in which the asset is managed. As an example of content-derived automation, a "Summary" metadata field might be populated automatically from controlled vocabulary found within the first paragraph of a document or by an AI-generated summary of the document in full. In an operations-derived example, a "Date Created" field could be automatically stamped when the asset is created, and the "Publisher" field could be automatically populated based on the credentials of the authenticated user who created the asset. Automatic metadata tends to be more valuable for system operations and requires SME validation and design alignment in order to be effective for the purposes of findability or data analysis.

Metadata exists to solve many different problems. For example, content and data professionals have long used metadata for analytics, personalization, findability, and data quality. We typically categorize the purpose and use of metadata into five key areas:

- **Descriptive**—Descriptive metadata provides information about a knowledge asset. Description fields include "Title," "Author," "Topic," and comments about the data. This metadata supports the interaction between people and assets, allowing users to know and identify what a specific asset is or is not. Therefore, descriptive metadata is most visible to an end user and is most employed for purposes of findability and discoverability.
- **Structural**—Structural metadata helps to explain the structure of the asset and how it relates to other assets. Examples include the type of document or the domain that the knowledge asset belongs to.
- **Administrative**—Administrative metadata is a type of metadata that provides information about the management of a knowledge asset. This can include information such as who created the asset, when it was created, when it was last modified, and who has access to it. Administrative metadata is important for tracking the history of an asset and for managing access to it (Taylor 2004).

- **Operational**—Operational metadata is that which the system needs to function. This is often what we'd call "back-end" metadata, meaning that a user would not see or interact with it. An example of operational metadata would be a unique, auto-generated ID or code for each document.
- **Records**—Records management provides additional information about the tracking and controls of a specific subset of organizational content that is officially considered a record. A **record** is a piece of content or document that contains policies, decisions, or other official or legal actions taken by an organization that must be preserved to ensure its memory. The official designation of "record" requires that it be handled differently than other documents and tracked through its lifecycle. Records metadata might include information such as who created the asset, when it was created, when it was last modified, and who has access to it. Records management metadata is important for tracking the history of an asset and for managing its access.

Of these five types, a semantic layer may use all or only some. Descriptive, structural, and administrative metadata are most commonly used (Fig. 2.7).

Though there are many standards for metadata, the most famous is the Dublin Core. The Dublin Core was developed in Dublin, Ohio in the 1990s by a group of librarians and computer scientists to describe web content. The group is now known as the Dublin Core Metadata Initiative (DCMI) and continues to iterate and update its standards, now including elements that support linked data and semantics. The Dublin Core details metadata fields including "Title," "Creator," "Subject," "Description," "Format," "Rights," and more. Because of its thorough documentation, we consider it a strong starting point for an organization to use, adapting it to their specific needs and use cases.

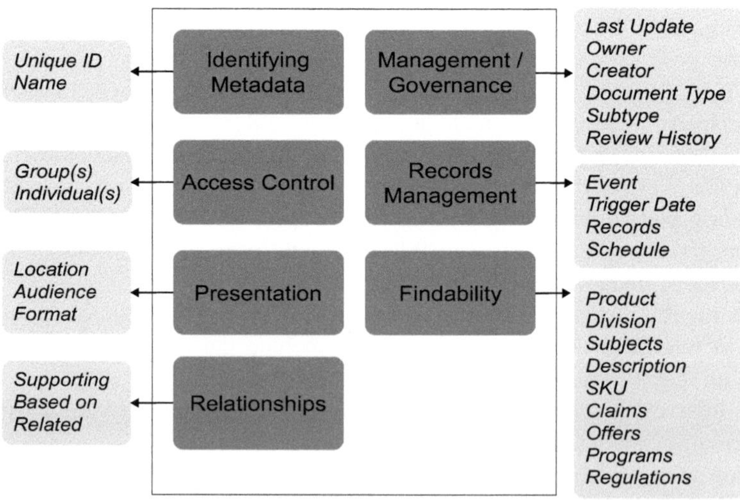

Fig. 2.7 Types of metadata

The Value of Metadata

As we have defined, the critical function of metadata is to apply additional information to a knowledge asset. A classic example of this purpose comes from the field of Digital Asset Management (DAM). Long before features like object detection, scene recognition, facial recognition, and text extraction existed, metadata was the primary means by which an image could be enhanced for better management and findability. Though AI and machine learning (ML) have come a long way, metadata continues to play a foundational and valuable role in how assets are managed, found, used, and reused. The most common uses of metadata are:

- **Findability and Discoverability**—Metadata can translate into navigation or faceting, improving search results through weighting and driving other features like recommendations.
- **Interoperability**—Metadata applied consistently across multiple repositories greatly improves interoperability between these systems.
- **Quality and Management**—Because metadata may include information about the source, owner, dates of creation, and dates of review, it can support quality and content governance. Since different types of content can each have a prescribed set of metadata requirements, this facilitates different levels of governance on an asset-type basis.
- **Workflow and Automation**—Metadata can include tags that allow data teams to automate standard data quality processes. For example, a metadata attribute could flag datasets that come from external sources and require regular review. If the common problems with those datasets are known, this review process can even be automated. Metadata fields that identify business units or the status of a dataset can be used to drive workflow as data is passed down between business units within a standard data analytics process.
- **Security**—Metadata can help protect data by providing information about how and by whom it should be used. It should be noted, however, that metadata is not a replacement for security, nor is it security itself. Some organizations try to use metadata as a replacement for poor security or lack of enterprise entitlements. This approach should be avoided at all costs.

Its Role in the Semantic Layer

Metadata plays a multifaceted role in the semantic layer, acting as a bridge between physical content, data, and business users and translating technical information into business-friendly terms and relationships. By working alongside taxonomy, ontology, and business glossaries, metadata brings clarity, context, and intelligence to raw content and data. This ensures that data within the semantic layer is not just stored but is truly understood and actionable.

As a component of the semantic layer, metadata accomplishes all of the things that content and data professionals previously used it for and more. Metadata blurs the distinctions between how structured and unstructured information are handled by shifting the focus from the physical nature of the data to its meaning and description. Acting as the descriptive layer, metadata captures the essential "who, what, where, when, why, and how" of data, enabling both humans and systems to understand its origin, purpose, usage, and connections to different domains.

Within a semantic layer architecture, metadata works in harmony with taxonomy, ontology, and business glossaries to ensure that data is not only technically accessible but also semantically meaningful. Where taxonomy answers the question, "what type of thing is this?" by *structuring and classifying* content and data, metadata *describes* the underlying content/data to answer "what is the context of this specific thing?" Thus, metadata forms the connective tissue linking semantic structures to real-world knowledge assets, powering discoverability, governance, lineage, and trust across the organization. There are five key areas in which metadata drives value for the semantic layer. They are:

- **Findability and Discovery**—Metadata within a semantic layer labels data elements in a business context, showing the implicit relationships between labels. For example, a data element labeled "customer" will interact with data elements labeled "product" or "revenue." By exposing these interactions and using terms that business users understand, metadata enables these users to find and manipulate data without needing to navigate complex database structures. Additionally, metadata supports the effective management and findability of data products, a structured and curated collection of data assets, along with its associated metadata, semantics, and templates, designed to address specific business needs.
- **Context and Understanding**—Metadata provides crucial background information about data, such as its source, when it was last updated, its status in a workflow, and any known quality issues. This information communicates how to analyze a data element and whether or not it's trustworthy for business use. Knowing that a dataset comes from a legacy system, for example, or that it hasn't been updated recently can influence decisions about its relevance or reliability.
- **Data Abstraction and Accessibility**—The semantic layer is valuable for its ability to abstract complex data systems, and metadata powers this abstraction. Metadata defines how data should be presented, regardless of where or how it is stored. This allows business users to access, analyze, and report on data without needing any technical knowledge of the actual data-containing systems, facilitating data accessibility.
- **Data Governance, Quality, and Security**—Metadata is essential for enforcing data governance policies. Building metadata simplifies and streamlines the management of the semantic layer. Additionally, it enables data discovery, governance, consistent data cataloging, and lineage tracking. These data governance practices, backed by strong metadata management, are able to protect sensitive data, enforce usage standards, and meet regulatory requirements. Many of the organizations that we work with employ metadata to provide a centralized view

of data definitions, access permissions, operational context, and data quality rules.

- **Enabling Automation and AI**—When machines understand the meaning of and relationships between data, they can generate more accurate predictions and recommendations. Rich, well-structured metadata provides this foundation for automation, artificial intelligence, and ML. For example, a semantic layer enriched with medical terms and metadata can help a **large language model (LLM)** interpret nuanced patient symptoms and recommend diagnoses based on medical knowledge. An LLM is an advanced AI model that, after processing large amounts of text, is able to generate natural, human-like language for question-and-answer and other generative chatbot functions.

Supporting Technologies

Within an organization, key technologies for managing metadata include modeling tools, metadata storage repositories, ETL and data integration platforms, and AI/ML capabilities that augment these tasks. Together, these solutions help create, manage, align, and connect metadata across assets more effectively. Many of these systems, and other enterprise applications, offer common metadata management capabilities such as:

- **Syndication**—Systems can "push" metadata to third-party tools, helping establish standardized metadata across multiple platforms.
- **Lineage and Security**—Management applications track the history of changes, allowing administrators to see who made what modifications and to revert to earlier versions if needed. These tools can also manage user permissions, ensuring appropriate access and control, which is especially valuable in large, distributed environments.
- **Governance**—Beyond lineage, governance features allow organizations to enforce metadata standards, such as limiting term length or restricting the use of acronyms, ensuring consistency and quality across systems.

Of course, virtually every system that stores knowledge assets has some level of metadata management capability, whether explicitly labeled as such or not. In other words, metadata can be managed and stored across a wide variety of technologies. Adding another layer of complexity, data assets themselves can contain embedded metadata. Rather than being stored in a separate system (like a card catalog), this metadata resides within the asset itself, though it's rarely used in practice.

For a more detailed discussion and specific solution recommendations for managing and integrating your organization's metadata within a semantic layer, see "Create Metadata Model and Assess Current-State Technology."

Metadata Implementation within a Semantic Layer

Metadata serves as the backbone of an effective semantic layer, as it supplies the ability to identify data and other knowledge assets with semantics. Feeding business glossary terms and taxonomy and ontology concepts into metadata fields allows you to tag a knowledge asset with machine-readable business language and logic that will allow the semantic layer to interact with that asset. Without metadata, knowledge assets remain unknowable to the semantic layer and its front-end applications and thus inaccessible to the business users who need it.

Create Metadata Model and Assess Current-State Technology

While your organization may already have some sort of metadata and metadata system in place, this system typically will need to be adjusted to encompass the specific semantic requirements of your use case and then integrated with the necessary data models, knowledge asset repositories, and front-end applications.

The first step in aligning this technology with your semantic layer use case is to define and identify the business terms, concepts, and processes relevant to this endeavor. At this stage, you may wish to conduct some profiling of the content and data within those relevant repositories to best understand the characteristics of this data, its structure, content, and relationships. This analysis will inform the business language, concepts, and processes identification, as the content and structure of this data will illuminate how it will need to be described and which metadata fields will be required to do so. Existing data dictionaries, business glossaries, and taxonomies that support the prioritized use cases or interact with associated data assets should also be analyzed to determine their relevance and the existence of gaps. This analysis and the resulting integration of benevolent features will further guide the operating model and future governance requirements for metadata management within the semantic layer.

The resulting understanding of concepts related to your use case can then be organized into the structured schema that will become your metadata model. This conceptual structure should define how your metadata will describe the knowledge assets or data elements like tables and content like documents and images. For example, if your organization's use case is to improve search on your website that sells books, your metadata fields will be related to common book properties like the cover image, the author, the publisher, the title, the year published, its genre, whether it is a bestseller or not, and its in-store location, as the book is the knowledge asset being searched for and described.

You will also want to identify the state of your organization's current metadata system and its technology. Effective metadata models should align and support multiple users and systems within an enterprise. As such, your metadata model will need to be managed to avoid duplication and semantic drift. We recommend that this management takes the form of a combination of tools, platforms, and features that can store and support your metadata model and its standards (Dublin Core,

ISO/IEC standards, RDF, etc.) at scale. Specifically, your metadata technology should not only store your metadata, it should also support its integration with existing data systems, databases, and applications, and should host features such as data cataloging, metadata discovery, data lineage tracking, and automated metadata capture. To encapsulate all of this functionality, we recommend that your organization invest in the following accompanying technology solutions:

- **Design and Metadata Definition**—Metadata modeling involves both data structure and semantic modeling capabilities. These tools are used to create conceptual, logical, and physical data models that define data structures, content descriptions, and relationships. Ontology and taxonomy design and management tools further standardize vocabulary and classification, ensuring that metadata remains consistent, meaningful, and aligned across different systems and business groups.
- **Metadata Storage and Management**—Metadata can be stored in several ways. It can be embedded within data files or maintained in centralized repositories such as data catalogs or term stores. Although the storage and sharing approach largely depends on an organization's data architecture and metadata management strategy, dedicated repositories, including data catalogs, master data management (MDM) systems, and metadata stores in data warehouses or data lakes, enable scalable management, integration, and governance actions like lineage tracking and editing. These repositories are essential for managing controlled vocabularies, defining relationships, and supporting labeling and tagging to ensure metadata completeness and consistency.
- **Metadata Integration**—The most effective metadata model is one that can be accessed and utilized across the enterprise through multiple channels, meeting users and applications where they are. This flexibility ensures that metadata is not siloed but readily available for integration and use throughout the organization. To this end, organizations use integration tools such as ETL (Extract, Transform, Load) platforms to automate the extraction, transformation, and loading of metadata from various sources into a central repository. Meanwhile, built-in connectors within knowledge asset sources provide direct interfaces to extract metadata from databases, data warehouses, and enterprise applications. Many modern platforms also offer metadata exchange APIs, enabling seamless integration and synchronization across the data ecosystem. In addition, AI and ML capabilities are continuing to enhance metadata management by automating key tasks such as profiling, tagging, classification, data observability, and lineage tracking. Adopting these intelligent features is increasing minimizing the manual burden on data teams and making metadata management more dynamic and scalable.

Such metadata management tools facilitate the consistent creation and application of metadata components (definitions, labels, and data quality rules) standardizing data across an organization, regardless of the complexity of its data landscape. For organizations in highly regulated industries, these tools are an absolute necessity.

The key takeaway is that these technologies will provide a structured approach to managing business context, data lineage, and the accessibility of knowledge assets, which is beneficial for data governance and findability.

Apply Your Metadata Model

Once you have created your metadata model and integrated it with these recommended technologies, you can begin applying metadata tags and labels to underlying knowledge assets and linking the business glossary into relevant metadata fields. Taxonomies can also be linked from their management systems into metadata field dropdowns. This enables a standardized, unified view of your content and data, allowing users to easily navigate and query through various business assets. The linkage between taxonomies and metadata ensures that assets are classified consistently and helps users find related content more effectively.

To further streamline metadata management, automating metadata tagging is a key next step. Modern tools like AI-driven auto-tagging, NLP, and machine learning algorithms can be leveraged to automatically assign tags and metadata to new data assets as they are created or ingested into the system or pushed to source systems. These automation techniques drastically reduce manual effort, ensuring faster and more accurate tagging, while also scaling the metadata management process across vast data environments. For instance, using NLP for NER, we typically automate the tagging of common or shared metadata such as customer names, product details, or financial terms within documents, transforming unstructured data into rich, searchable metadata.

Linking metadata to the business glossary is equally important to ensure consistency in how business terms and concepts are understood across the organization. The business glossary provides a formal definition of metrics, terms, and key performance indicators, which can be embedded directly into the metadata model. This alignment allows stakeholders across different teams to work from the same terminology, reducing confusion and improving collaboration. Additionally, metadata from upstream applications (such as databases, CRM systems, or data lakes) can be pulled into the metadata model via automated connectors or ETL processes. By capturing metadata at the source, you ensure that the data lineage and context are preserved, which is crucial for data governance, auditing, and compliance purposes. With this approach, metadata management becomes a streamlined and integral part of your organization's knowledge and data ecosystem.

Govern Your Metadata

Metadata governance is typically considered an afterthought, but it is just as important as designing and developing your metadata model. Metadata and taxonomies are living tools that evolve with the content they describe, and without a forward-thinking governance plan, metadata initiatives will stagnate and end up abandoned.

Organizations that invest in metadata management can mitigate risk and liability and realize more and more complex use cases. The most successful metadata governance contains the following components:

- **Roles, Responsibilities, and Operating Model**—Successful metadata governance defines ownership and accountability of metadata management, ensuring that the right stakeholders are involved in the decision-making and enforcement of governance practices. "Ownership" should involve data stewards, design leads, business stakeholders, and/or a system admin who can lead metadata creation, management, and maintenance and can enact changes in a metadata management tool or in an integrated system. An **operating model** is a blueprint that defines how an organization delivers value by outlining its structure, processes, technology, and people. The purpose of an operating model is to help an organization achieve its strategic objectives. It is important to note that these roles are moving away from strict oversight and regulation and toward enablement. This means that ownership roles should increasingly focus on establishing frameworks that support transparency, collaboration, and compliance across a more data-centric enterprise.
- **Process Automation**—Organizations can implement tools and processes to automate metadata collection, updates, and management, reducing manual effort and ensuring accuracy and efficiency. Governance plans that are augmented by automation technology, are seamless to the end user, and succeed. In other words, the most effective governance doesn't have to be learned or followed, it just happens when using the system, because that's how the system was designed.
- **Standards and Policies**—Standards allow for governance to be baked in from the design stage. Governance involves, too, the establishment of a clear set of standards, consistent guidelines and rules for how metadata should be created, managed, and maintained, to ensure uniformity and compliance across the organization. Organizations should consider adopting industry standards such as Dublin Core Metadata Specification, Metadata Object Description Schema (MODS), etc. and augment their existing policies with these tools, depending on use case needs.
- **Align with Data Governance Framework**—Organizations should integrate their metadata strategy into their overall content and data governance framework. This ensures that metadata management aligns with broader data management objectives and supports the organization's data quality and compliance goals.

To effectively manage and leverage metadata, it's essential to implement structured systems that enhance clarity and consistency across an organization. This is where taxonomy and a business glossary play a critical role as complementary components within the semantic layer. A well-defined taxonomy organizes metadata into a clear hierarchical structure, making it easier to categorize, search, and navigate large datasets. Meanwhile, a business glossary ensures that all stakeholders, both technical and non-technical, share a common understanding of key terms and concepts.

Taxonomy

A taxonomy is a hierarchical structure that categorizes concepts and terms according to their characteristics. The concept of taxonomy is far from new and dates a lot further back than semantic layers. One of the earliest known taxonomies was developed by Aristotle in the fourth century BCE. Aristotle's taxonomy divided animals of the natural world into two categories, those with blood and those without blood, and further subdivided these kingdoms into genera and species ("Aristotle" n.d.). Like modern taxonomies, each level shares the traits of the parent categories but increases in specificity and detail. In the last century, taxonomies have taken on much broader usage, being applied in a variety of fields beyond biology. For example, taxonomies now classify diseases, chemical compounds, fields of study, and even stars. In the most recent decades, taxonomies have become a standard tool for organizing and understanding information, leveraged in libraries, museums, businesses, and governments around the world. Within the field of information science, too, taxonomies now play a critical role. And it is this application of taxonomy that comprises part of the semantic layer (Fig. 2.8).

This brief history is important in distinguishing traditional taxonomies from what we call "business taxonomies." Traditional taxonomies are designed and used by scientists and librarians. They are deep and detailed hierarchical structures, commonly possessing thousands of terms. Highly rigorous in their designs, these scientific taxonomies exhibit "mutually exclusive, collectively exhaustive" (MECE) qualities, ensuring that all possible options and no possible duplications exist. Mutually exclusive means that each term is distinct and that no overlap or ambiguity exists between terms. For example, the terms "mammal," "bird," "reptile," and

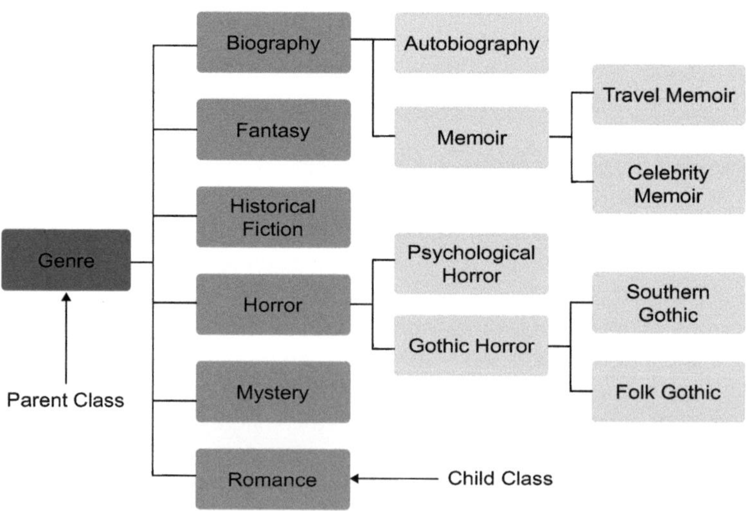

Fig. 2.8 Book genre taxonomy

"amphibian" are mutually exclusive because an animal can only belong to one of these categories. Collectively exhaustive means that all possible options are included in the taxonomy and that no omissions exist. For example, if you are to create a list of all of the countries in the world, you must ensure that every country is included. Put in more colloquial terms, these traditional taxonomies are designed so that there is a place for everything, and everything is in its (singular) place.

Business taxonomies, on the other hand, are designed specifically for business users, meaning that they need to be focused more on usability and simplicity rather than conforming to rigorous MECE principles. Businesses are often messy, using conflicting language and duplicate terms. Business users most likely do not want to click through twenty layers of a taxonomy hierarchy to find the right term, nor do they have the need or capacity to search through thousands of terms to properly tag a document with the single correct possibility. But business taxonomies must still be designed with sufficient rigor and detail for them to accomplish their express purposes, creating a delicate balancing act for taxonomy design professionals.

An organization's business taxonomy design will balance the art, science, and organizational politics of taxonomy to deliver a clear structure to organize and connect knowledge assets of all types. Within the frame of the business taxonomy, there are several terms and types of which to be aware. First, taxonomy, metadata field, metadata, and their related terms (all of which comprise a cohesive enterprise taxonomy design for an organization) should be clarified.

Taxonomies, as described above, are the controlled vocabularies used to describe knowledge assets. For the purposes of this book, the term "taxonomy" is used broadly to encompass both controlled vocabularies and thesauri. It is important to note that a single taxonomy design will typically have multiple taxonomies, each containing a specific set of terms with its own purpose (i.e., Topic, Product, Location, Intended Audience, etc.). For example, a "Topic" taxonomy would include all business topics, while a "Product" taxonomy would list businesses products, and so on.

Though taxonomies are typically hierarchical, with parent and child values, each level possesses additional degrees of specificity while inheriting the qualities of the parent. Business taxonomy designs can include flat taxonomies, also known as picklists, which consist of categories that are all considered equal. As taxonomies become increasingly surfaced as front-end navigation, and, as modern systems allow for more discrete management of taxonomies and metadata fields, flatter and simpler taxonomies are becoming more popular. This means that, although hierarchical taxonomies remain salient, flat taxonomies should exist as part of an enterprise design.

More advanced taxonomies can include synonyms, also known as non-preferred terms or lead-in terms. Though it quickly becomes convoluted, advanced taxonomies might also include related terms or fuzzy matches, where meaning is not identical but similar. Some organizations may define each term within their taxonomy, but we prefer to employ a business glossary for this purpose.

Metadata fields are often populated by taxonomies. In these cases, the metadata field will correspond with the taxonomy: a "Topic" metadata field will be populated with values from the "Topic" taxonomy, and a "Product" metadata field will be populated with values from the "Product" taxonomy. Given the interdependent nature between metadata fields and taxonomy, additional design considerations exist: should a metadata field be populated with a single taxonomy value or multiple values?

Metadata are whatever tags, terms, phrases, or values are placed within a metadata field. While these are often terms from a taxonomy, they may also be "free-text entry," words simply typed into the field, or automatically extracted text from the knowledge asset or other source.

In more complex enterprise designs, a complete taxonomy typically includes conditional metadata, meaning that some of the fields and associated taxonomies will only be applicable to a subset of content, depending on its type or nature. We typically describe this in terms of primary fields, those that should be applied to all content, and secondary fields, those that should only be applied to a subset of content. For instance, "Topic" or "Subject" is an example of a primary field in that any piece of content will possess one or many topics/subjects. On the other hand, length or time are examples of secondary fields because questions like, "how long is it?" or "what is the running time?" are not relevant to all content (Figs. 2.9 and 2.10).

To summarize, many metadata fields will be populated using taxonomies, wherein the taxonomy terms will exist as metadata within the metadata field. Another way of thinking about this is that the metadata field is a question that can be asked about the knowledge asset; the taxonomy includes all of the potential answers; and the metadata is the answer specific to the knowledge asset:

Question What is the genre of the book?
Answer The genre is "Gothic Horror."

In this example, the metadata field is "Genre," and the metadata, selected from a taxonomy of genres, is "Gothic Horror."

The Value of Taxonomies

Taxonomies, specifically business taxonomies, play many roles in the fields of knowledge management, content management, and data management in addition to their role as a component of the semantic layer. In most instances, taxonomies enable findability for an organization, making it easier for end users to locate the materials they're seeking. Beyond findability, taxonomies also play a role in discoverability, meaning that they identify, make available, or even advance content that may not have been explicitly searched for.

The most common uses for a taxonomy are:

- **Enterprise Search and Querying for Information**—Taxonomy can support findability of information and knowledge assets in several ways. First, taxonomies can impose alignment when a taxonomy design is deployed across multiple repositories, allowing disparately located content to be more easily related

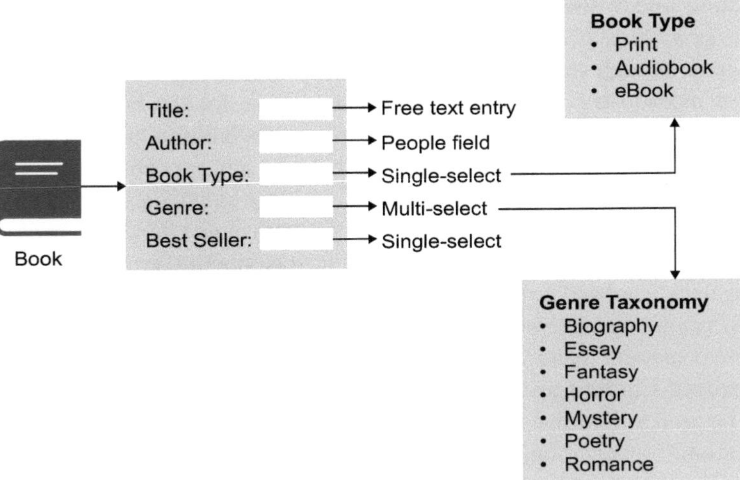

Fig. 2.9 Book metadata

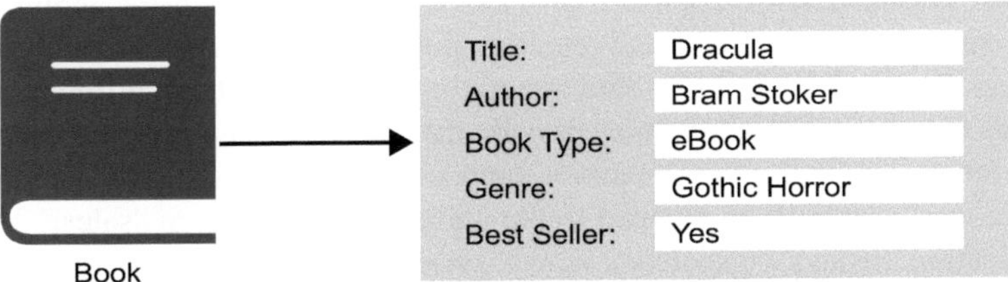

Fig. 2.10 How taxonomies populate metadata

through a search experience. This alignment can also actuate faceting within a search tool, enabling end users to narrow down potentially large result sets. Taxonomy design and associated faceting can reduce a result set from thousands to ten or so documents in just a few clicks. And, when a taxonomy is applied as metadata on content, that metadata can be used for search weighting, surfacing the most pertinent documents toward the top of the results.

- **Browse and Navigation**—A front-facing taxonomy or taxonomies can also be implemented as the actual information architecture for a search tool. In these cases, users directly interact with the taxonomy of a repository, clicking through it to find and discover knowledge assets.
- **Recommendations and "Like" Content**—Taxonomy terms applied as metadata can suggest similar content to a user. For instance, if a user finds content on a particular topic, the system can identify other content that possesses the same topic tags and recommend that material. While there are many ways a recommendation feature can be implemented, varying in maturity and value, taxonomies often play a key role in their design.

- **Business and System Alignment**—As we discussed above, when multiple repositories or systems leverage the same taxonomy design, those systems are easier to integrate through search or other means, including being used to link data across siloed repositories. This same concept holds true for the broader organization, influencing not only technologies and repositories but also how people within an organization communicate. A taxonomy helps to align vocabulary even when it's unrelated to technology or digital content, enabling individuals within an organization (or beyond it) to communicate and collaborate more effectively. In cases where different departments or agencies use distinct taxonomies, crosswalks, which map equivalent or related terms across vocabularies, are often used to bridge semantic gaps, a common and essential practice in large institutions or government agencies where consistent interpretation across jurisdictions or programs is critical.
- **Improved Content and Document Management**—In some cases, a taxonomy can be used to improve the management of content by providing consistent classification, organization, and location of that content, bettering governance and visibility.
- **Data Governance and Compliance**—Data teams are increasingly adopting taxonomies to strengthen data governance by labeling data assets with standardized terms. This structured approach provides a clear foundation for applying business rules, access controls, and retention policies. This plays a more critical role especially when it comes to data integration. When data from different systems needs to be merged, taxonomies provide the standardized terms that align disparate labels. For example, a finance system's "POS revenues" and a sales system's "revenues" can both be mapped to the unified taxonomy term "sales." This normalization ensures consistency across systems and improves the accuracy and reliability of downstream analytics and reporting.

Its Role in the Semantic Layer

In essence, taxonomy functions as the semantic backbone of a semantic layer, supplying the structure, consistency, and context necessary for users to effectively access, interpret, and leverage enterprise data and information. Taxonomy serves as a core component of the semantic layer by providing a structured framework to represent business concepts and their relationships. This framework is essential for creating a unified and meaningful view of organizational knowledge assets, delivering context, and supporting controlled vocabularies that foster business alignment.

More specifically, taxonomies organize and classify content, documents, business terms, and data, establishing the semantic foundation upon which the semantic layer is constructed:

- **Organizing Information**—Taxonomies define the fundamental units for structuring information within the semantic layer, providing a system for managing the framework's metadata. This metadata describes the characteristics and context of data, improving its quality, consistency, and reusability.

- **Standardizing Terminology**—By enforcing consistent naming conventions and terminology, taxonomies reduce ambiguity and promote a shared understanding of business concepts, crucial for establishing a reliable and coherent semantic foundation.
- **Reference Data and Schema for Analytics and AI**—Taxonomies provide a hierarchical framework that helps data teams organize, classify, and standardize information across the enterprise. They serve a dual purpose: as a schema, a taxonomy enforces structure and consistency, and as reference data, it offers a trusted set of controlled values used to categorize data. For example, by acting as a single source of truth for reference information such as product categories, geographic locations, or employee titles, taxonomies help prevent common data quality issues like misspellings, inconsistent abbreviations, or duplicate labels that can undermine analysis and reporting.
- **Enhancing Data Annotation for Advanced Applications**—Taxonomies improve data labeling, annotation, and organization, which enhances the accuracy and consistency of training data used in analytics, machine learning (ML), and NER. These taxonomy capabilities are central to the value of the semantic layer in aggregating, contextualizing, and connecting diverse knowledge and data assets for advanced solutions.

At its core, taxonomy delivers consistency and categorization for the semantic layer, helping to ensure the artificial barriers between systems and content types can be traversed and understood.

Supporting Technologies

The key supporting technology for taxonomies is intended for designing, storing, and integrating taxonomies in an organization. This includes specialized taxonomy management software and/or data management platforms that enable centralized governance, automated processes, and the streamlined integration of taxonomies with other enterprise systems or availability for users. These solutions play important roles within the semantic layer. The first role is that of managing the taxonomy design and syndicating its appropriate elements to the systems that house knowledge assets. The second role is that of auto-tagging content based on the taxonomies models and applying those taxonomy terms as metadata.

In the next subsection, we'll discuss the potential ontology capabilities of some taxonomy management solutions, but, for now, we'll focus on the functions of discrete, taxonomy-specific capabilities. The following are the core technical features required:

- **Delegated Administration and Collaboration**—In large enterprises, it would be unlikely and unwise for a single individual to manage a complete taxonomy design. Instead, different divisions, functions, and geographic locations of an organization should manage separate taxonomies within the complete taxonomy design or even manage different branches or nodes within a single taxonomy. Delegated administration and collaboration functions allow different groups to manage their own taxonomies without enabling edit access and other privileges (i.e., add/delete a synonym, add/delete a node, etc.) to the taxonomies of other organizations.

- **Support for SKOS and Other Standards**—The field of taxonomy design has evolved to include key standards for interoperability, including SKOS, a format that captures individual taxonomy elements, and Resource Description Framework (RDF) which is designed to simplify the exchange of information across different repositories and systems, including the Internet as a whole. Specifically, **Simple Knowledge Organization System (SKOS)** is a W3C recommended standard for representing knowledge organization systems such as thesauri, classification schemes, subject heading systems, and taxonomies in a machine-readable format that can then be exchanged between computer applications and published on the Web. Technologies with RDF capabilities can ingest existing, curated, public lists of information to extend its taxonomy designs.
- **Synonyms and Polyhierarchies**—Managing enterprise taxonomies is never a one-time effort. As synonyms and other relationships are added, it becomes essential to implement solutions that can effectively govern and manage the entire taxonomy design, with all of its nuance and complexity. Synonyms enhance context and help tune auto-tagging capabilities offered by systems; polyhierarchy is when one term possesses two or more parents within a taxonomy. Synonyms, fuzzy synonyms, acronyms, and polyhierarchies are all common in large and complex enterprises.
- **Multilingual Capabilities**—Organizations that operate in more than one language require a taxonomy design that supports each language. Unfortunately, the strategy of simply translating each term in a taxonomy may not accommodate all words in all languages. Solutions with built-in capabilities to handle semantics in various languages, with embedded generative AI capabilities, can help map multilingual taxonomies and manage this particular challenge.
- **Application Program Interfaces (APIs)**—A taxonomy management needs to not only manage the taxonomy design but syndicates this design to all repositories of knowledge assets through APIs. This means that if a modification is made to a taxonomy design within a shared model, the modification will proliferate in all connected systems. APIs also play a major role in auto-tagging content.
- **Consistent Application of Taxonomy (Auto-Tagging)**—Another critical role of a taxonomy management solution is the automated application of the standardized terms or controlled vocabularies through auto-tagging. In earlier decades, organizations seeking to apply metadata to their content were left with an unenviable choice: time-intensive human tagging efforts, highly unreliable auto-tagging, or leaving content untagged. Even when an organization invested in human tagging efforts, the results were rife with inconsistencies given differing definitions and assumptions. In the last several years, accuracy has improved in auto-tagging capabilities, making the feature now highly trustworthy and compelling for organizations (Salminen et al. 2019). The potential value is significant.

Taxonomy Implementation within a Semantic Layer

Like a business glossary, a taxonomy establishes a common vocabulary that bridges the gap between technical data and business users. Taxonomies play a critical role as part of the semantic data model by providing structure, organizing data hierarchically and in a consistent and meaningful way that reflects the way business users think. By defining clear hierarchies and classifications related to your use case, a well-structured taxonomy can support metadata in enabling the capture of unstructured and semi-structured data.

If your use case involves content tagging, faceted search, basic reporting or analytic features, and navigation functions, you will want to consider incorporating a taxonomy into your semantic layer data model. These use cases are typically applied to content management repositories such as intranets, learning portals, or other front-facing interfaces like retail websites. Advanced taxonomy use cases can also include text parsing, automated classification, predictive analytics, insight inference, chatbots, and recommendation engines. In these cases, taxonomies are primarily utilized by machine learning processes and are therefore extremely encompassing, including polyhierarchies and other semantic relationships that complicate their usability in other scenarios. A well-designed taxonomy not only helps with data classification but also enhances the usability of business and operations tools by enabling quick, meaningful, and intuitive interactions.

Define Core Concepts, Categories, and Source Data

When designing a taxonomy, the first step is to define the concepts and hierarchies that will structure your content and data. Taxonomies are essentially classifications of terms or concepts into a hierarchical structure or categories that reflect the relationships between them. For example, in the previous retailer use case, the hierarchy or classification might start with broad categories like "Store Operations," "Sales Performance," and "Employee Metrics," which are then further broken down into more specific subcategories such as "Revenue by Region," "Sales by Product Category," and "Employee Headcount by Store." This clear categorization helps ensure consistency in how data is organized and ensures that metrics like "revenue" or "store performance" are uniformly defined across the organization. These categories should be intuitive and designed with your business in mind to ensure that data can be easily navigated and understood, ultimately reducing discrepancies and improving usability and efficiency.

Once the concepts and categories are defined, the next step is to categorize terms within the taxonomy. It's important to ensure that terms are consistent, well-defined, and mapped to business objectives. Categories should be structured in a way that aligns with organizational functions or use case needs. A key best practice is to avoid ambiguity in terms. This doesn't necessarily mean each term should have a single meaning, rather, the definitions for multi-meaning concepts or terms should be managed by respective functions and domains within context. For example, large organizations often have multiple definitions of a term like "customer," depending on the business context. A best practice is to anchor definitions contextually (for instance, distinguishing between how "customer" is defined in marketing versus sales) and manage these through a well-maintained business glossary. The use of controlled vocabularies further supports this effort by enforcing consistent terminology, avoiding duplication, and reducing the risk of conflicting definitions across systems and teams.

In organizations with existing or mature taxonomy environments, the goal should be to formalize and enrich existing reference data rather than starting from scratch. This may involve refining and optimizing the current model: overly broad categories might need to be broken down into more specific subcategories, while redundant or overly narrow terms can be merged or aligned with broader concepts to improve clarity, usability, and governance. Figure 2.11 illustrates how to assess and adapt existing information models based on their current state and maturity.

The task of organizing all of the business processes and terms related to a business unit or use case can seem daunting. Business taxonomies are not necessarily straightforward to design, as one user may see one concept as separate and not as part of another. This is why it is critical to have a taxonomist on your team who has experience thinking about how to organize knowledge and understands Simple Knowledge Organization Systems (SKOS). Once a conceptual taxonomy model has been outlined, real business users can then interact and experiment with the concepts, running test tagging and sorting activities to ensure that the taxonomy is actually usable and intuitive.

Taxonomy Application and Integration

When building a taxonomy, you want the value of the model to extend across the organization, rather than being confined to a static spreadsheet or siloed within a single program. To achieve this overarching goal, the taxonomy must be integrated

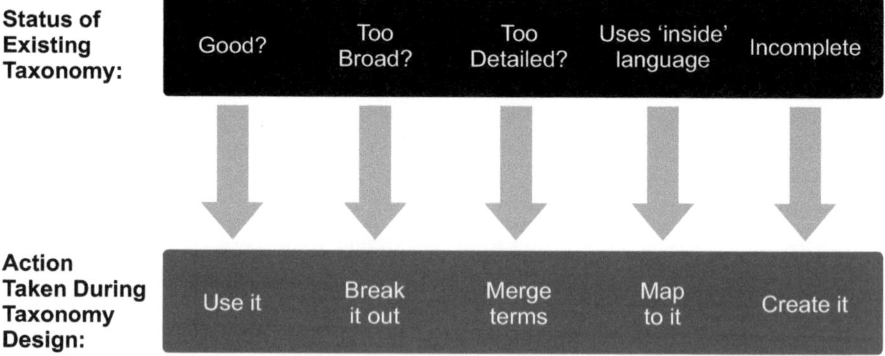

Fig. 2.11 Common modeling decisions

consistently into knowledge assets through methods such as auto-tagging and supported by an appropriate technical architecture.

Based on your use cases and technical infrastructure of your organization, you can choose to implement the taxonomy directly within a knowledge asset repository (such as a CMS or DMS) or use a dedicated taxonomy management tool that connects to multiple systems via APIs. The best approach depends on the complexity of the taxonomy, the number of use cases, and the systems involved. Equally important is weaving the taxonomy into the everyday workflows of different departments, including content creation, customer relationship management (CRM), and data analytics.

Effective taxonomy management solutions (TMS) are crucial for integrating and handling large and complex taxonomies across an enterprise. TMS enables centralized control over the taxonomy, offering features like version control, metadata enrichment, and collaborative tagging. Taxonomy management tools also play a critical role in ensuring that taxonomies remain up to date as your business evolves. With integrated version control and audit trails, TMS allows teams to track changes to the taxonomy over time, ensuring that modifications are made in a controlled manner and that historical changes are documented for transparency. Additionally, most TMS platforms come with workflow management capabilities, allowing for structured review and approval processes when changes are made. This level of governance helps mitigate risks associated with misclassification and ensures alignment with the organization's overarching objectives.

When it comes to the consistent and scalable application of taxonomy, many organizations today turn to auto-tagging solutions. These solutions span a spectrum of customizability, allowing businesses to select the best fit for their needs. On one end, there are ready-made auto-tagging solutions (typically embedded within TMS) and offer quick setup, user-friendly features, and low-code or no-code interfaces, making them ideal for standard use cases. On the opposite end, custom AI-powered auto-tagging solutions are tailored to a business's specific data, addressing more specialized tagging needs. While these solutions still require human validation and oversight, they provide high levels of customization, greater accuracy for particular data types, and full transparency into the model's design and performance (EK Team 2025).

A well-designed taxonomy design, a complete architecture, and quality content can result in auto-tagging accuracy of up to and beyond 80–90%, meaning nine out of ten tags are deemed "correct" by a human expert (EK Team 2021). This increased reliability creates a realistic situation in which millions of documents of different types and sizes can be auto-tagged with humans overseeing and quality controlling only critical or high-value content, minimizing the previous cost and human effort of metadata initiatives. Auto-tagging becomes even more reasonable and accurate when it is used during the content creation or uploading process, wherein a TMS, complemented by LLMs, NER, or hybrid, analyzes the content and recommends tags for the content owner or uploader to immediately review, edit, and amend. In both cases, these auto-tagging solutions (including the TMS) leverage APIs to connect to the asset repositories, inspect the content, and then populate the appropriate metadata fields in the repository with the recommended taxonomy terms.

In addition to knowledge assets and consuming applications, integrating the taxonomy with metadata systems further enriches the overall management strategy. The integration of taxonomies with other semantic organizational frameworks, such as ontologies, business glossaries, and metadata, is essential for creating a unified and coherent ecosystem. Taxonomies often serve as the backbone of ontologies, which are more complex, formalized structures that define relationships between different concepts. By linking taxonomy to ontology, you can create richer, more meaningful connections between terms, enabling semantic interoperability across various systems. Similarly, aligning the taxonomy with the business glossary ensures that business terms are consistently defined and understood across the organization. This reduces ambiguity and helps establish a common language between business and technical teams.

Taxonomy Governance and Best Practices

Taxonomy governance is essential for ensuring that the taxonomy remains consistent, scalable, and aligned with the organization. The governance model should establish clear roles and responsibilities for taxonomy management, including who is responsible for adding, modifying, or deprecating terms. A strong governance framework also includes review cycles to assess the relevance of taxonomy categories and terms, ensuring they reflect evolving business needs and market conditions. For effective governance, you should consider integrating the taxonomy management system with data governance processes, particularly in terms of data quality, compliance, and security. This helps prevent issues like the misapplication of terms or the use of outdated categories, which can undermine the accuracy and reliability of the model.

Best practices in taxonomy governance include adopting a collaborative approach to taxonomy development, ensuring that both business and technical teams contribute to its design and ongoing maintenance. Regular training and communication are also critical, as employees at all levels need to understand the taxonomy's structure, the meaning of terms, and how they should be used. Additionally, establishing a taxonomy stewardship program, where designated individuals or teams are responsible for overseeing and maintaining the taxonomy, ensures ongoing alignment with organizational goals and keeps the taxonomy flexible enough to adapt to new needs, tools, or business processes. Finally, as with all content and data-related initiatives, continuous monitoring of metrics and feedback loops from end users will help you identify areas for improvement and ensure that the taxonomy remains a valuable resource for the organization.

Ontology

Ontologies are a structured framework that define and relate knowledge concepts. Unlike taxonomies, ontologies do not express hierarchical relationships but rather *all* of the existing relationships between concepts. Ontologies define the structure for future knowledge graphs and provide a foundation for improving reasoning and decision-making processes, enabling explainable AI. Ontologies can be thought of as a structure-defining component of the semantic layer, providing guidance on how graph databases are designed (similar to the way that entity relationship diagrams help define the structure of relational databases) and working in concert with taxonomies to define, categorize, and structure knowledge assets across an enterprise.

Like taxonomy, ontology began as a philosophical concept, originating from the Greek words *ontos* (being) and *logos* (study). *The Categories*, one of the first recognized uses of ontology, is a work by Aristotle that describes every possible thing as either the subject or the predicate of a proposition. Ontologies remain a critical component of modern philosophy.

Ontologies were first used in computer science in the 1950s. Early efforts at building artificial intelligence relied on ontologies as a structure to represent the knowledge that would drive AI applications. By the 1980s, ontologies were formalized as the knowledge representation for AI. The Cyc project, which began in 1984, is a long-term artificial intelligence project, aiming to assemble an ontology that captures the rules and concepts dictating how the world works.

Tim Berners-Lee championed ontologies as a critical component for the Semantic Web in the late 1990s (Berners-Lee et al. 2001). He correctly envisioned that ontologies could serve as the translation layer that would enable machines to understand and process web content, and his early efforts led to the creation of standards such as RDF and OWL (Weinberger 2009). These important standards have continued to mature and are now critical enablers of the semantic layer and its ability to communicate both business users and machines.

Today, ontologies are used to enable knowledge graphs, data integration, and AI/machine learning:

- **Knowledge Graphs**—Knowledge graphs are instantiated ontologies, meaning that they take an ontology and embed knowledge assets into its structure. Google popularized the use of knowledge graphs with the introduction of their knowledge panels (Sullivan 2020). Knowledge panels aggregate information about a person, place, or thing from massive datasets into a single, consolidated view of that entity. These knowledge panels are now used by every major information supplier, including Amazon, Facebook, and LinkedIn. Ontologies aggregate the information presented in knowledge panels and graphs through their structure, which defines the relationship between domains of information and associates information with other relevant information.
- **Data Integration**—Domain-specific ontologies are being developed in nearly every major industry to standardize terminologies and to enable data interoperability. These domain ontologies serve as a map, identifying how diverse information assets relate to each other, ultimately helping to align datasets that have differing information structures. Organizations employ these domain-specific ontologies across their data lakes to relate and combine data not just for end users but also in a machine-readable way so that ETL processes can manage and integrate data in a consistent fashion.

- **Machine Learning**—Ontologies can be manipulated to enhance machine learning and AI concepts, and they are gaining traction within generative AI initiatives. **Retrieval-augmented generation (RAG)** describes an organization querying their own repositories for information and then sending the most relevant documents to an LLM for processing. This approach allows organizations to prioritize information specific to their business while taking advantage of the vast knowledge gathered by the LLMs. Originally, search and vector technologies facilitated RAG, but tech-savvy organizations now implement Graph RAG, where a graph handles this internal retrieval, minimizing hallucinations (Barry et al. 2025).

The Value of Ontologies

Ontology serves organizations by creating a shared, formal map of their domain knowledge, fostering a common understanding of knowledge assets (content, people, data, processes, etc.) and their relationships. This structured framework eliminates ambiguity, enabling a standardized aggregation of assets across. New purposes for ontologies continue to arise. For example, we have seen ontologies wielded as aggregators for the modern knowledge portal and exercised as a tool for proving standardized data schemas as a product for inter-industry data exchanges.

The most common uses for an ontology today include:

- **A 360-View of Organizational Entities**—Ontologies define key business concepts and their relationships, so organizational teams, departments, and systems use shared definitions. Ontology used within enterprise applications today such as knowledge/data portals today defines the important entities of an organization (for example, a manufacturing organization's entities may be products, factories, parts, people, partners, and customers) and provides a structure that illuminates how these entities are related to the organization's knowledge assets. Entities are then mapped to their associated knowledge assets, exhibiting to the viewer a complete picture of any given entity. This approach automates the assignment of information: entity extraction tools associate documents and information automatically with an entity, eliminating the need for someone to continuously curate the portal and its links. Additionally, no department biases exist because each individual user can view whichever entities are relevant to their work. The best way to envision the function of the modern knowledge portal is like that of the Google knowledge panel which provides users with relevant information about whatever it is that they have searched for, and further reading is available in just a click.
- **Improve Data Management and Aggregation**—Organizations are also employing ontologies to standardize the integration of information assets. The financial services and pharmaceutical industries, for example, are working to develop industry standard ontologies that simplify the sharing of information between organizations. Financial Industry Business Ontology (FIBO) was devel-

oped by the EDM Council, a trade organization focused on elevating data management and analytics in business ("FIBO GitHub Space" n.d.). FIBO is the most comprehensive ontology for the financial industry, covering concepts such as:

- **Legal Entities**—Models how entities are owned, their hierarchical structure, and the relationships between them.
- **Business Entities**—Shows how different parties participate in financial transactions and includes financial institutions and counterparties.
- **Financial Instruments**—Identifies the most common financial instruments, such as securities, loans, bonds, and derivatives to provide an understanding of their characteristics and how they work in context.
- **Market Data**—Provides definitions of common market data such as pricing and economic indicators.
- **Compliance Requirements**—Structures data to align with regulatory reporting requirements and standardizes common risk factors.

Benefits of FIBO include faster regulatory reporting and standardized modeling of financial data and information. Because FIBO provides consistency to data formatting, organizations that adopt the ontology can simplify data sharing within their enterprise, share information with other financial institutions or regulators, and implement software products that support the FIBO ontology. Additionally, the Global Legal Entity Identifier Foundation (GLEIF) was created after the 2009 crisis to support the global Legal Entity Identifier (LEI) system to address regulators' inability to identify parties in cross-market financial transactions (GLEIF 2025).

- Ontologies are also common in the pharmaceutical and life sciences industries. These industries benefit greatly from standard structures that simplify the sharing of information about drugs and research efforts. The Drug Ontology (DrOn) is a great example of this. DrOn classifies drugs based on their ingredients, mechanisms of action, relationships with other products, and by whom they are produced. The standards provided by DrOn allow researchers, healthcare systems, and regulatory agencies to analyze relationships between drugs (and their ingredients) for adverse events, allow healthcare professionals to cross-reference different drug products, and enable large scale drug research activities. This standardization of information allows for collaboration across all of the entities involved in life sciences in a way that would not be possible without ontologies (Fig. 2.12).

- **Map for AI and ML**—Ontologies are increasingly being adopted to power AI and ML by providing a structured, transparent framework for understanding and reasoning. They enable explainable AI by making AI decision-making traceable which is vital for the adoption of AI across many organizations and industries. This enrichment of data with context and relationships through ontologies also improves model accuracy and relevance. Moreover, as of this writing, ontologies are beginning to guide autonomous AI agents, offering them a clear map of business processes to ensure their actions remain consistent with organizational goals and rules.

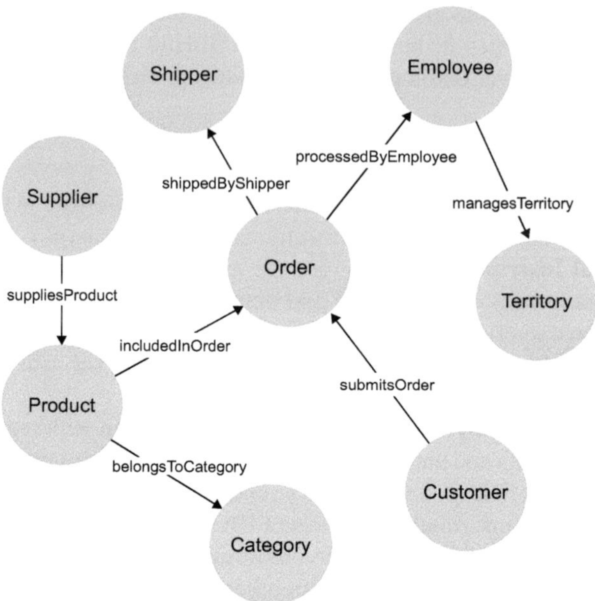

Fig. 2.12 Ontology

Its Role in the Semantic Layer

One of the core purposes of an ontology is to provide the structure for a semantic layer by providing explicit *relationships*. But the ontology's value exists beyond this simple function, too. When most people think of database structures, they think of entity relationship diagrams (ERDs). ERDs are used in relational databases to define the structure of, and relationships between, data tables. In the case of an ERD, the purpose of the structure is to maximize the capture and performance of data when it is queried and reported on.

When designing a semantic layer, developing the ontology is another great place to begin. The process of designing the ontology provides significant benefits that will guide the overall design of the semantic layer, including:

- **Aligning Business Concepts**—Ontologies are made up of nodes (things) and edges (relationships). Identifying the most important "things" within an organization and the relationships between those things is a great way to align business users with the data they are looking for. Much like what emerges when a business team gets in a room and sketches how their world works on a whiteboard or a mind map, that kind of exercise of drawing entities, processes, and relationships in a diagram is essentially a tacit knowledge modeling activity. It is informal, intuitive, and human-centered. Ontologies take that same process and formalize it in a machine-readable, logic-based structure. For example, within a manufacturing company, those things might be the products, parts, suppliers, and customers. Meanwhile, an investment bank's "things" may be deals, investments, companies, investors, funds, and employees. Businesses and their users can and should collaborate to define the nodes of their ontology and their natural interactions, agreeing upon what "things," or soon to be defined, structural categories, are important to their work and existing knowledge assets. This work simplifies the rest of the mapping process.

- **Translating Natural Data Structures**—Once the basic ontology is in place, existing data can be categorized by the resulting salient and agreed-upon categories so that users have a view of the data not in its native structure, but rather in a way that aligns with how they naturally think about their work. In this way, the ontology functions like a picture on a puzzle box: you can visualize the full puzzle and can use it as a reference to put the puzzle pieces (or in this case, information assets) together. The instantiated ontology, which has been populated with real enterprise data, comprises a knowledge graph. This knowledge graph serves as an automated translation layer between the business view of information and the native information stores. This translation layer can be used to dynamically generate visuals of information or as a rule engine for ETL processes to pre-process data in a consistent fashion. It is also one of the biggest reasons that organizations are implementing a semantic layer approach to their enterprise information. What previously existed only in the heads of data developers and data scientists now exists for all business users, democratizing and delivering information access within an enterprise.

- **Enabling Inference**—Another advanced application of ontology within the semantic layer is allowing humans and systems to derive new knowledge from existing data based on defined relationships and rules. For example, the most common use case for ontology within the pharma space is if the ontology defines that all "Clinical Trials" must have a "Principal Investigator," and a dataset links a specific person to a trial. Then, an inference engine can deduce that the person is a Principal Investigator, even if that label isn't explicitly stated in the data.

- **Providing Semantic Layer Scope**—The final benefit of an ontology as part of a semantic layer is that it can be used to control scope. Defining a semantic layer that maps information assets across an entire enterprise is a massive and arguably indefinite undertaking. The ontology can identify only the most important mappings and requires discussions about and agreement on the scope of the semantic layer implementation. The best semantic layer projects are implemented incrementally, and ontology makes this incremental progress possible, allowing both business and technical teams to keep tabs on what is currently usable and what still needs to be completed, all in their own business terms.

To summarize, ontology is not a tool or product; there are, however, products that enable their design. Ontology functions as the structure of the semantic layer, its design and capture of relevant business concepts later allowing for the mapping of an organization's data onto those business concepts. The power of ontology is in its individualized, language-based approach, which delivers alignment across their organization and transforms information into usable knowledge.

Supporting Technologies

The standards developed to support Tim Berners-Lee's vision of the Semantic Web greatly simplified the development and management of ontologies in the 1990s. These standards (RDF, OWL, SHACL, and SPARQL) endure today as integral to the success of an ontology.

Resource Description Framework (RDF) is a standard model for interoperable XML data exchange on the Web, organizing data structures logically to capture the representation, access, constraints, and relationships of objects in a given domain. Specifically, it represents data in an ontology in triples. A **triple** is defined as the subject, predicate, and object. For example, Subject: Cow, Predicate: Jumps, Object: Moon is the triple of a children's nursery rhyme. Many tools used to model ontologies, including graph databases, store information within the RDF structure. This consistent structure enables data interoperability and allows for the existence of OWL and SPARQL (Fig. 2.13).

OWL or, the W3C Web Ontology Language (OWL), is a Semantic Web language designed to represent knowledge. It is built on top of RDF, facilitating more complex modeling. Unlike RDF, OWL supports class hierarchies and properties within its structure. Classes refer to concepts or categories, and hierarchies define the relationships between classes. A golden retriever is a dog (class), and a dog is a mammal (class). Like in taxonomy, the class inherits the properties of its parent class within the hierarchy: a golden retriever is both a dog and a mammal. This hierarchical structure provides valuable information about how concepts relate to one another. Properties are descriptive metadata that extend or differentiate the instances of a class. The color of the golden retriever is an example of a differentiating and descriptive property. These and other features of OWL extend the capabilities of RDF so that RDF-based solutions can more accurately model information assets.

SPARQL (pronounced "sparkle") is a W3C semantic query language that is used to retrieve and manipulate data stored in RDF format. SPARQL, which is analogous to structured query language (SQL) in the database world, queries triple stores. While RDF and OWL provide a mechanism to store and structure information, SPARQL makes that information accessible through a standard query language. SPARQL reveals the real value of creating ontologies and storing them in RDF format. Industry ontologies can be implemented on any RDF compliant platform and queried in a consistent and repeatable fashion by researchers, regulators, and data scientists.

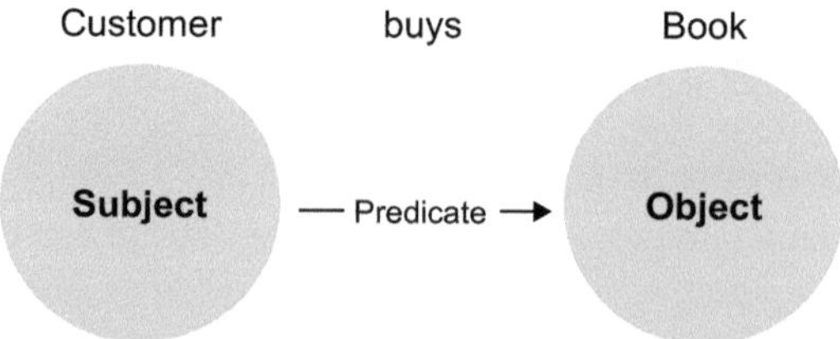

Fig. 2.13 Ontology in RDF

SHACL (Shapes Constraint Language) is a W3C standard for validating and describing the structure of RDF knowledge graphs against a set of conditions (called shapes). SHACL is particularly essential for enforcing consistent data standards as a governance toolkit for semantic models that manage large-scale, complex, and disparate data sources. By enforcing business roles and automated data validation, modeling and documents, SHACL shapes provide and ensure that the data conforms to expected structure, types, cardinality, and relationships.

RDF, OWL, SPARQL, and SHACL are the foundation for many graph databases and taxonomy and ontology management solutions and applications found in the market today. Because these tools are standardized, organizations can invest in them knowing that these standards will protect their investment and increase the interoperability of their data.

Ontology Implementation within a Semantic Layer

To review, ontologies define the relationships between concepts and entities within a business domain, providing more structure to the semantic layer data model. This structure surpasses that of the taxonomy in that it uses business vocabulary and logic to not only capture hierarchical relationships within a business process but also establish rules and visualize *all* relationships between entities. To distinguish between taxonomy, ontology, and business glossary, let's use an event like a conference as an example (Fig. 2.14):

Ontologies are important because they capture business logic and structure data intuitively in a machine-readable format, powering semantic search engines and artificial intelligence functions like text mining and content recommendation. Consider developing an ontology to realize your use case if your use case involves the following goals:

- **Personalization and Related Content Recommendations**—An ontology can map the relationships between similar content and shared attributes (like the topic or author of a document) to support a recommendation engine that surfaces relevant content to users.

Ontology	Taxonomy	Business Glossary
A *"Speaker"* gives a *"Talk"* A *"Talk"* belongs to a *"Session,"* which is part of a *"Track"* A *"Talk"* is about a *"Topic"*	All *"Sessions"* are categorized by *"Topic"* Each *"Session"* falls under a *"Track"*	*"Speaker"* - The person presenting a talk at the event. *"Track"* - A theme or subject area of the event, which sessions are categorized by.

Fig. 2.14 Ontology, taxonomy, and business glossary

- **Semantic Search and RAG**—By applying RDF and storing the ontology in triples, the model can be instantiated with data and traversed via relationships by asking natural language questions. This enables semantic search capabilities, where users can ask questions in plain language, and the system can return contextually relevant results. To put "semantic search" into practice, it is important to ensure that your taxonomy definitions include both "description" and preferred labels or "prefLabel" (validated by SHACL shape rules) and that you run the text of these through embedding models, e.g., in vector stores or vector indexes within graph databases.
- **Data Integration and Interoperability**—Ontologies enable data integration across different systems by defining how data is related across platforms. This is especially useful in industries with complex data environments, like healthcare or financial services, where data is often siloed and requires frequent exchange between applications and organizations.
- **Product Lifecycle Management**—Ontologies help manage and track products and processes through their lifecycle stages, such as design, manufacturing, distribution, evolution, and retirement. In industries like drug development, automotive, aerospace, or consumer goods, where the lifecycle of a product spans multiple departments, suppliers, and systems, an ontology is used to define the relationships between components, processes, and stakeholders.

Types of Ontologies

Before designing an ontology, it is important to first understand the different types of ontologies and the purposes that they each serve. This understanding will allow you to make a decision about which ontology will best support your use case. The key difference between types of ontologies lies in their scope, level of detail, and purpose each serves. Next, we detail the different types of enterprise ontologies and when to use them:

- **Upper Ontology**—Upper, or top-level, ontologies define the most general concepts that apply across various domains and industries. While upper ontologies don't focus on a specific industry, they aim to provide common categories that can be applied universally, creating a shared foundation or vocabulary that can be used across multiple domains to help standardize the different ways these domains understand broad, abstract concepts. For example, "Product," "Customer," and "Transaction" can all be generalized across retail, finance, healthcare, and other industries, through an upper ontology.
  - **When to Use**—Use an upper ontology when you need a broad, overarching framework to unify different systems, departments, or industries. Upper ontologies are especially useful when integrating diverse data sources or working across different business domains.
- **Domain Ontology**—Domain ontologies are more specialized than upper ontologies in that they focus on one specific domain or industry. Domain ontologies

define and relate more detailed concepts within a business sector or functional area, helping to improve the precision and consistency of data within that domain. For example, retail entities such as "Product," "Customer," "Purchase," "Shopping Cart," and "Order" would be mapped on a different ontology than healthcare-specific concepts such as "Patient," "Diagnosis," "Treatment," "Appointment," or "Prescription."

- **When to Use**—Use a domain ontology when focusing on a specific industry or business area. Domain ontologies are ideal for tasks like data integration within a particular field, as it ensures that the data used within that sector is consistent and accurately described.

- **Process Ontology**—Process, or task, ontologies define the steps, actions, processes, or workflows involved in the completion of a specific business task and represent the interactions involved in the task in a formalized way. Process ontologies describe how things happen within a business, sequencing activities to formalize business processes and ensure that tasks are repeatable and reliable. Task ontologies also facilitate the automation of workflows. For example, these ontologies could map the relationships between customer support tasks like "Create Support Ticket," "Assign Agent," "Resolve Issue," and "Close Ticket."

  - **When to Use**—Task ontologies are valuable when a business wishes to improve or optimize its processes, workflows, and task completion. Task ontologies can be used for process automation, system integration, and tracking the performance of tasks or activities within an enterprise.

- **Application Ontology**—Application ontologies describe how specific business concepts are represented and used within software applications or systems. These ontologies provide a way to map the business world onto the digital world, aligning business logic and data requirements with technical architecture. Application ontologies standardize the use of data and allow systems to communicate. For example, within an inventory management system (IMS), application ontologies help define and relate entities such as "Stock Item," "Supplier," "Warehouse," and "Order," within the system.

  - **When to Use**—Application ontologies are useful when integrating business processes into specific software applications, as they ensure that data is represented and used most accurately. Application ontologies are also essential when designing or applying semantics within enterprise software.

- **Event Ontology**—Event ontologies capture and define the occurrence of and relationships between business events and their entities, allowing businesses to track changes and activities over time and the influence that events have on one another. For example, an event ontology could map retail events like "Customer Purchase," "Payment Processed," "Order Shipped," and "Refund Requested."

  - **When to Use**—Event ontologies can monitor, track, and manage events within business operations. This function is especially useful in systems with event-driven architecture or for data analysis that requires an understanding of a sequence of business events.

Now that you have an understanding of the types of ontologies that may be applicable to your project, we will next discuss important ontology design considerations such as using standards, how to define your ontology's entities, classes, and relationships, and finally, the technology necessary to support your ontology.

Start by Reusing Standards and Existing Specifications

As organizations increasingly recognize the value of ontologies and other semantic models, the rapid proliferation of ontologies has often led to their siloed, uncoordinated development. This has created new challenges, such as semantic drift or stovepipes, which can hinder effective data integration and reuse. To counteract this, best practices for ontology development have emerged, offering guidelines that promote consistent, non-redundant models that facilitate cross-system collaboration and ensure semantic clarity. Additionally, leveraging existing industry ontologies provides an excellent foundation for designing and integrating new ontologies, streamlining the development process and enhancing interoperability.

The World Wide Web Consortium (W3C) has sanctioned several languages for ontology development, with the Web Ontology Language (OWL) being one of the most prominent. These standards have fueled the rise of powerful open-source tools for creating and reasoning with ontologies, furthering the adoption of semantic technologies (Fig. 2.15).

Ontology Standards	Ontology Specifications
Ontology Standards are formalized, widely recognized frameworks or guidelines for structuring and defining terms within a domain. These standards ensure consistency in how concepts and relationships are represented across different systems, facilitating interoperability. An ontology standard typically includes: • Formal definitions of concepts. • Relationships between concepts (e.g., hierarchies, part-whole relationships). • Formal rules about how concepts can be combined and linked. **Examples** • **Web Ontology Language (OWL):** A standard for creating and defining ontologies on the web. • **Resource Description Framework Schema (RDFS):** A standard for defining basic relationships and structures within an ontology.	**Ontology Specifications** are documents or sets of rules that specify the practical implementation of ontologies in specific domains or use cases, often leveraging existing ontology standards but providing more targeted, application-specific instructions. Specifications typically define: • How an ontology should be used in practice (e.g., in a specific domain, application, or platform). • APIs, data formats, and other implementation-specific details. **Examples** • **FIBO (Financial Industry Business Ontology):** A practical guide for using ontology standards (like OWL/RDF) to model and represent financial industry concepts, and how they can be applied to financial data and business processes.

Fig. 2.15 Ontology standards and specifications

We recommend starting by leveraging ontology development standards that define the rules and structures for conceptualizing relationships, alongside adopting specifications that guide the practical implementation of ontologies within your domain. There are numerous publicly available starter ontologies and ontology libraries that organizations can use to design domain-specific ontologies. By importing relevant existing ontologies into your design, you create a solid framework to build upon. This approach not only simplifies transferring an ontology between tools (enhancing interoperability), it also allows you to reuse existing models, and ultimately save development time, all while embedding governance through semantic consistency.

For example, an organization in the financial services industry could import the Financial Industry Business Ontology (FIBO), which defines and structures entities found in financial business applications; meanwhile an organization in the veterinary industry could import terms like "Procedures," "Clinical Findings," and "Events" from the Veterinary Extension of SNOMED CT from the Veterinary Terminology Services Laboratory Browser (VTSL Terminology Browser). Another industry-specific model is the Unified Medical Language System (UMLS), which contains biomedical and clinical vocabularies in one web browser interface.

One resource for finding industry or domain-specific models is Linked Open Vocabularies, a collection of open-source vocabularies ("Linked Open Vocabularies" 2025). Implementing these term catalogs or ontology structures ensures that an organization is aligned with its industry before further business specification occurs. Additional, non-industry-specific resources include DBpedia, Wikidata, Friend of a Friends (FOAF), Schema.org, and W3C's OWL and Resource Description Framework Schema (RDFS). Generally speaking, utilizing existing tools is an incredible way to create a deep ontology on a limited budget, and we recommend their use for this reason as well as for reasons of industry alignment.

There are a number of factors that may affect an organization's selection of a particular ontology resource for integration, including the types of features necessitated by a use case, industry standards, and the type of ontology management tool that your organization wishes to use. For example, SKOS supports simple, hierarchical ontologies, much like taxonomies, while OWL and RDF better define relationships between people, places, and things. If the organization's goal is to create an ontology that can express more complex relationships, the organization should use OWL or RDF standards. Before designing an ontology, you should also research and refer to the standard most commonly used in its industry to ease alignment and interoperability, allowing your organization to integrate existing public ontology frameworks. Finally, ontology management tools often already support a specific standard. If your organization has already purchased a tool, you may choose to use the standard supported by that tool to avoid additional costs and the challenge of integrating incompatible systems. The opposite is also true: if your organization has selected a standard for its ontology design, you should purchase a management tool that supports this standard. Often, management tools support more than one standard.

Finally, look for existing taxonomies and glossaries, which are also excellent starting points for ontology development, as they provide foundational structures for organizing terms and concepts within a specific domain. As you start your design process, taxonomy will offer a hierarchical classification of terms, helping to define relationships between concepts, while a business glossary provides clear definitions. You can expand on these resources to formalize into more complex ontologies, serving as a blueprint for capturing deeper relationships and adding richer semantic meaning. Building on existing taxonomies and glossaries, will help you accelerate the ontology development process while maintaining semantic consistency in terminology across systems.

Identify Classes and Concepts

The important components of an ontology design are as follows: classes, concepts, instances, attributes, and relationships. These components help to organize, classify, and define data in a meaningful way, resulting in the structure or model of the ontology, which is later instantiated with data instances. We will discuss the process of instantiation in the next section on knowledge graphs (Fig. 2.16).

Classes	Instances
Classes, also known as concepts, are abstract categories that contain similar entities based on definitions. Entities are deemed similar based on shared characteristics. Classes organize knowledge in an ontology and can be used across contexts, providing a reusable structure. For example, a consulting company's ontology classes might include Consultant, Service, Expertise, Client.	**Instances** are the specific occurrences, individual items or real-world objects, of a class. Instances populate the ontology as concrete data to be manipulated and queried. For example, if Consultant is a class in our consultancy's ontology, then individual consultants like authors Joe Hilger, Lulit Tesfaye, and Zach Wahl will be underlying data instances.
Attributes	**Relationships**
Attributes, properties and characteristics, represent the specific features of a class or instance. Attributes describe the qualities associated with an entity or define and differentiate instances of a class, allowing more precise identification and understanding of these categories. For example, attributes on the Consultant class in our sample ontology might include: • **Expertise Area:** "Semantic Modeling" • **Location:** "Arlington, VA" • **Phone Number:** "(555)-666-7777"	**Relationships**, or predicates, explicitly define how classes or instances are connected to and interact with one another to machines the way humans see the world. A predicate is a grammatical clause that contains a verb and refers to the subject. The triple statement – subject, predicate, object – provides the structure of the ontology, connecting data points with semantic meaning. For example, relationships might appear as: • Consultant "*is expert* in" topic. • Service "*requires*" expertise. • Client "*receives*" service.

Fig. 2.16 Classes, instances, attributes, and relationships

When designing a new ontology, the differences between class and instance can be tricky to define, especially if an organization is building off of an existing taxonomy or glossary. In many cases, the highest classes in a well-constructed taxonomy can be repurposed as the classes of an ontology: organizations can transition taxonomy metadata fields like "Content Type," "Role," and "Department" into ontological classes, making narrower terms like "Project Report," "Ontologist," and "Knowledge and Data Engineering" into instances of those classes, respectively. Before attempting this, it is important to understand which of your taxonomy terms are candidates for ontology classes, subclasses, or instances. A good rule of thumb is to organize terms as types of things versus individual things. For example, a quarterly report is a type of report. Therefore, "Quarterly Report" is a subclass of "Report"; meanwhile, the "2020 Q3 Quarterly Report" is an instance of the "Quarterly Report" subclass. These distinctions are important to the organizational success of your ontology.

OWL and RDFS provide useful axioms that allow ontologists to express relationships in a way that machines/applications can infer from the model:

- **rdfs:subClassOf**—This axiom defines a class as a child class of another, inferring the subclass's inheritance of class properties.
- **owl:equivalentClass**—This axiom indicates that a class is equivalent to another, stipulating that the instances within the two classes are the same. This is not the same as saying that a class is owl:sameAs another class, meaning that they have the same intensional meaning.
- **owl:disjointWith**—This axiom can restrict classes from containing the same instance as another class, which reduces ambiguity for automatic tagging and recommendation. For example, if we have an ontology with classes "Animal" and "Car," we can disjoint them, preventing the same instance of Jaguar from appearing in both classes.

These axioms ensure that an ontology models classes in an accurate and detailed way, further characterizing their instances and relationships.

Define Attributes and Relationships

Once you have defined the classes and instances that are relevant to your ontology, the next step is to identify the attributes of each class, specifying data types and other constraints. When designing attributes, it is important to ensure that they are relevant, meaningful, and consistent in describing specific classes. Important considerations include:

- **Relevant Characteristics**—Ensure that attributes include those features that are essential to describing each class. For example, "Product" class attributes might include "Price," "Name," "Stock Keeping Unit (SKU)," and "Description."
- **Data Types**—Each attribute must have a data type that specifies the kind of value it can hold. Common data types include: string (e.g., Name, Description),

integer (e.g., Quantity), decimal (e.g., Price), date (e.g., Date of Birth, Order Date), and Boolean, which is simple data type that can only have two possible values: true or false (e.g., IsAvailable or IsActive).

- **Constraints and Validations**—Attribute values should conform to specific rules. For example, a Price attribute should always be a positive number, while an "Order Date" should always be a valid date.
- **Attribute Relationships**—Sometimes, attributes need to be related to other classes. For example, a "Product" might have a "Manufacturer" attribute, which could itself be a class with its own attributes (e.g., "Manufacturer" with attributes like "Name" or "Country)." In this case, the attribute "Manufacturer" refers to another class, not just a simple value.

The next step is to define the relationships between classes. In ontology models, relationships specify the interactions, dependencies, and associations between classes. Relationships are typically directional, one entity relates to another, and may have cardinalities that determine how many entities can be involved, such as "is a," "has part," and "part of." When defining relationships, you should consider:

- **Key Relationships**—How are the entities in the ontology actually related? The fundamental interaction between entities can be represented by a verb or verb phrase, as in the Customer "places" an Order, or a Product "belongs to" a Category. Creating these relationship statements will help you narrow down the specific interaction that is occurring between two entities.
- **Relationship Types**—There are three main relationship types: simple, hierarchical, and causal. Simple relationships are direct associations, such as "Customer places Order." Hierarchical relationships indicate a hierarchy within two entities: "Category contains Product." Finally, causal relationships represent cause and effect. For example, "Product generates Revenue."
- **Directionality**—Most relationships are also directional, which means that one entity acts upon another. In the previous example, where the Customer "places" an Order, the Customer acts upon the Order. To establish directional relationships, **cardinality** must be defined. W3C defines cardinality as describing the "numerical restrictions or relationships an instance of a class can have with other instances through properties, such as the exact number, minimum, or maximum number of values for a property" ("OWL Web Ontology Language" 2004). Common cardinalities include:
  - One-to-One (1:1)—An instance of one class is related to exactly one instance of another class. For example, a Person "has" exactly one Social Security Number.
  - One-to-Many (1:N)—An instance of one class is related to many instances of another class. For example, a Customer "places" many Orders, but each order is placed by only one customer.
  - Many-to-One (N:1)—Many instances of one class are associated with a single instance of another class. For instance, many employees work for one business unit.

– Many-to-Many (N:M)—Instances of one class are associated with many instances of another class, and vice versa. For example, a Student "enrolls in" many Courses, and each Course can have many Students (Fig. 2.17).

Unlike traditional data models, the key differentiator of an ontology-based approach is its ability to relate concepts directly and descriptively. This reduces the need for intermediate or linking tables typically required to model relationships in relational systems using SQL joins (used to combine rows from two or more tables based on a related column between them). By capturing relationships in a more natural, flexible, and semantically rich way, ontologies enable more intuitive data exploration, reasoning, and alignment with real-world business concepts.

Create a Formal Representation

The next step of the ontology design is to formalize this conceptual model into a usable ontology that can be applied to data and content systems by selecting languages like OWL or RDF to represent classes, relationships, and attributes in a

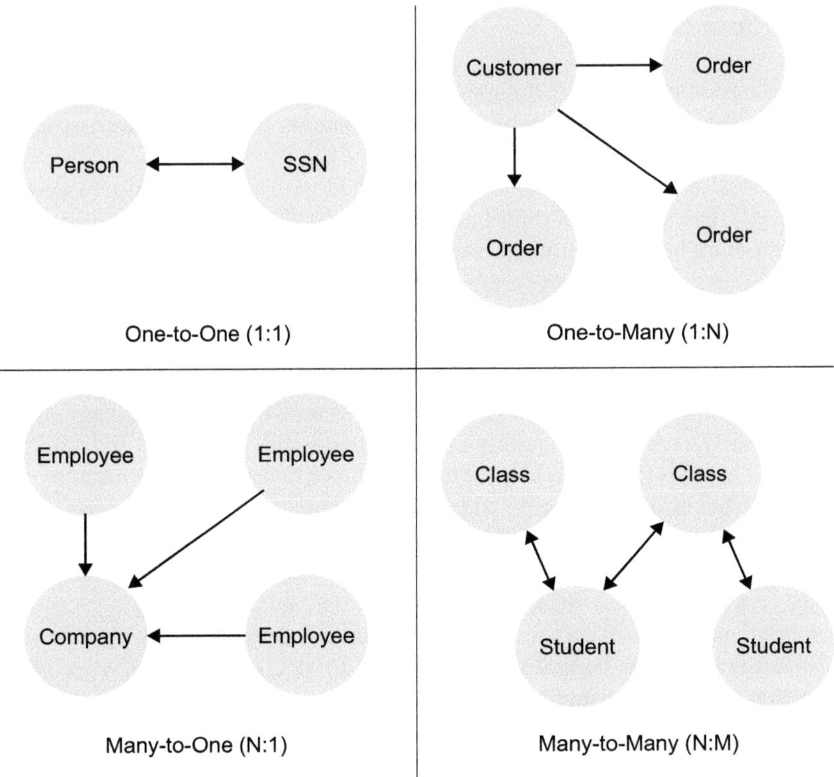

Fig. 2.17 Cardinalities

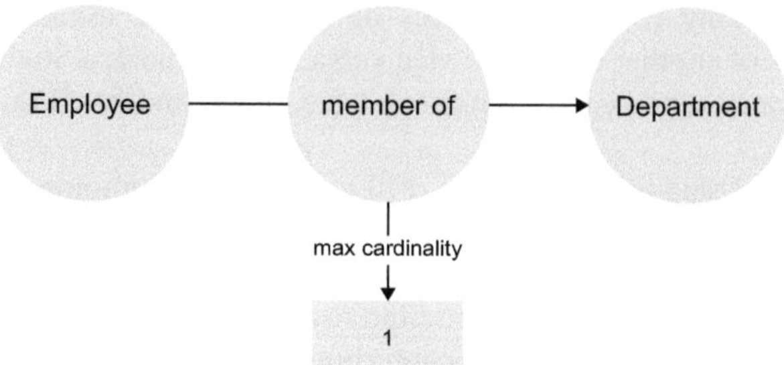

Fig. 2.18 maxCardinality

machine-readable way. Formal ontology languages like OWL represent relationships as object properties, which relate two instances, or data properties, which link an instance to a literal value. We recommend that, when formalizing relationships, cardinality constraints should be represented explicitly. For example, an OWL ontology might use properties like minCardinality, maxCardinality, or cardinality to define how many instances of a related class are permitted (Fig. 2.18).

Publish Your Ontology

The ontology is of no use if it cannot be queried or consumed. There are several ways to make an ontology available for use by ensuring that they are well-structured, validated, and documented.

Once finalized, ontologies should be published with a stable **Uniform Resource Identifier (URI)** and hosted either publicly—via web servers, shared code repositories like GitHub, or ontology registries such as Linked Open Vocabularies (LOV)—or internally within enterprise management platforms (LOV, (n.d.)). Proper metadata, clear documentation, and version management are needed to ensure the ontology is discoverable, maintainable, and usable by both humans and machines.

Once published, an ontology can be queried and integrated into applications through standards. The W3C defines SPARQL as an RDF query language. In other words, SPARQL is a semantic query language that is able to retrieve and manipulate data stored in RDF format. When formalizing an ontology, it is important to ensure that knowledge or data engineers within your organization understand the basics of SPARQL for interacting with and extracting meaningful insights from the ontology. Familiarity with SPARQL enables engineers to formulate and automate complex queries, retrieve specific data points, and manipulate the underlying knowledge graph efficiently. This expertise is crucial for maximizing the utility of the ontology and ensuring that it can be leveraged effectively for decision-making, reporting, and integration with other systems.

Once you have designed and have made the ontology model available for your use case, the next step is to begin mapping data sources onto the ontology, instantiating the ontology using graph technology. Leveraging ontologies to define relationships and connections between your organization's knowledge assets lays the foundation for mapping your knowledge into data and serves as the blueprint for creating a knowledge graph. Next, we discuss the practical steps and best practices for knowledge graph design and implementation to help guide this process.

Ontology Management Technology and Integration

As a standard framework that models real-world business entities and their relationships, an ontology should be treated as an enterprise-wide capability and a shared resource. While you may have started with a small or contained use case, you should have a clear plan for integrating and scaling the ontology across the organization from the start. This ensures that the ontology can deliver its full value as a unified framework for understanding data and processes throughout the enterprise.

Part of your initial design process should be the consideration of an effective ontology management solution that can facilitate enforcement of web standards, track changes, maintain consistency, and support the lifecycle of the ontology. Without a management solution, your organization runs the risk of creating a disconnected, siloed model that becomes difficult to use, particularly as the complexity of your systems and data grows. Scaled ontology management tools are designed to aid in the creation, integration, and governance of ontologies across an organization, helping to connect data, systems, and processes. Using ontology management tools will enable your organization to enforce consistent policies, reduce ambiguity, and ensure that the ontology evolves in alignment with business needs.

Especially today, when AI tools and other advanced technologies are increasingly integrated with business operations, data, and content, ensuring the capability to manage your ontology at scale becomes even more critical. Adopting enterprise-grade ontology solutions and model management platforms enables you to integrate ontologies with enterprise systems, aligning them with key business processes and data sources. This empowers your organization to link and govern both structured and unstructured data efficiently. These solutions also facilitate programmatic integration with other semantic components, particularly knowledge graphs, and enhance metadata management by providing tools for semantic metadata modeling, ensuring that business concepts are consistently defined, connected, and reused.

Knowledge Graph

An enterprise knowledge graph is a machine-readable representation of an organization's knowledge assets that leverages semantic components to describe and relate data. It is, in other words, a metadata, taxonomy, or ontology inscribed with a specific organization's knowledge domain.

Knowledge graphs allow us to model the human understanding of concepts and processes as entities, with connections between entities illuminating their dependencies and relationships to other entities. Organizational knowledge assets are then mapped to the graph as "instances" of entities. This encodes the human understanding of a knowledge domain such that it can be understood by business users and

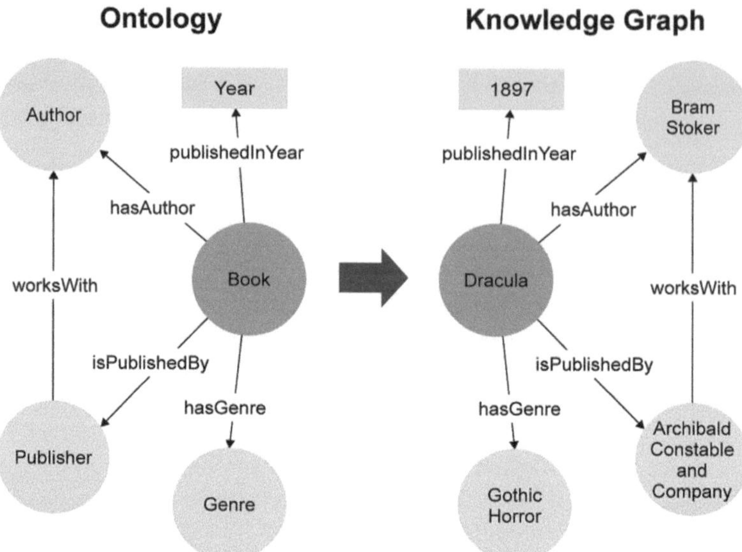

Fig. 2.19 Ontology and knowledge graph

reasoned over by machines. Knowledge graphs are also powerful for mapping content and data sources onto a structure that reveals business meaning to power enterprise search, content recommenders, enterprise AI applications, and more. As depicted in Fig. 2.19, knowledge graphs use other semantic layer components (such as taxonomies, controlled vocabularies, metadata, and ontologies) as foundational building blocks to provide structure, context, and semantic meaning to instantiate the concepts and relationships over underlying data.

The history of knowledge graphs is closely aligned with the history of ontologies. In the 1980s, knowledge graph structures captured domain knowledge in support of expert systems. These expert systems lacked the power or data that are foundational to today's expert systems, but they were a good starting point and a reminder of the importance of structuring data in a knowledge-first format.

Knowledge graphs were next used in Tim Berner's-Lee's Semantic Web (Yu 2024). The vision of creating machine-readable content that was structured in the way we actually think was critical to the rise of the standards that many of the most common knowledge graphs are built upon today, such as OWL and RDF. These standards ensure that non-mainstream technologies like graph databases can be safely adopted by large organizations and that information can be shared between systems. DBPedia, a structured version of Wikipedia, was one of the most well-known knowledge graphs in the early 2000s.

In the early 2010s, Google launched a knowledge graph to enhance its search results (Singhal 2012). The Google knowledge graph linked people, places, and things, displaying these relationships in the right-side panel of their search results. Searchers could now see a consolidated picture of everything that they needed to know about the person, place, or thing that they were searching for. This single, coordinated picture proved much more helpful than the list of links that Google was previously known for. Organizations (and technology solutions) around the world quickly recognized the power of knowledge graphs and began implementing them for a wide range of purposes. Facebook, Amazon, and Microsoft all created knowledge graphs on their primary sites to link people together, improve sales, and make information more accessible.

Today, knowledge graphs power a wide variety of solutions to improve the employee and customer experiences for businesses around the world. In the data space, knowledge graphs are helping data engineers and scientists provide organizational context to structured data and make connections. These knowledge graphs have primary nodes that represent the most important entities of an organization, and the edges capture the relationships between these entities and their associated data elements, which persist in a repository. Once implemented, a knowledge graph serves as a machine-readable map between business concepts and the data that users wish to collect. The graph can explain to users how information should be combined for analysis, and machines can automatically read the graph to aggregate information from multiple, disparate data sources in a consistent and reliable manner. These capabilities solve one of the hardest problems faced by data professionals, one that they have been dealing with for decades: a fully implemented knowledge graph allows business users to ask questions about their business without having to understand how the underlying data is structured.

The Value of Knowledge Graphs

Knowledge graph solutions have gained momentum over the past 5 years because of their ability to enhance information retrieval, data exploration, and the validity of artificial intelligence models, in support of use cases like personalization, fraud detection, predictive analytics, and supply chain optimization. At a summit in March 2025, the global research firm Gartner predicted that knowledge graphs will be integral to the success of AI initiatives, recommending their use in the innovation and implementation of future models (LoDolce 2025). Additionally, they predict that, in 2026, graph technologies will be used in 80% of data and analytics innovations, up from 10% in 2021.

In addition to enhancements in KM, data engineering, and AI, knowledge graph solutions support a wide range of applications across multiple industries:

- **E-Commerce**—E-commerce companies are employing knowledge graphs to link products, user preferences, and browsing history. By understanding user interests and connections, knowledge graphs provide tailored recommendations, personalized content, news feeds, and other online experiences, ultimately improving customer satisfaction and retention and thereby driving sales. Because customer data is typically spread across multiple applications, departments, and even regions with each department and system containing diverse sets of data about their customers, the business user experience is often siloed. A knowledge graph solution allows the organization to create a layer of connection that blankets these disparate systems and departments, facilitating the consistent aggregation and ingestion of diverse information types from sources, internal or external, to the organization's business users. The next, critical step after analyzing and understanding customers through their data is to personalize and recommend content to them. With the size of data and changing consumer preferences, digital personalization has become one of the top priorities of today's business models (Stein et al. 2025). Organizations looking for innovative ways to understand and target online customers, and knowledge graphs provide the solution.

- **Financial Services**—Organizations focused on advanced analytics and business intelligence are leveraging knowledge graphs as the foundation for a data fabric. Like the semantic layer, data fabrics provide a flexible and reusable layer of translation between data and business users, responding to complex queries across disconnected systems to create a unified view of data for analysis and decision-making. Within the financial industry, where operation consists of a network of markets and transitions, a risk issue in one financial institution could have a negative impact on many others. Risk analysis continues to suffer from its inability to scale the understanding of how data is interrelated. Graph solutions enable institutions to model and visualize these connections as a collection of nodes and points, specifying the exact link between financial concepts. Specifically, knowledge graphs excel in detecting fraud by uncovering suspicious patterns and relationships between accounts, transactions, and entities in real time. Regulatory entities of financial institutions are increasing the adoption and use of knowledge graphs to assess creditworthiness, detect fraudulent activities, and evaluate operational risk (Zhang 2024). By linking customer data, transaction histories, and regulatory requirements, knowledge graphs are providing the industry with a comprehensive view of their information, improving decision-making and preventing costly errors.

- **Healthcare and Life Sciences**—Knowledge graphs are revolutionizing how data is used for discovery, patient care, and insight. For example, many organizations within the drug development and patient care spaces are integrating clinical trial data, biomedical research, and real-world evidence to speed up research and drug development. Researchers are leveraging graphs to model complex biological systems, such as the interactions between genes, proteins, and diseases, which helps to identify new drug targets. When applied to patient data and treatment records, knowledge graphs enable more personalized care and deeper insights into disease progression.

- **Manufacturing and Logistics**—Knowledge graphs offer a powerful way to visualize and optimize supply chains. A major challenge across industries is often the lack of standardized vocabulary, leading to inconsistent understanding of key business and supply chain concepts. By mapping the entire supply chain, from suppliers to distribution, knowledge graphs reveal inefficiencies, enhance transparency, and support sustainability goals. Knowledge graphs continue to provide a framework for continuously reconciling and integrating data from diverse sources, enabling interactive queries and providing a graphical representation of supply chain components. This visual and semantic modeling aids in pathfinding and enriches complex ML algorithms, ultimately driving better decision-making.

- **Artificial Intelligence**—With the developments in the AI space, knowledge graphs are gaining more adoption by ML and AI teams to derive new knowledge from existing data and as a framework for understanding how AI models arrive at their decisions, making them more transparent and trustworthy. Techniques like knowledge graph embedding are able to represent knowledge in a way that is suitable for machine learning models, enhancing their reasoning and performance in various tasks.

Its Role in the Semantic Layer

The knowledge graph ties together all disparate asset sources to create a business-centric view of an enterprise's structured and unstructured information. In most cases, it is the instantiation of an ontology, modeling the entities of an organization and how business users think about them. As such, the knowledge graph becomes one of the best ways in which business users can find and interact with their organization's data. Knowledge graphs are typically used in the semantic layer to improve the findability of information assets, model how information should be constructed, understand how it's connected, and serve as a "map" for AI integration.

- **Information Aggregation**—The first, most common way in which knowledge graphs are used as part of the semantic layer is to improve aggregation of assets. The entities of a knowledge graph are the people, places, and things that business users recognize and typically look for. A query or glance at the schema of a knowledge graph can surface aggregated results for these entities with the addition of salient, contextualized, and relevant information. For example, we implemented a knowledge graph for an investment banking organization so that its employees could search for deals made by their organization and retrieve a single search result containing the deal along with relevant information. In this project, the knowledge graph aggregated information from 20 different repositories to create relevant and easy-to-use search results, giving business users a quick and efficient way to find the most important information about a specific deal. Once launched, the graph search became the primary way in which all business users within this organization researched deal information, and the graph was extended to aggregate results about investments, banks, and the employees working on the deal.
- **Understanding Relationships Between Knowledge Assets**—The second most common use for the knowledge graph within a semantic layer is to document the relationships between data in a machine-readable way. Historically, an ERD diagram represented, or a data catalog documented the relationships between datasets in a data lake. Primary and foreign keys related data between tables but contained no usable understanding of the created relationship or of the resulting

meaning of the linked tables. As a result, most organizations were overly reliant on packaged queries, views, or ETL processes created by a single developer. This approach elicits expensive lead times for new data reporting and inconsistent results when developing new reports. Because the knowledge graph identifies and defines relationships between business entities, rules for relating data elements can be stored within the knowledge graph itself so that it is both business user and machine-readable. The impact of machine readability cannot be under-emphasized. Queries and views for your reporting tools can read the graph to automatically create the SQL to display datasets. This can also be done to ETL processes. Once this modern approach is in place, changes to the graph will automatically change the way in which data is aggregated. This ensures that business users get a consistent result each time that organizations are not reliant on a single developer, and that changes can be made quickly in one spot without having to update code in multiple locations.

- **Reporting and Analytics**—Because of their unique structure, knowledge graphs also allow for more advanced reporting and analytics. For example, knowledge graphs enable the quick traversal of information and across a series of relationships, which organizations can use to identify faster methods of getting from one point to another. This function is frequently used to analyze supply chains, identifying faster ways to complete the supply process. Knowledge graphs can also help identify fraud. The nodes and edges of a graph can display the frequency of relationships between entities. Entities with infrequent or unusual relationships in the graph can suggest fraudulent activity. This would not necessarily be clear without a graph-based view. Graphs also excel in their ability to infer. Data scientists employ the graph's power of inference to identify a relationship or important point that was not specified in the original data. For one organization, we used the knowledge graph to develop a recommendation engine that suggested product marketing ideas that combined existing products through inference.
- **Grounding for AI**—Knowledge graphs also drive the way in which the semantic layer improves the efficacy of ML and LLMs. Knowledge graphs provide the context that especially allows GenAI and LLMs to provide the best possible answers. Because graphs capture the entities of an organization and associate these entities with the most important information about an organization, the graph can feed information to the LLM that could not as easily be delivered otherwise. For example, as a consultancy, we developed a knowledge graph that stored information about our clients, the projects we did with them, who was on each project, and what skills were used. We integrated the knowledge graph with its LLM to ask and answer questions about who worked on what projects and in which industries, which would not have been possible without the graph. This ended up being a solution we were able to provide to three of the big-four consultancies. Additionally, a properly integrated graph and LLM solution not only answers questions but also shows the source of its response. This audit trail minimizes hallucinations and builds trust between business users and the tool.

Knowledge graphs play a very important and highly visible role in the semantic layer. As our use of semantic layers continues to grow, we will likely see other important uses for a tool that ties information together across an enterprise so well.

Supporting Technologies

A knowledge graph is most often persisted or stored in a graph database. However, knowledge graphs often require more than just a graph database to function properly. Because we have discussed additionally relevant tools such as business glossaries, metadata, taxonomy, and ontology management systems in the previous sections of this chapter, our description of supporting technologies will focus on graph databases.

There are two main types of graph storage solutions on the market: RDF graph databases and labeled property graph (LPG) databases, simply known as property graphs. While RDF graph databases are based on original RDF standards, property graph databases are a newer custom model that is faster and typically more scalable.

- **RDF Graph Databases**—RDF is the most common database format for knowledge graphs. This is because RDF requires ontologies for design and can administer constraints to ensure that the ontology is followed. Their structure allows for more complex relationships as well as inferencing, which is when a new fact is understood based on the relationship between two other facts, identifying relationships among existing relationships. Inferencing is a powerful tool often encountered in AI programs because of its ability to discern relationships that are not explicitly captured. Finally, because RDF follows W3C standards, interoperability and integration into existing systems are much easier, and there is a wide array of tools that work with RDF graphs.
- **Property Graph Databases**—LPG graph solutions store information as nodes (entities) and edges (relationships). They are not standards based, so integration with other tools in the graph space is more complex. But, LPG databases are more efficient at storing and querying data in that they are significantly faster and are able to handle large datasets through distributed storage and processing. As a result, these databases are typically used for applications that require fast querying and traversal of the graph. Some organizations use LPG databases for their knowledge graphs, which, while more uncommon, typically occurs when the organization already owns licenses to the LPG database or when there is a need to store lost information in the graph rather than reference the information at its source.
- **Graph Query Engines**—It is important to note that the graph database market is continuing to develop, reflecting the growing need for more connected, contextual, and flexible data architectures. One notable trend that is emerging is the shift toward graph query engines rather than tightly coupled graph data storage. While persistent graph databases store data in native graph formats, emerging solutions are increasingly focused on querying graph-like relationships over

existing data sources (without requiring organizations to store or duplicate their data). This trend is being driven by the rise of knowledge graphs and AI applications that require deep contextual understanding but can't afford the complexity or latency of migration.

These trends indicate that the focus is shifting from graph as a storage model to graph as a query and reasoning model, enabling more agile and interoperable architectures that can serve both operational and analytical needs.

Knowledge Graph Implementation within a Semantic Layer

Knowledge graphs leverage semantic components like taxonomies and ontologies to capture relationships, hierarchies, and context in a machine-readable format, providing a foundation for more intelligent data interactions. If your use case requires the capabilities and business needs discussed above, you should consider modeling a knowledge graph within your semantic layer (Fig. 2.20).

Understand Knowledge Graph Types

Before investing in the modeling and implementation of a graph solution, it is important to understand that there is never a single, enterprise graph for an organization. There are typically multiple graphs which have different usage that can be used within an enterprise, the distinct purposes they serve, and the specific business needs that they address. **Metadata graphs**, **knowledge graphs**, and **analytics graphs** are the three most common graph applications ("What are the Different Types of Graphs?" 2025). Collectively, we refer to these graphs as a "**semantic network**," as they all represent interconnected entities and their relationships in semantic context, allowing for richer data interpretation and analysis. Essentially, the semantic network is a web of information where the connections between data

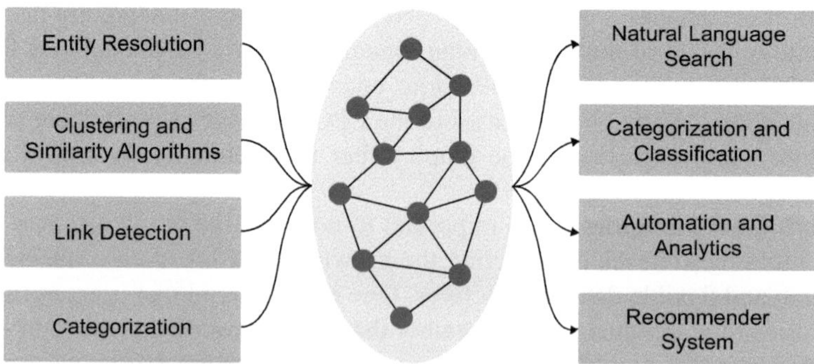

Fig. 2.20 Knowledge graph functions

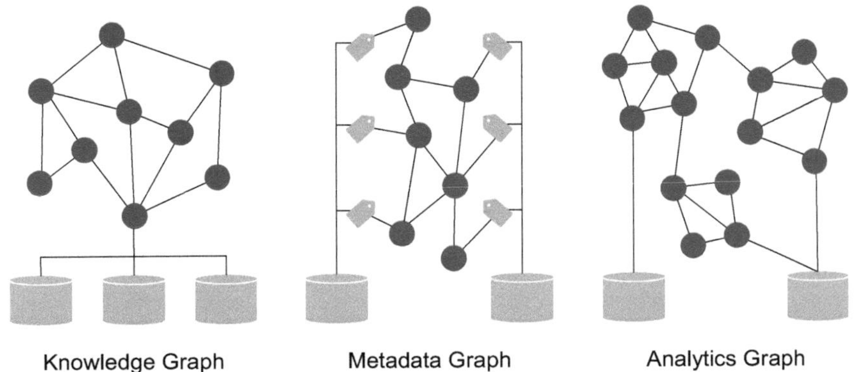

Fig. 2.21 Types of graph

points hold meaning. Next, we explore these three graphs and their respective business uses (Fig. 2.21).

- **Knowledge Graph**—Recall that a knowledge graph is simply an ontology model instantiated with enterprise knowledge assets. Using ontologies and standards like OWL and RDF, knowledge graphs organize and link information based on its business meaning and context, representing entities (people, products, places, things) and the relationships between them in a way that is understandable to both humans and machines. By integrating heterogeneous data from multiple touchpoints and systems into a unified knowledge model, the knowledge graph serves as a semantic abstraction layer over enterprise data.
  - **When to Use**—A knowledge graph is a key solution in enterprise knowledge and data management and is best suited for semantic understanding, contextualization, and insight. Knowledge graphs allow organizations to capture, store, and retrieve tacit and explicit knowledge in a structured way and provide a holistic view of organization-specific domains such as customers, products, services, etc., ultimately supporting customer 360, sales, and marketing efforts. Additionally, enterprise knowledge graphs power AI capabilities such as NLP by providing context-aware knowledge that can be used for machine-specific tasks like entity recognition, question answering, and content and data categorization.
- **Metadata Graph**—Metadata graphs capture the structure and descriptive properties of data by tracking business, technical, and operational metadata attributes, such as process, ownership, security, and privacy information across an organization, providing a unified repository of metadata and a connected view of data assets. Building a metadata graph entails organizing metadata in a graph format to create a structured, interconnected representation of the data assets for your organization. As such, a metadata graph specifically focuses on organizing "data about data" (its structure, properties, and context) to manage and track data assets, providing a unified view of an organization's data landscape for better accessibility, governance, and understanding.

- **When to Use**—A metadata graph is best used for managing and tracking the metadata across an enterprise. It helps ensure that data is properly classified, stored, and governed and is accessible to data users. This approach is particularly valuable for use cases such as data discovery, governance, data cataloging, and lineage tracking, as it enables you to easily trace data flow and improve overall data accessibility and understanding across the organization.

- **Analytics Graph**—Analytics graphs support analytics by connecting and modeling relationships between data entities to uncover insights and identify trends, patterns, and correlations, enabling users to perform sophisticated queries on large, complex datasets with interrelationships that may not be easily captured in traditional tabular models. Analytics graphs are only as valuable as the data they represent. Without a strong understanding of the domain, analytics graphs can misinterpret the meaning of data relationships, leading to misleading or incomplete insights. Moreover, if the analytics team doesn't work closely with SMEs, the graph may not fully capture critical context or domain-specific nuances, reducing the effectiveness of its use.

  - **When to Use:** Analytics graphs support advanced analytics use cases including advanced data exploration, which enables analysts to identify trends, anomalies, and correlations that are not immediately apparent through standard reporting tools, and recommendation systems that require analyzing user behavior, preferences, and interactions. We have seen most success when analytics graphs are implemented to power personalized recommendation engines in domains like e-commerce, media, and content delivery; predictive analytics in manufacturing and engineering; and fraud detection use cases for our financial institution clients.

In many of our enterprise solutions, a combination of these graphs is employed to achieve more comprehensive outcomes. For example, with the financial institution client case study we briefly discussed above, its risk and compliance department is one of the key users of its semantic layer, and a metadata graph is used to track regulatory data and compliance requirements across 20+ systems and 8+ lines of business. Meanwhile, a knowledge graph contextualizes this data by linking it to business operations and transactions. The data and analytics team then utilizes an analytics graph to analyze historical data for potential risks and non-compliance patterns, alerting management to any emerging issues. This integrated approach helps the organization ensure both regulatory compliance and proactive risk management.

Next, we will detail the step-by-step design and implementation of the semantic layer's knowledge graph. While this discussion will focus on the knowledge graph, design elements shared by metadata graphs and analytics graphs will be addressed.

Model Your Knowledge Graph

In the previous subsection, we discussed how to design an enterprise ontology. The goal of the ontology is to structure data in a meaningful way. Without this structure, the knowledge graph is not a graph; it is mere data. Building a sound ontology and taxonomy will provide the basis for implementing advanced applications later on that can query and understand the data, discover explicitly defined facts, and infer and reason about data (Tesfaye 2019).

When designing a knowledge graph, a key consideration is whether to start from scratch, building a custom model that is specifically geared toward a single use case or an organization's domain, or manipulate pre-designed and highly used ontologies to fit the organization's needs. We recommend starting by integrating existing semantic models (taxonomy, ontology, metadata, etc.) as it forms your organization's foundation for creating a knowledge graph. This approach will provide you with the structure and semantics needed to create a rich knowledge graph. As established in the previous section on ontology, we also find that exploring existing, open-source semantic models serve as a low-risk, high-value starting point.

One benefit to this approach is that it ensures data interoperability through the incorporation of W3C standards and alignment of business terms with industry definitions. W3C standards are data description frameworks that provide a formalized set of rules for representing data. This formalization assigns natural language meaning to data, making it both machine and human readable. These standards also provide a proven approach to the management and sharing of data and flexible logic that allows for mapping of knowledge, relationships, and hierarchies. Finally, these standards encompass semantic query language which allows data from natural language and artificial intelligence systems to be accessed and analyzed.

The success of the semantic layer heavily depends on the skills and training of the teams that will be asked to model, implement, and operationalize the solution. It is critical to ensure that the project team tasked with supporting these initiatives understands Semantic Web standards such as RDF, OWL, and SPARQL. This knowledge ensures that the data models will integrate with existing systems, which is optimal for development cycles, minimizing performance issues, and facilitating scalability.

Map, Organize, and Enrich Your Asset Sources

The next step in developing a knowledge graph is to ensure that the knowledge asset sources required of your use case are ready for integration. For data to be instantiated into an ontology, forming a knowledge graph, the data itself must be organized and machine-readable. Unstructured knowledge assets, those in the form of emails, articles, text files, presentations, etc., must be manipulated by taxonomies and metadata to allow for effective classification and categorization, thus facilitating

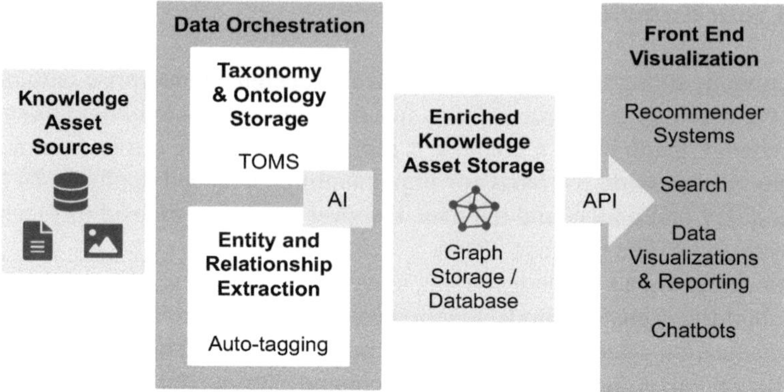

Fig. 2.22 Solutions architecture for scalable knowledge graph

findability and discoverability. Specifically, developing a business taxonomy provides structure to unstructured information and ensures that an organization can effectively capture, manage, and derive meaning from large amounts of content and information.

There are a few approaches to inventorying and organizing enterprise content and data. If you are faced with the challenging task of inventorying millions of content items, consider using tools to automate the process. We recommend conducting a user- or SME-focused design session. This coupled with bottom-up analysis of selected content will help you determine which aspects of content are important to your use case and which are not. Taxonomies and metadata that are most intuitive and close to business process and culture tend to apply more useful terms faster to structured content. Organizing content and data with machine readability in mind will lay the foundation for the semantic model that you are developing to understand and use the organization's vocabulary and start mapping relationships that add context and meaning to disparate data. The goal is to create a knowledge graph schema that offers a rich, structured, and usable representation to your knowledge (Fig. 2.22).

Identify Graph Data Storage and Management Technology

Much akin to the discussion above regarding the need for scaled and standards-based management of other semantic components, graph data requires a fit-for-purpose solution that can handle the complexity, scalability, and interconnectedness of data relationships. This is where graph data storage and management technology (discussed above) play a key role based on its ability to support the specific use cases for your organization. This includes handling complex queries, ensuring data consistency across large datasets, and enabling real-time access to graph data. A key consideration when selecting graph databases is their ability to efficiently model, store, and query interconnected data, as traditional relational databases often fall short in representing complex relationships. When designing and implementing graph solutions, it is also important to understand the differences in capabilities between LPG (Labeled Property Graph) and RDF (Resource Description Framework) graph storage tools.

When it comes to implementing a graph, LPG graphs are ideal for highly connected data that requires fast traversal and flexibility in modeling properties on nodes and relationships. They excel in scenarios like social networks, recommendation engines, or fraud detection, where entities (e.g., users, transactions) and their direct relationships (e.g., friends, purchases) are key to performance.

On the other hand, RDF graphs are more suited for applications that demand rich semantic standards and data interoperability, such as linked data, Semantic Web applications, or enterprise data integration. RDF's standardized structure and the use of SPARQL for querying make it ideal for use cases where data provenance, compliance, and formal reasoning are important, like in healthcare or research data management.

Depending on your organization's core use case, we recommend adopting a hybrid model that combines the strengths of both RDF-based models and LPG graph storage. Use RDF standards and management tools to manage and integrate data models, for ensuring consistency, governance, and semantic interoperability. For analytics at scale, leverage LPG graph storage to take advantage of its performance and flexibility in handling large volumes of data and complex queries. This hybrid approach allows you to optimize both data integration and high-performance analytics based on your needs.

Working collectively, the components of knowledge assets, business glossary, metadata, taxonomy, ontology, and knowledge graphs comprise our semantic layer framework solution. Each offers its own unique value, both to an organization and to the semantic layer, if designed and integrated properly. In Chap. 3, we will cover the key steps and methods necessary to integrate these components into a complete, cohesive, and highly functional semantic layer framework.

References

"Aristotle" *University of California Museum of Paleontology.* https://ucmp.berkeley.edu/history/aristotle.html.

Barry, Mariam, Gaetan Caillaut, Pierre Halftermeyer, Raheel Qader, Mehdi Mouayad, Fabrice Le Deit, Dimitri Cariolaro, and Joseph Gesnouin. "GraphRAG: Leveraging Graph-Based Efficiency to Minimize Hallucinations in LLM-Driven RAG for Finance Data." *Proceedings of the Workshop on Generative AI and Knowledge Graphs (GenAIK)*, 2025: 54–65, Abu Dhabi, UAE. International Committee on Computational Linguistics.

Berners-Lee, Tim, James Hendler, and Ora Lassila. "The Semantic Web," *Scientific American*, May 1, 2001. https://www.scientificamerican.com/article/the-semantic-web/.

EK Team. "System Migration and Enterprise Search Design Powered by Enterprise Taxonomy, Automated Tagging, and Content Governance," *Enterprise Knowledge*, August 10, 2021. https://enterprise-knowledge.com/system-migration-and-enterprise-search-powered-by-taxonomy/.

EK Team. "A Guide to Selecting the Right Auto-Tagging Approach," *Enterprise Knowledge,* January 15, 2025. https://enterprise-knowledge.com/a-guide-to-selecting-the-right-auto-tagging-approach/.

"FIBO GitHub Space", *EDM Council.* https://spec.edmcouncil.org/fibo/.

GLEIF. "10 Years of GLEIF," *GLEIF.* 2025. https://www.gleif.org/en/about/this-is-gleif/gleif-anniversary.

Hilger, Joseph and Zachary Wahl. *Making Knowledge Management Clickable: Knowledge Management Systems Strategy, Design, and Implementation.* Springer, 2022: 93.

Linked Open Vocabularies (LOV), (n.d.). Linked Open Vocabularies. https://lov.linkeddata.es/dataset/lov/.

LoDolce, Matt. "Gartner Data & Analytics Summit 2025 Orlando: Day 3 Highlights," *Gartner.* March 5, 2025. Orlando, Florida.

OWL Web Ontology Language, W3C. February 10, 2004. https://www.w3.org/TR/owl- ref/.

"Semantic Versioning 2.0.0," (n.d.) SemVer. https://semver.org/.

Salminen, Joni, Vignesh Yoganathan, Juan Corporan, Bernard J. Jansen, and Soon-Gyo Jung. "Machine Learning Approach to Auto-Tagging Online Content for Content Marketing Efficiency: A Comparative Analysis between Methods and Content Type." *Journal of Business Research* 101, August 2019: 203–17. https://doi.org/10.1016/j.jbusres.2019.04.018.

Serrat, Olivier. "Notions of Knowledge Management," *Knowledge Solutions.* Springer, 2017. https://doi.org/10.1007/978-981-10-0983-9_30.

Singhal, Amit. "Introducing the Knowledge Graph: Things, Not Strings," *Google.* May 16, 2012. https://blog.google/products/search/introducing-knowledge-graph-things-not/.

Stein, Eli, Kelsey Robinson, Alexis Wolfer, Gaelyn Almeida, and Willow Huang. "Unlocking the Next Frontier of Personalized Marketing," *McKinsey & Company.* January 30, 2025. https://www.mckinsey.com/capabilities/growth-marketing-and-sales/our-insights/unlocking-the-next-frontier-of-personalized-marketing.

Sullivan, Danny. "A Reintroduction to Our Knowledge Graph and Knowledge Panels." *Google.* May 20, 2020. https://blog.google/products/search/about-knowledge-graph-and-knowledge-panels/.

Taylor, Arlene. *The Organization of Information.* Westport, CT: Libraries Unlimited. 2004.

Tesfaye, Lulit. How to Build a Knowledge Graph in Four Steps: The Roadmap From Metadata to AI, Enterprise Knowledge. September 9, 2019. https://enterprise-knowledge.com/how-to-build-a-knowledge-graph-in-four-steps-the-roadmap-from-metadata-to-ai/.

Weinberger, David. "The Dream of the Semantic Web," *KMWorld.* March 1, 2009. https://www.kmworld.com/Articles/ReadArticle.aspx?ArticleID=52764.

Yu, Fanghua. "The Future of Knowledge Graph: Will Structured and Semantic Search Become One?" *Neo4j,* April 25, 2024. https://neo4j.com/blog/developer/knowledge-graph-structured-semantic-search/.

Zhang, Haozhe. "Research on the Application of Knowledge Graphs in Bank Risk Management," *Advances in Economics, Management and Political Sciences.* November 2024: 62–69. https://doi.org/10.54254/2754-1169/2024.17745.

Methodologies for Designing and Integrating the Semantic Layer 3

In this chapter, we take you step-by-step through the efforts necessary to conceive, design, and implement the semantic layer. There is no one way to implement a semantic layer, and we present multiple approaches and design considerations. This chapter will proceed as follows: first, we outline our methodology for the semantic layer's implementation; we detail the important step of defining your organization's vision, goals, and use cases to ensure that a human-centric and value-oriented approach throughout the effort is maintained and that your organization is focused on solving real business problems and not simply implementing "cool" new technology. We also detail methods of assessment that will allow your organization to adjust the scope and feasibility of these goals to your existing technology and current-state knowledge assets. In the next section, we discuss the best practices for the design and modeling of the core semantic layer components. Then, we explore three semantic layer architectures and discuss the engineering required to integrate the semantic layer into your organization's existing infrastructure. Finally, we focus on the need for governance and organizational structure to support the long-term iteration and operation of the framework. In short, this chapter walks through the quintessential steps of strategy, design, implementation, operation, and iteration. After finishing this chapter, our goal is that you feel prepared for large-scale initiatives and have a comprehensive understanding of the considerations of the scope, intricacy, key steps, and activities necessary to design and implement a semantic layer.

Methodology Overview

Our methodology for designing, implementing, and maintaining the semantic layer is grounded in our collective experience across the professional domains of knowledge, information, and data management, application development, and data and AI engineering. Through numerous initiatives, both successful and unsuccessful, we

J. Hilger et al., *Bridging Knowledge, Data, and AI*,
https://doi.org/10.1007/978-3-032-17178-8_3

have learned that building a semantic layer is never an individual endeavor. Instead, it requires a cross-functional task force: a dedicated group within your organization composed of technical teams, knowledge asset wranglers, and subject matter experts (SMEs). This team is essential for leading and coordinating the design, development, implementation, and ongoing governance of the semantic layer. Such a task force will require the expertise and time of various business users and managers throughout the process, especially in the initial assessment and discovery period, but will, at the end of the day, be fully responsible for the semantic layer and the activities detailed in this chapter.

In this chapter and throughout the book, we use the term "stakeholders" to holistically refer to business leaders or end users who will be impacted by the design and implementation of the semantic layer or are needed to influence it by providing domain or technical expertise. These may be technical SMEs who work directly with existing metadata, taxonomy, ontology, or graph systems and functions, or who maintain applications like enterprise intranets and search portals. Meanwhile, "business users" or "end users" are those who rely on accurate, consistent information for decision-making and are directly impacted by the semantic layer's implementation, like data analysts who access data through BI tools, or HR managers who post training material on the intranet.

The implementation team should be a blend of business, data, information science, and technology specialists. At its core, the team should include an implementation lead or project manager, a technical or business analyst, a taxonomist, an ontologist, a semantic or graph data engineer, and one or more data scientists, application developer, and an architect. This cross-functional team is crucial to ensure the integration of complex enterprise systems, provide the required expertise to develop scalable solutions, facilitate alignment of technical build with business and use case objectives, and ensure the successful execution of the project.

Additionally, the term "stakeholders" also defines those people in leadership positions within your organization who will be overseeing the project and from whom you will receive funding for the semantic layer initiative. The reality, one that we find integral to our methodology, is that these initiatives take time, cost money, and require the expertise and effort of real people. Our methodology for implementing a semantic layer encompasses this reality that you will need to prove again and again, at every step, the value of the semantic layer to leadership, to stakeholders who will fund this initiative, with time, resources, staff, and money. Not only do we disclose a step-by-step guide to technically crafting a semantic layer, we also divulge those best practices for this effort that will keep you honest and true to the business reality behind the technology.

When it comes to technical architecture, many of the organizations that we work with support an enterprise architecture that is based on relational databases, data warehouses, or a wide range of content management, cloud, or hybrid cloud applications. These existing applications act to drive knowledge engineering and analytics capabilities, and we believe that it is not necessary for organizations with these existing models to overhaul their entire enterprise architecture to adopt the semantic layer. On the contrary, existing models enhance the capture of business meaning and context with the addition of the semantic layer's components and standards.

With this integration principle in mind, it is important to remember that the semantic layer and its incorporation into existing enterprise architecture is not a theoretical concept; it is a framework that requires finesse, strategy, and real knowledge experts to orchestrate. Over the last 10 years, we have worked with a diverse set of organizations to fine tune the design and implementation of the semantic layer and its components and have identified these five key steps. We note here that, in the beginning, the implementation of the semantic layer is not a one-and-done activity or a single solution that will solve every business problem related to your organization's knowledge assets. Our methodology is centered around the incremental growth of the semantic layer (Fig. 3.1).

1. **Define Vision, Goals, and Use Cases**—The first step in designing and implementing a semantic layer is to define your organization's vision, goals, and use cases. You should have a wide-scale view of the needs of the business and the organization when identifying the ultimate vision or target state for knowledge and data, and then brainstorm small, individual use cases that iteratively fulfill this vision. Use cases identify the individual business problems that the semantic layer will ultimately tackle, providing inspiration for the semantic layer's construction and outlining design requirements. Once you have articulated the collection of business challenges into use cases, your organization will then be able to construct an order for their incremental implementation.

2. **Develop Semantic Data Model**—The second step in designing and implementing a semantic layer is to develop the semantic data model. A **data model** is a formal, visual blueprint that defines and standardizes the structure, relationships, and rules of data within a system, serving as a conceptual representation for organizing and managing information. It outlines what data an organization collects, how it is related, and the methods for storing, accessing, and analyzing it, ensuring data consistency, quality, and efficient management. In this step, your organization will identify the semantic components required to solve the business problem outlined in your initial use case. The semantic data model defines

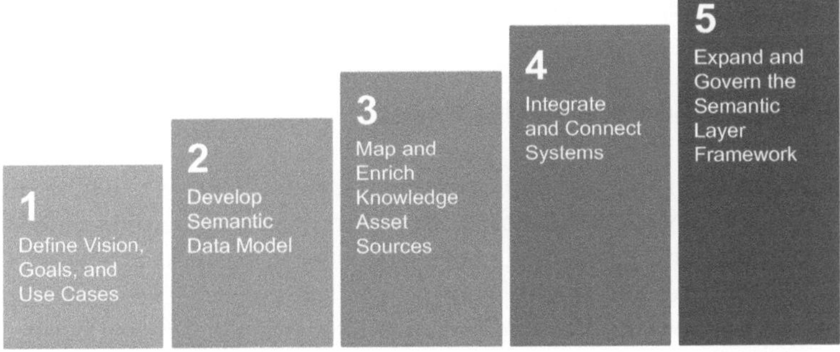

Fig. 3.1 Five key steps to implementing a semantic layer

the core concepts, properties, and relationships of your data using business language and context and links components like the business glossary, metadata, taxonomy, and ontology/knowledge graph to deliver on your organization's use cases and vision. For more detail about modeling specific components, see Chap. 2.

3. **Map and Enrich Knowledge Asset Sources**—The third step in designing and implementing a semantic layer is to map and enrich the organization's data sources. To do this, organizations should define the existing metadata and data sources (structured, semi-structured, and unstructured), that are relevant to the initial use case. Data concepts can then be enriched, tagged, and connected via metadata, taxonomy, and ontology labels. As the semantic layer is developed use case by use case, the data model can slowly expand its coverage to other sources and domains.

4. **Integrate and Connect**—The fourth step in designing and implementing a semantic layer is to integrate and connect the layer with the organization's existing technology. The semantic data model, created in step two, should be incrementally integrated with upstream and downstream applications and treated as a modular component that can be implemented in multiple systems throughout an organization.

5. **Expand and Govern**—The fifth and final step in designing and implementing a semantic layer is to expand and govern the architecture once it is implemented. Governance keeps the semantic layer's knowledge assets, components, terminology, and technology up to date, while expansion allows the semantic layer to solve more business problems. Expansion is based on the incremental use case plan and will recycle steps two, three, and four to enable new capabilities and applications. Global data standards and embedded governance can be leveraged to support expansion and consumption across data assets. We recommend that, as with any large-scale enterprise initiative, organizations adopt an Agile delivery approach for semantic model development, data stewardship, and staff enablement, supported by well-configured governance workflows.

In the next five sections, we explore and expand on each one of these five steps, respectively, explaining why each is critical to building a scalable semantic layer and taking into consideration the fabric of enterprise architecture, processes, and most importantly, people and culture.

Define Vision, Goals, and Use Cases

The first step in designing and implementing a semantic layer is to define your organization's vision, goals, and use cases. To do so, it is necessary to understand the current state of your organization's knowledge assets, business processes, technology and architecture, and finally, your people and culture. This understanding is important because organizational efforts that lack grounding in real business problems cannot deliver real business solutions. In 2024, Gartner predicted that, by

2027, 80% of data and analytics governance initiatives will fail because they do not "prioritize business outcomes" and have no grounding in "real crisis" (Gartner 2024). While Gartner is specifically speaking to governance here, the logic remains pertinent: business solutions that do not come out of real problems will not solve anything, especially in a changing data landscape that has swiftly pivoted toward AI capabilities. To define the goals and projected outcomes of the semantic project and to outline potential use cases, an organization must first assess its current state of knowledge and data maturity. In other words, an organization cannot plan to solve a problem that it doesn't know exists. To effectively articulate key business challenges, develop corresponding use cases, and model the semantic layer, we recommend initially limiting this scope to two or three business units or departments.

In this section, we define three strategies for discovering potential use cases for the semantic layer, assessing your organization's current-state data systems, its existing capabilities, processes, opportunities, strengths, and weaknesses, and validating these findings. The three discovery, assessment, and validation methods are user personas and journey maps, top-down and bottom-up analysis, and conceptual domain modeling. These assessment activities should all focus on the people, processes, knowledge assets, success metrics, and technology within an organization, ensuring that all factors are not only considered in this process, but also that the assessment team has a detailed understanding of the needs and goals of the initial solution focus. Finally, we will discuss additional design considerations that will inform this discovery and planning phase of your semantic layer initiative, including how to imbue your design with key performance indicators and measures of success.

Use Cases, User Personas, and Journey Maps

In addition to solving real business problems, the semantic layer should serve real business users. It is true that the semantic layer can benefit a myriad of business units, applications, and processes, and it is easy to view the semantic layer as a single technology that will solve all of your organization's business problems, but this perspective will ultimately tarnish the functionality of the framework. Instead of biasing a technology-first perspective, the design and implementation of the semantic layer should be user-centric, preferencing those who use the technology over the technology itself. Therefore, the design and implementation of the semantic layer should focus on end users, what they want to accomplish, and what problems they want to see solved, so that they can be more effective at and excited about their work. This user-centric model not only aligns more sustainably with business goals, it also significantly limits the scope of the design and modeling process, ultimately benefitting the functionality and setting the foundation for the adoption of the semantic layer. To craft a user-centric model, we suggest that the semantic layer task force or delivery team develop use cases, user personas, and journey maps to discover the potential avenues for the semantic layer's design.

Use Cases

A **use case** is an outline of an interaction between a hypothetical user and a system, technology, or application (What is a Use Case? n.d.). Use cases allow experts tasked with developing a technology to understand a user's goals and all of the ways in which a user might interact with the technology to achieve these goals, allowing the developers to establish the scope of the technology and the potential errors and inefficiencies a user might experience. With this description in mind, the purpose of a use case is to:

- Establish the scope and necessities of a technology including what it should and should not ultimately accomplish and what is required for its development.
- Identify potential errors, misuse, risks, and inefficiencies within the user-technology interaction.
- Provide a framework that can be used as a point of reference to verify the effectiveness of the technology once created.
- Communicate the business value of the technology.

Use cases foreground users and the organization's overarching needs, and because our methodology is based on upfront business alignment, use cases are foundational to the design and implementation of the semantic layer. Use cases allow technical stakeholders to really understand the needs of the organization and business users to address those needs specifically when designing the semantic data model and integrating the semantic layer into existing technologies. We also value use cases in the context of the semantic layer because the value of the semantic layer is hard to quantify and thus challenging to justify to C-suite executives who are removed from the daily frustrations of business users. The descriptive outline provided by a use case explicitly communicates the needs and goals of business users, ultimately expressing the value of the semantic layer to these users and to the organization as a whole. Use cases also provide a sort of success metric (e.g., does the technology meet the criteria and need outlined in the use case?) and allow technical stakeholders to predict costs, necessary resources, and a timeframe for the semantic layer's design and implementation, all valuable information when pitching the initiative. Foregoing this foundational step may harm ROI.

To create a use case, the task force should assess business needs through approaches like top-down and bottom-up analysis and user personas and journey maps, all of which are detailed in the coming sections, define the features and functions necessary of the technology to fulfill the identified business need, and create a map of the design process based on the priority of these features. It is important to note that use cases themselves are not intended to be overly prescriptive, and they should leave sufficient flexibility for the design and implementation teams to actually construct the semantic data model. We suggest that this team identify a plethora of potential use cases for the semantic layer and assemble these use cases in order of their proposed deployment. In this way, you can think of the semantic layer as a marathon and a use case as your workout regimen. To run a marathon, you will need to go on more than one run, just as, to construct a semantic layer, you will need to realize more than one use case. And, running a marathon requires stamina. Instead of running the same distance every day, you may alternate between long and short runs, experimenting with pace and distance. You will want to construct your use case deployment plan like a workout regimen, taking into consideration the technical requirements and the ease or difficulty of a use case's realization within your existing technology ecosystem. Because the state of an organization's data is typically disparate, varying from source to source, we recommend starting with a small use case. Starting small will allow the stakeholder team to most quickly see and share the results of their efforts, allowing them to assess the project timeframe and value (Fig. 3.2).

In addition to brainstorming a backlog of use cases, the team should also identify multiple key performance indicators (KPIs) that vary in complexity and avoid success measures centered around short-term ROI or immediate performance improvements. We will cover KPIs in more detail later in this section. The semantic layer often becomes more valuable over time, as it uncovers deep, complex relationships to generate insights that may not be immediately obvious. Having a long-term vision for the semantic layer and an incremental use case design will ultimately guide the success of the effort.

Project	Project Name: Investment Portal	Business Unit: Investments	Sponsors: Zachary Wahl, Joe Hilger
Technical Use Case	Name: Semantic Search	Target Persona(s): Investment Manager	
	Use Case Type: Discovery Through Relationships	User Story: As an investment Manager, I want to know everything about the investments I manage (contact information, investment ID, related documents, etc.) so that I can make more informed decisions on how to handle them, monitor their performance, and report on them to my bosses.	

Specifications	Systems / Data Assets:
	• Investment ID Spreadsheet
	• CRM
	• Investment Project Folders
		Inputs/User Actions/Queries:
		• Select Investment
		• Filter Related Documents
			Key Concepts:
			• Investment Entity
			• Investment ID
			• Contact
			  • Name
			  • Email
			• Related Document

		Outputs/Expected Outcomes: Investments and their associated IDs, contacts, and documents.	Business Use Case: Data driven decision making based on holistic information from structured and unstructured data.

Fig. 3.2 Semantic layer use case builder

Common Semantic Layer Use Cases

Use cases are not specific to the semantic layer; they are used for a myriad of design processes. So, in the specific context of brainstorming use cases for your organization's semantic layer implementation, as you use user personas and journey maps, it is important to note that each use case should be outlined from two different user perspectives:

- **Semantic Layer Consumers**—The first, more important use case perspective is that of users of semantic layer-powered applications. We refer to these users as business users or end users, employees whose job is not to support the semantic layer but to use the semantic layer for their business purpose. Semantic layer consuming applications also include advanced search, chatbots, recommendation engines, and more. This user perspective will drive the usability of the semantic application and provide important design constraints. When drafting potential use cases, the semantic layer task force should start with these types of inputs.

- **Semantic Layer Operators and Admins**—The second perspective is that of the owners, administrators, and designers of the components of the semantic layer. These users are responsible for creating and maintaining the semantic layer. The purpose of this perspective is to ensure that the proposed use case design is intuitive and most easy to update and administer. We refer to these users as operators or administrators, as their job within the organization is directly related to the semantic layer.

To best understand the function of use cases in semantic layer development, we will detail five common semantic layer use cases: search and knowledge discovery, data product enablement, data interoperability, advanced analytics, and reliable artificial intelligence.

Search, Information Retrieval, and Discovery

Over the past decade, we have completed between 50 and 70 semantic layer projects. In nearly every one of these cases, the core business challenge was an age-old data and knowledge management question: how do I make my organizational knowledge and data findable and discoverable? Organizations' search portals are often outdated and no longer meet the demand of today's fast-paced work environments. Traditional search methods fall short in delivering the depth, context, and relevance business users need to make timely, informed decisions. Moreover, the landscape of data consumption has evolved, it's no longer just human users seeking information. This is where the semantic layer becomes critical. While human users require intuitive access to data within the context of their specific business needs, machines and AI algorithms demand structured, contextualized, and explainable data to drive advanced capabilities such as intelligent search, chatbots, recommendation engines, and automated decision-making.

The semantic layer addresses this dual need by organizing and connecting data with business context. It bridges the gap between raw data and organizational context, enabling both humans and machines to interact with information in a consistent, actionable, and context-aware way. For business users in particular, the goal is no longer just retrieving files or datasets: it's about getting clear, meaningful answers that are directly tied to their objectives. Unlike traditional keyword-based search, semantic search understands the intent and context behind a query. By leveraging a shared business vocabulary and the relationships between business concepts, semantic search delivers more accurate and relevant results.

Case Study Organizations in the pharmaceutical and healthcare sectors, particularly clinicians and researchers, have long faced the challenge of locating relevant medical research, patient records, and treatment protocols, much of which exists in unstructured formats such as documents and PDFs. In this use case, the semantic layer plays a critical role by connecting disparate sources of information, including clinical data, research articles, treatment guidelines, and clinical trials, regardless of their format or origin. By extracting and classifying key entities such as "Patient Names," "Diagnoses," "Medications," and "Procedures" from unstructured medical records, the semantic layer enables previously inaccessible documents to be understood and retrieved in search results. This structured layer of meaning transforms traditional search, allowing users to pose natural, context-rich questions like "What are the side effects of drug X?" or "Which pathways are affected by drug Y?" instead of relying on rigid, keyword-based queries such as "Glycogen synthase kinase" vs. "GSK." Traditional systems often failed to distinguish between similar terms (e.g., the enzyme GSK vs. the company GSK), resulting in irrelevant or inaccurate outcomes. The true value of structuring unstructured knowledge through entity tagging and semantic enrichment lies in its ability to support clinical research and improve patient care outcomes. Ultimately, this use case is brought to life through the semantic layer's core components; business glossary, taxonomy, metadata, and ontology, creating a unified, intelligent framework for search and find, knowledge discovery, and decision-making (EK Team 2025).

Semantic Layer as a Data Product

Most organizations face the problem of disconnected data, that is data spread across multiple **legacy systems**, or outdated applications and custom-built or proprietary software still in use within an organization. Despite well-intended investments in enterprise knowledge and data management efforts, data repositories often become outdated. These repositories include not only legacy applications, but also email, shared network drives, folders, and information saved locally on desktops or laptops. Some organizations even have physical records and archives that remain undigitized. Global investment banks, for instance, struggle with multiple outdated record management, risk, and compliance tracking systems, while healthcare organizations are up against electronic health record (EHR) systems and electronic medical records (EMRs). These legacy systems hinder organizations' ability to integrate or share data with newer, more advanced systems and are typically not designed to handle the growing demands of modern data, like its connection and storage. As a result, organizations have to spend manual time and effort extracting knowledge.

The use case for this kind of data ecosystem would treat the semantic layer as an abstracted data product, standardizing and connecting fragmented data from legacy systems with metadata and semantics. This approach not only streamlines decision-making but also modernizes data infrastructure without requiring a complete overhaul of existing systems or incurring expensive migrations.

Case Study A global financial firm asked us to transform their risk management program. The firm managed over 21 legacy applications across 8+ business lines, each handling a different aspect of their risk process. Compiling a comprehensive risk report typically took up to 2–3 months, and answering questions like, "What are the related controls and policies relevant to a given risk in my business?" was a complex and time-consuming task. The firm engaged with us specifically to augment their data transformation initiatives with a semantic layer. We began by piloting a conceptual graph model of their risk landscape, defining core risk taxonomies to connect disparate data across the legacy ecosystem. We used ontologies to explicitly capture the relationships between risks, controls, issues, policies, and more. Finally, we leveraged large language models (LLMs) to summarize and reconcile over 30,000 reported risks, which had previously been described manually using free text. In this use case, various components of the semantic layer are being delivered as data products, enabling multiple use cases across the organization. While metadata and taxonomies are used to classify different aspects of terminology for risk operations, the ontology and knowledge graph provide contextualization by linking data from legacy systems to business operations and transactions. This results in an end-to-end, connected view of the risk assessment process.

Ultimately, through the semantic layer, the firm is able to build a simplified, intuitive view of risk through a centralized risk library, enhanced by semantic search and knowledge panels. This allows users to quickly look up a specific risk and access relevant information via a graph-powered, front-end search application. Beyond the risk library, the semantic layer also supports four recommendation engines and a comprehensive risk analytics dashboard that includes threshold and tolerance analysis. This integrated approach is enabling the organization to meet regulatory compliance requirements while also supporting proactive risk management. It reflects a growing trend and emerging best practice: a use case-driven semantic layer, providing semantic data products for legacy systems to deliver a holistic view of enterprise knowledge assets, support data governance, and scale incrementally to accommodate both advanced and evolving analytical use cases.

A key factor in the early success of this initiative was the firm's strategic decision to treat the semantic data model as a stand-alone data product, rather than attempting to retrofit it into existing legacy applications. This modular approach allowed risk assessors and applications to leverage semantic layer components like "Lego bricks," enabling faster, more flexible access to critical insights without disrupting existing systems.

Data Interoperability

The average tenure of an S&P 500 company is predicted to be just 12 years in 2027. This is a drastic shift from 2000, when the median age of the top ten companies was 85 years (Hillenbrand et al. 2019). This trend reflects the challenge of constant technology and vendor solution turnover. The ability to adopt new tools and systems, while still maintaining operational continuity and reducing risk, is an enterprise challenge. One key solution to this challenge is to use the semantic layer to make organizational data interoperable, offering the flexibility to navigate changing vendors, technologies, and tools.

Case Study A few years ago, one of our clients faced a significant problem when their graph database vendor was acquired by another company, leading to a sharp increase in both license and maintenance fees. To mitigate the impact of this change, we were able to methodically migrate all of the company's semantic data models from their old graph database to a new one within less than a week. This move saved the client approximately $2 million over 3 years. The success of the migration was due in part to the fact that the original data models were all built with Semantic Web standards RDF and related W3C specifications. Because the underlying data models and ontologies adhered to these widely accepted standards, they were vendor-agnostic and inherently interoperable. More importantly, this experience demonstrated a critical strategic advantage of implementing a semantic layer based on open standards: the ability to retain control over your data architecture, regardless of changes in the vendor landscape. By decoupling the data model from the underlying technology stack, the client avoided long-term vendor lock-in and preserved the flexibility to pivot quickly when external conditions changed.

This case study serves as a compelling proof point for why data interoperability is considered as a core use case when building a semantic layer. In an increasingly volatile technology ecosystem, organizations are investing in standard-based, modular, and portable architectures to be better positioned to manage risk, reduce costs, and maintain business continuity. Ultimately, this example illustrates a broader shift in data management strategy: toward open, interoperable systems that prioritize long-term agility over short-term convenience, and place the semantic layer at the center of organizational resilience at times of high uncertainty.

Advanced Analytics

For many large-scale organizations, it can take weeks or even months for analytics teams to develop "insights": reports and dashboards that fulfill data-driven requests. This is because these organizations often work with a myriad of complex systems, ranging from customer relationship management systems (CRMs) and enterprise resource planning systems (ERPs) to data lakes and cloud platforms, where data is fragmented and locked away in tables and applications with little to no business context. Without a coherent, integrated view of these systems, navigation, extraction, and management of their data is incredibly difficult. Thus, organizations often come to us seeking a way to more easily use their data for advanced analytics. Using the semantic tools that make up the semantic layer, this raw data can be transformed with meaning and extracted from disparate systems. Semantically infused data is easier for both data teams and business users to query, analyze, and visualize. By standardizing terminology, it also decreases the likelihood of reports with incorrect or inconsistent data.

Case Study To avoid the problem of disparate data systems, a global retailer migrated its data to a data lake in an attempt to centralize their data assets. Despite this investment, the organization was still challenged by requests for data from leadership, particularly metrics related to store performance. Each time a leadership team requested a new metric or report, and the data team had to spin up a new project and develop new data pipelines. It took 5–6 months for data analysts to understand the data related to these metrics, as each request could involve petabytes of raw data. The process of creating these reports also involved the management of 1500 ETL pipelines which led to inefficiencies. The cost to produce a single metrics dashboard for C-level executives exceeded $900,000. And, even after completing the dashboard, teams would often discover that the metrics were defined and used inconsistently. Terms like "revenue," "headcount," or "store performance" were frequently misunderstood and dependent on who worked on the report. Thus, these costly, complex reports were ultimately and often unusable.

As this global retailer's data and analytics teams worked to integrate siloed data and unstructured content, we partnered with them to build a semantic ecosystem that streamlined reporting processes. First, we developed standardized metadata and vocabularies in the form of a business glossary to describe key enterprise data assets, especially store metrics like sales performance and revenue. The purpose of this step was to ensure that every business user within the organization used the same definitions and language when discussing key metrics. Next, we employed ontologies and knowledge graphs to explicitly define the relationships between various domains such as products, store locations, store performance, etc. This created a logical and standardized model that allowed data teams to work with a shared understanding of how different data points are related. Finally, we helped the retailer integrate these semantic models into a data catalog that made data available as data products. This allowed analysts to access predefined, business-contextualized data directly, without having to start from scratch each time a new request was made.

This approach reduced report generation steps from seven to four and cut development time from 6 months to just 4–5 weeks. Most importantly, however, the semantic layer enabled the discovery of previously hidden data, unlocking valuable insights that optimized operations and continues to drive business performance.

Reliable AI

The final, most common semantic layer use case is artificial intelligence. Emerging technologies like generative AI (GenAI) are democratizing access to information, but they are also contributing to the "dark data" problem. **Dark data** refers to the information assets organizations collect, process, and store during regular business activities but generally fail to use for other purposes, such as analytics, business relationships, and direct monetizing. It is that which exists in an unstructured and accessible form but contains valuable or sensitive information. Without the organizational context provided by the semantic layer, raw data or text is often messy, outdated, redundant, and unstructured, making it difficult for AI algorithms to extract and meaningfully use. This organizational context cannot be sourced solely from structured data. Unstructured data, shared language, expertise knowledge, and best practices must be—and increasingly become—machine-readable.

While LLMs have garnered widespread attention and use in content generation, organizations are realizing that their data management challenges require a more specialized approach that will address gaps in explainability and precision and improve issues of alignment between AI and business-specific goals, rules, and context, all of which are reasons why enterprise AI initiatives "fail." With GenAI chatbots and other applications as a foregrounding use case, the semantic layer can be implemented to provide this enterprise AI initiative with a programmatic framework for making knowledge assets machine-readable. The semantic layer can facilitate this machine readability through techniques such as data labeling, taxonomy development, business glossaries, and ontology and knowledge graph creation.

Case Study A global foundation experienced a failed AI experiment after a mandate from their CEO required data teams to "figure out a way" to adopt LLMs to evaluate the impact of the organization's investments on strategic goals by synthesizing information from publicly available domain data and internal investment documents and data. The challenge of the failed initiative lay in connecting diverse and unstructured information to structured data. Additionally, the insights generated needed to be precise, explainable, reliable, and actionable for executive stakeholders.

To address these challenges, we took a hybrid approach that leveraged LLMs augmented with advanced graph technology and a semantic retrieval-augmented generation (RAG) agentic workflow. **Retrieval-augmented generation (RAG)** describes an organization querying their own repositories for information and then sending the most relevant documents to an LLM for processing. Our solution also leveraged an investment ontology as a semantic backbone, ensuring that all investment-related data, from structured to narrative reports, was harmonized under a common language. This semantic backbone supports both precise data integration and flexible query interpretation. To effectively convey the value of this hybrid approach, we implemented a chatbot to serve as a user interface, toggling back and forth between the basic GPT model and the graph RAG solution.

The result is a solution that consistently outperformed the basic LLMs, demonstrating the value of semantics for providing organizational context and alignment. We ultimately delivered an AI model that, through semantics, bridged structured and unstructured, internal and external investment data, and provided coherent and transparent insights that could be traced, allowing stakeholders to see exactly how each answer was derived.

In addition to these five common use cases, there are many additional use cases for the semantic layer that exist. In Fig. 3.3, we outline additional uses for the semantic layer through the lens of a specific business challenge.

Semantic Enablement	Business Challenge	Semantic Challenge	Process Challenge	Technical Challenge
Data Discovery	It is difficult to find and discover data. Business users waste their time searching for data or re-make work that already exists.	Data that is discovered is difficult to understand because it is not tagged with metadata.	There is no recommended process for data discovery.	There are no applications or interfaces that foster a connection between data and business users.
Data Integration & Aggregation	Siloed data sources prohibit business user access to existing data.	Semantically meaningless data models impair effective analytics.	Data models that are developed are not entirely or consistently semantically meaningful.	There are no effective self-service analytics applications leveraging semantically connected data to generate valuable insights.
Access & Consumption	No organizational understanding of why certain datasets were created resulting in their duplication.	Data is not meaningfully connected across teams and systems to facilitate shared understanding.	When datasets are created, appropriate documentation and metadata are not immediately applied or managed.	The process of applying and maintaining metadata is not automated.
Governance	Lack of data governance delays data utilization for product research and development, negatively impacting company revenue.	Tacit knowledge is uncaptured.	Inconsistent and unrefined data governance processes lead to duplication and inaccuracies.	No centralized system exists to capture tacit knowledge.

Fig. 3.3 High-level use case examples

Now that we have defined what a use case is and discussed some of the most common semantic layer use cases, we can delve into the process of identifying use cases that are specific to *your* organization and its business problems. While AI chatbots, semantic search, data interoperability, and BI tools are all tried and true semantic layer use cases, there are a plethora of other technologies, workflows, and applications that can function as productive use cases for your organization's semantic layer implementation. To develop use cases that best reflect your organization's business needs, the next step is to craft user personas and journey maps.

User Personas

Constructed from real research and data, a **user persona** is a fictional character that represents a specific group of business users. Like use cases, user personas are employed by teams who have been tasked with developing a new system, technology, or application, and their purpose is to provide a documented and formulaic understanding of users' needs, goals, motivations, and frustrations, thus informing the team's decisions about which features, functions, and overall design elements the system should accommodate. Ultimately, by understanding users' needs, organizations can design business-intuitive and easy-to-use technology that will more likely result in user adoption (Figs. 3.4 and 3.5).

To design a user persona, the task should begin by categorizing users from the chosen two or three business units by their types of interactions with semantic applications. These user personas should be an abstraction of a type of user, representing a specific activity, experience, responsibility, or interaction. These categories of users should also represent interactions at all stages of the semantic layer, from knowledge asset creation and curation to metadata tagging and knowledge graph maintenance, and front-end use. Specifically, the following users or user actions should be represented:

- Users who *create* or *curate* knowledge assets, depending on whether the semantic layer will leverage only existing knowledge assets.
- Users who *design* semantic models (taxonomies, ontologies, knowledge graphs, business glossaries, and metadata) for the semantic layer.
- Users who *use* semantic layer-powered applications.

Persona	Action	Goal
Who is the user? A persona is a business user archetype who will be interacting with the semantic layer. The persona should be a specific role, like Customer Representative.	**What is the user doing?** How will the persona interact with the semantic layer? This should include the specific systems that the user will interact with, such as a website or customer management system.	**What is the user's goal?** This is the persona's purpose for using the semantic layer. Their goal should be a specific objective or action, such as "to identify products a customer has purchased."

Fig. 3.4 Persona design

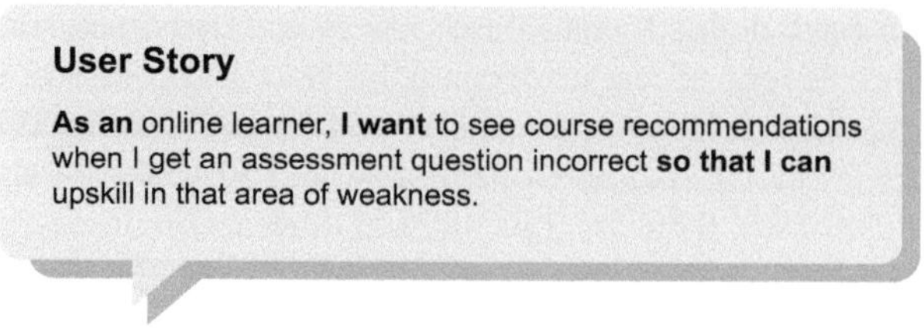

Fig. 3.5 Sample user story

Representing these users will require their identification within your organization. For example, does your organization have an information architect, a dedicated taxonomist, and an ontologist? Which data analysts are responsible for the knowledge assets within the initial project locus? What applications does this data currently serve, and which users use these applications for what purposes? This last question should be the focus of your discovery and user persona design effort, as these users will have the most impact on the scope and overall semantic layer experience. In most cases, these diverse personas help uncover the various ways different design components will be used, each potentially requiring its own supporting technology and tailored user experience.

There is incredible value in designing highly detailed user personas. Instead of making inferences or trying to guess at your users, gather as much information about users demographics (tenure, education, language, etc.) as possible, and document users' technical savvy, areas of responsibility, expectations for the semantic layer, component, or application, as well as their needs, wants, and frustrations. Tenure, for example, may indicate the technicality of the language that can and should be used to inform the semantic layer. The more tenure the user, the more advanced the business vocabulary could be. Technical savvy, on the other hand, may influence the complexity of the interface design and other semantic processes. If the user persona is relatively technology-averse, developers may wish to sacrifice detail or granularity in the name of simplicity and usability.

Finally, documenting the needs, wants, and frustrations of your users will inform your use case development and help define your current state. This research can be conducted through interviews with a sample of users within a domain or through the review of employee documentation. In our experience, workshops and small group exercises, moderated by the task force, are most effective for designing personas as part of a semantic layer initiative. This is because, unlike one-on-one interviews, workshops allow for collaboration and conversation, as users work through their perspectives and opinions to align on those most important features. With this in mind, it can also be helpful to have multiple groups work independently on the same persona so that even more experiences are taken into consideration (Fig. 3.6).

Journey Maps

Journey maps are a visual representation of a user's, or persona's, interaction with a system, application, or technology, often incorporating the amount of time and the emotions of the user over the course of the interaction. In this way, journey maps are

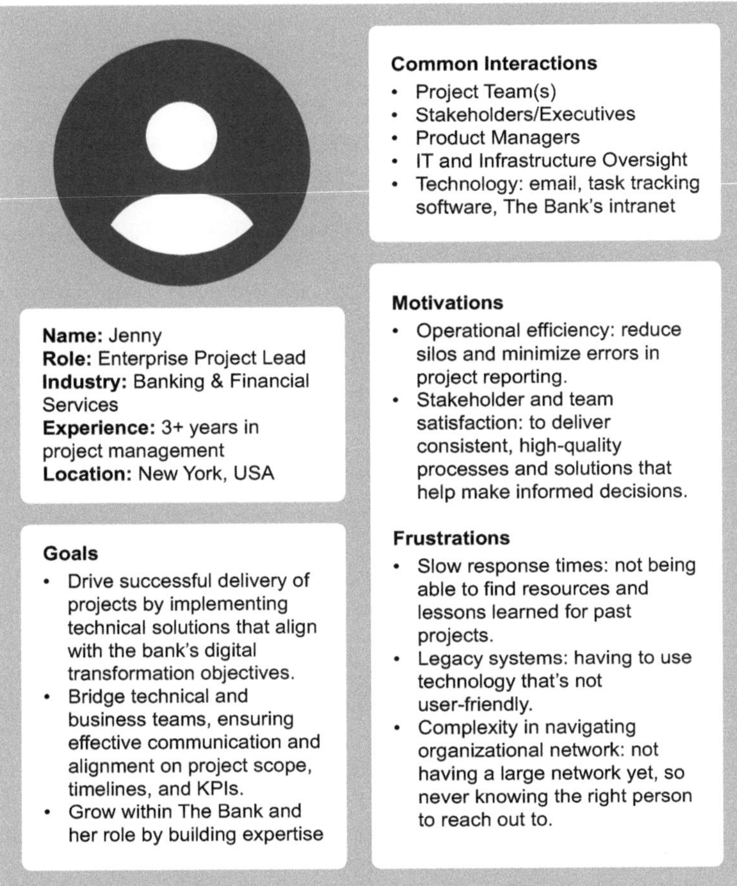

Fig. 3.6 Sample user persona

very similar to use cases, as they outline user-process interactions, but differ in that journey maps express individual stories or narratives, like user personas. We use journey maps to create a current and target-state view of the specific activities or processes supported by the semantic layer. Because the semantic layer is at times both nebulous and esoteric, journey maps clarify the functionality of the semantic layer through its visual representation of user-process interactions. Journey maps, for example, can more specifically show what will change when the semantic layer is implemented, and, like a use case, can demonstrate savings and improvements to user experience.

Additionally, the "before" and "after" view provided by journey maps acts as a meaningful way of actually explaining what the semantic layer is and does, helping to build support and buy-in from leadership. Thus, the purpose of journey mapping is to:

- Understand and empathize with your users and what they currently perceive as difficult or impossible.
- Identify opportunities for improvements to user experience and create a list of product development priorities.
- Communicate current-state user experiences to executives, product managers, and other designers to ultimately ensure business alignment and buy-in.

As with user personas, we recommend that the creation of journey maps occur through facilitated exercises with groups of stakeholders and business users. Once the user personas, representing fictional users, categorized by shared characteristics, demographics, behaviors, motivations, and goals, have been crafted, we assign each group to a persona that they feel familiar with. Next, we instruct groups to create a current-state map for a common, semantic layer-related task associated with their persona. These semantic layer tasks identified for journey mapping can be marked as potential use cases. The resulting journey map should discretely detail each step required to complete the task in the current state, the user's overall satisfaction or dissatisfaction at each step, based on the experiences of the real business users in the room, and the total amount of time it takes the user to complete the task journey. The exercise is repeated to create a target-state map, representing how the same task could be completed with a semantic layer in place.

The semantic layer should be leveraged here to address the challenges faced by the current-state user, enhancing the user's experience of the task with its known capabilities. Workshop participants can ask questions like, "What if there was a tool that recommended relevant documents?" or "What if the user could search for employees based on the projects they have worked on?" The instructions are to "think big" and not worry about technical limitations or change friction. The expectation is that the user satisfaction will improve over the journey, the required steps shrinking in number, and the overall time decreasing. The scale at which these improvements occur visually on the map is up to the perceptions of the business users and stakeholders: If the semantic layer could recommend relevant documents, how much time would that save the user? (Fig. 3.7)

Of course, there are other approaches to creating journey maps, but we find that using your organization's own users and stakeholders, in our experience, yields the most reliable results. The additional benefit of this approach is that, now, you have engaged members of your organization in the process of designing the semantic layer, empowering their early and excited adoption of its applications. In short, involve your users, and many of them, early and often in your semantic layer initiative.

Assess Technical Capabilities

To brainstorm and realize semantic layer use cases, the task force must also understand the current state of the organization's technology and existing systems architecture. It is important to note that assessing technical capabilities and defining use

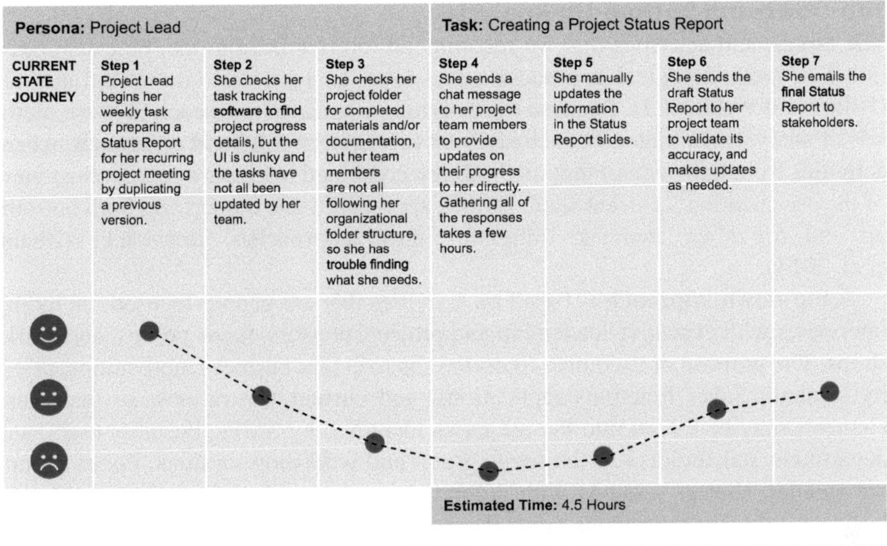

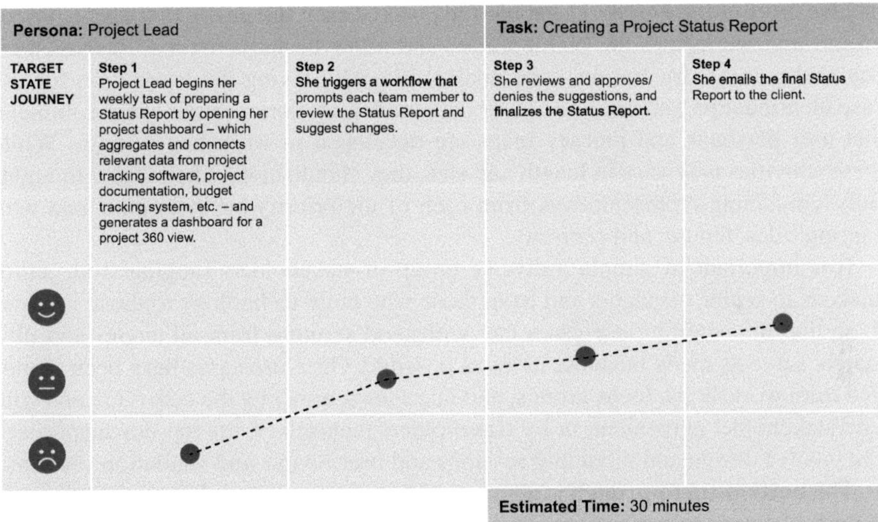

Fig. 3.7 Sample journey map

cases and business vision are not mutually exclusive parts of the semantic layer design and implementation process. The approach we propose next has aspects that inform use case, user persona, and journey map creation. Instead of perceiving these "steps" as chronological, it is better to think of them as simultaneous, as, for example, assessing the technical savvy of your business users will inform both your user personas and the technical realization of your use cases. Next, we detail our recommended approach to researching and assessing an organization's current-state technology, processes, culture, and content.

Top-Down and Bottom-Up Analysis

The assessment activities that we recommend to organizations can be categorized into two methodological approaches: top-down analysis and bottom-up analysis (Hilger and Wahl 2022). Because the activities associated with each of these methods of analysis are mutually exclusive, we recommend a **hybrid approach**, where activities from both assessment methods are combined to create a more robust view of the organization's current state. Hybrid approaches can outperform both bottom-up and top-down analysis, mitigating these approaches' drawbacks (Zhang et al. 2014).

A **top-down approach** is based on activities that are people-focused, including interviews with executive leadership and project sponsors, focus groups, and workshops. The purpose of executive interviews is to assess business motivations, priority semantic layer functions/applications, and current frustrations, so that these elements may be folded into the use cases identified by SMEs, business users, and department stakeholders in the focus group and workshop sessions. Focus groups are smaller, shorter sessions with around three to six employees from a specific business area. These sessions range from 1 to 3 h. Workshops are much longer and involve more users, around 15 people for a half or even full day of discussion. Focus groups and workshops are collaborative and allow business users to discuss their day-to-day tasks, frustrations, and goals, ultimately laying the foundation for use case identification and semantic layer data modeling. For example, we recommend that user personas and journey maps are developed in workshop settings. While these activities may vary in length and size, they should always be curated thoughtfully, containing representatives from each of the priority business units and with varying titles, tenure, and seniority.

It is important to sample a diverse group of stakeholders ranging from junior analysts to senior managers and from those who build technology to those who use it, so that the resulting use cases can withstand scrutiny from all angles and ultimately serve as many business users as possible. Once use cases have been identified from workshops, focus groups, and interviews, either by the task force and with user/stakeholder agreement, or by stakeholders themselves, the top-down approach can involve design and modeling sessions and user review and validation sessions.

The **bottom-up approach** is alternatively content-oriented. Its activities include document reviews, assessments of existing data models, analyses of sample data, and demonstrations of current-state systems. Part of the purpose of the bottom-up approach is to alleviate the time commitment of the top-down approach on stakeholders by prioritizing all of the other resources that exist and are related to semantic functioning. The semantic layer task force can, instead of interviewing stakeholders, review any previous plans for AI or semantic layer component implementation to assess documented goals, risks, and failures.

Additionally, in this assessment phase, the task force can and should make an inventory of existing systems, components, processes, applications, and technologies related to the semantic layer, assessing the functionality of each. The bottom-up analysis can also verify that an organization's knowledge assets are captured, organized, defined, and shared correctly and consistently in order to best support the semantic layer. To do this, it is important to inventory and then record which knowledge assets are managed where and connected to what. Again, it is necessary to start small, for example, within two or three business units, so that this type of analysis is feasible. Finally, the task force can assess the complexity of the systems connected to the relevant data sources by observing, for example, whether or not the system allows for the creation of different user types and permissions.

Now that we have identified the types of activities characteristic of each assessment approach, we can formalize our technical assessment recommendation. To facilitate this formalized assessment, technical stakeholders should demonstrate each system related to the chosen departments to showcase its capabilities. These system demonstrations will produce a comprehensive understanding of the organization's **system architecture**, a conceptual model that defines and visualizes the behavior and interaction of technologies that make up or support an application, and its maturity, assessing its readiness for semantic layer implementation and informing the next steps of design and semantic data modeling. Within the project locus, the task force should:

- Create an inventory of existing systems, components, processes, applications, and technologies related to the semantic layer.
- Map this inventory into a conceptual system architecture.
- Review up to date documentation of governance policies, existing architectural diagrams, and technical/maintenance requirements.
- Interview architecture stakeholders to better understand technical, security, and privacy mandates for system integration collected from document review.
- Identify gaps in the current system architecture, specifically within the data integration process and of governance capabilities, and strengths and weaknesses of user applications, assessed through employee anecdotes and documentation review.

As you can see, this evaluation recommendation is a hybrid approach, combining both top-down (employee interviews) and bottom-up (document review and system demos) activities. With this understanding of the types of activities that are necessary for assessment, there are several key questions that your team should aim to answer. Our recommendation is that these questions be asked of each component of the semantic layer (business glossary, metadata, taxonomy, ontology, and knowledge graph) and scored on a matrix rather than answered with simple "yes" or "no" responses. The questions are:

- Does the component exist within the enterprise, and if so, what is its level of coverage and usage within the organization?
- Has the component been built or purchased with the features appropriate and necessary for semantic layer integration?
- Is the component independent or integrated with other components?
- What is the component's state of design?
- For knowledge assets: What is the current state or asset quality, and what is its semantic layer readiness?

In Figs. 3.8 and 3.9, we illustrate a sample scoring matrix for each component's coverage and use, respectively. To answer the second question, you will need an understanding of the "appropriate and necessary" features of each component, which we detailed in Chap. 2. We generally recommend that an organization invest in enterprise-scale semantic model management solutions, such as a metadata repository to capture and store metadata and business glossary terms associated with structured data assets; a content management system to persistent and avail metadata associated with unstructured knowledge assets; and a graph database to store linked data used by the semantic layer's knowledge graph. Again, most organizations already have one or more of these tools in house. As you are outlining a plan for the implementation of the semantic layer, it is important that you identify which of these tools already exist within your organization and which need to be built or purchased. If these tools do exist within your organization, work must still be done to assess whether or not they meet the needs of your project and if the licensing that your organization owns will allow for access to data aggregated by the semantic layer.

Component	1	2	3	4	5
Business Glossary	Non-Existent	Limited to Small Group, Division, or Geographic Area	Large-Scale Deployment, Inconsistent Design	Large-Scale Deployment, Consistent Design	Enterprise Deployment and Integration
Metadata	Non-Existent	Limited to Small Group, Division, or Geographic Area	Large-Scale Deployment, Inconsistent Design	Large-Scale Deployment, Consistent Design	Enterprise Deployment and Integration
Taxonomy	Non-Existent	Limited to Small Group, Division, or Geographic Area	Large-Scale Deployment, Inconsistent Design	Large-Scale Deployment, Consistent Design	Enterprise Deployment and Integration
Ontology	Non-Existent	Limited to Small Group, Division, or Geographic Area	Large-Scale Deployment, Inconsistent Design	Large-Scale Deployment, Consistent Design	Enterprise Deployment and Integration
Knowledge Graph	Non-Existent	Limited to Small Group, Division, or Geographic Area	Large-Scale Deployment, Inconsistent Design	Large-Scale Deployment, Consistent Design	Enterprise Deployment and Integration

Fig. 3.8 Semantic model coverage

Component	1	2	3	4	5
Business Glossary	Limited Trial Usage	Production Usage by Expert Users Only	Widespread Usage by Stakeholders	Widespread Usage Related to Core Business Functions	Widespread Usage, Regarded as Critical Business Solution
Metadata	Limited Trial Usage	Production Usage by Expert Users Only	Widespread Usage by Stakeholders	Widespread Usage Related to Core Business Functions	Widespread Usage, Regarded as Critical Business Solution
Taxonomy	Limited Trial Usage	Production Usage by Expert Users Only	Widespread Usage by Stakeholders	Widespread Usage Related to Core Business Functions	Widespread Usage, Regarded as Critical Business Solution
Ontology	Limited Trial Usage	Production Usage by Expert Users Only	Widespread Usage by Stakeholders	Widespread Usage Related to Core Business Functions	Widespread Usage, Regarded as Critical Business Solution
Knowledge Graph	Limited Trial Usage	Production Usage by Expert Users Only	Widespread Usage by Stakeholders	Widespread Usage Related to Core Business Functions	Widespread Usage, Regarded as Critical Business Solution

Fig. 3.9 Semantic model usage

Conceptual Domain Modeling

A **conceptual domain model** is a visual representation of an organization's entities and the relationships between them. The purpose of the model is to capture and organize the observations gathered from the discovery and assessment phase of the organization's current-state technology, data, and business processes using a knowledge graph data modeling approach, which will ultimately serve as a component of the semantic layer. The model also acts as another mode of communication between the task force and leadership or other stakeholders external to the semantic layer implementation or as a mechanism for aligning modeling, engineering, and business teams. Conceptual models support understanding, problem-solving, and communication (Valle et al. 2025).

Even after creating an inventory of an organization's data sources and technical systems, even within just two or three business departments, it can be challenging to conceptualize how all of these different entities connect or work together. By visualizing these knowledge structures at scale, the task force will be able to more easily identify inefficiencies, gaps, and duplicative processes in the organization's information ecosystem. In this pre-modeling phase, the task force should propose candidate classes, entities, and relationships, as well as design a map of the key features of the organization's data domains. This semantic process yields a visual model that can validate the group's understanding of findings relevant to the semantic layer use cases, while also functioning as an outline for initial semantic data models. Additionally, conceptual models further facilitate conversations about prioritization, focus, and business value.

To create a conceptual model, we advise against traditional artifacts such as application architectures or entity relationship diagrams (ERDs) as these can be too complex or technical. Figure 3.10 shows a conceptual modeling framework designed to map knowledge assets and diagnose what exactly needs to be stored, managed, standardized, and connected. The reality is that, at this point of the discovery phase, there could be a hundred possible solutions for the semantic layer. Writing down and mapping out all of these possibilities through the conceptual model will allow you to see what is most feasible and will have the most impact on your existing architecture.

To conclude, the successful execution of the discovery, assessment, and validation process as part of the preliminary planning phase for an organization's semantic layer design and implementation endeavor will allow an organization to understand the current state of its semantic capacity, translation into the potential design and modeling requirements for the semantic layer. Use cases, created through a hybrid approach to user personas and journey maps, lay the groundwork for the semantic layer implementation within the proposed business locus. Infused with the findings of the current-state technology assessment, the starting use case will identify the scope for the semantic model (i.e., which components are necessary to incorporate), supporting technology that will need to be implemented, and identifying existing architecture and technology that will need to be connected to the semantic model once designed, all before requiring a large financial investment or a commitment to any software solution.

From here, the semantic task force can predict the cumulative ROI that could be generated from the realization of this semantic layer use case to make one final pitch for the actual implementation of the semantic layer. Or, if the investment has already been made, the identified use case can immediately be acted upon, as the task force can begin developing the semantic data models. Regardless, artifacts from this assessment stage will serve as supporting documentation that provides context and

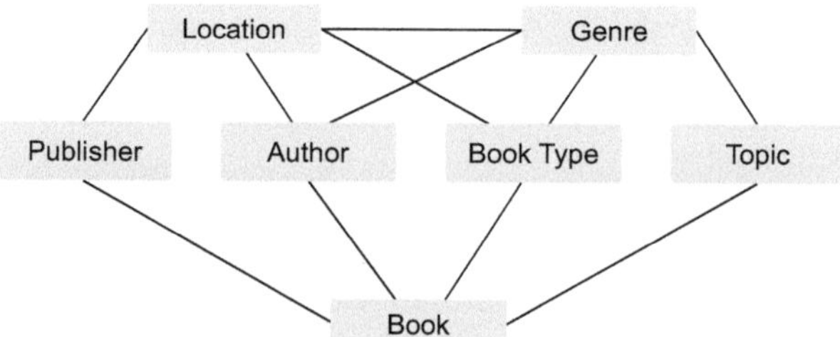

Fig. 3.10 Conceptual model

strategic guidance for the implemented semantic layer, facilitates stakeholder buy-in, communication, and leadership consensus building, and can solicit feedback regarding the proposed scope of the effort.

Knowledge Asset Readiness

In the previous section, we discussed the bottom-up approach and its value in assessing the readiness of these assorted knowledge assets for inclusion in the semantic layer. It is important to revisit this topic in more detail to ensure a clear understanding of the importance of knowledge asset readiness, especially traditional knowledge assets that fall into the two main categories of content (unstructured information) and data (structured information). These traditional forms of knowledge assets historically suffer from sprawl due to a lack of governance and controls. This has resulted in:

- Poor quality assets, generally compounded over time, resulting in a mass of duplicate, near-duplicate, outdated, or completely incorrect assets.
- Assets that are poorly tagged, incorrectly placed, or otherwise lacking the necessary semantic structure.
- Incorrectly secured assets, which haven't been noticed due to their lack of accessibility or visibility, but which may cause significant damage if exposed via a semantic layer.

Each of these knowledge asset issues will prevent the semantic layer from successfully surfacing information in a complete and trustworthy way. And, these issues may in fact introduce risk to the organization, with the semantic layer taking the blame. These issues will be most evident when the semantic layer is used for findability and discoverability purposes, and even more so when an AI solution is incorporated into the framework. Quality issues include:

- **Duplicate Assets**—Duplicate assets will affect the usability of the semantic layer in that they will cause the surfacing of multiple instances of the same asset. While this is not inherently risky if these duplicate assets are both correct, duplicate assets can skew results, creating an artificial view of the amount of assets existing on a particular topic. Additionally, duplicate assets can negatively impact performance and incur unnecessary costs.
- **Near Duplicate Assets**—Version control issues, working documents, and iterative reports can often lead to the creation of "near duplicate" versions of an asset. They can cause confusion and conflict, especially when versions represent improvements or changes in finding.
- **Outdated Assets**—While metadata can indicate creation dates and updates, this does not guarantee asset validity. Some semantic layer use cases, like generative AI, can inadvertently combine old and new assets, presenting outdated information as current. This can lead to inaccurate or unactionable results.

- **Incorrect Assets**—Many organizations maintain inaccurate assets. These inaccurate assets may have been wrong at their inception or became incorrect over time due to new findings or organizational changes. Regardless, these inaccuracies pose a significant risk to output quality, adhering the "garbage in, garbage out" principle.

Regardless of whether or not an organization's knowledge assets are of high quality, if these assets lack semantic structure, the semantic layer will be unable to properly connect, combine, contextualize, and leverage them. When planning to feed the semantic layer with diverse data, you should anticipate challenges related to data quality or consistency (such as varying definitions, granularity, and near-duplicate assets that require resolution), governance (such as access controls), and the technical integration of these assets. To ensure an accurate view of real-world entities across different data sources and diverse knowledge assets, we recommend establishing a metadata-first architecture (detailed in the next section, "Integrating and Implementing the Semantic Layer") and a shared business glossary. Additionally, your organization should plan for **entity resolution**, a process that determines if multiple, apparently different database records actually represent the same real-world entity, to create unified "approved records" for unique entities.

From our experience, organizations also often struggle with poorly secured assets. Old file drives or systems possess sensitive information, such as personally identifiable information (PII), salary or other financial information, or competitive trade secrets. These issues never directly arose from this unsecured information because it was buried deep in file repositories or databases where no one would be able to find it. But, new technologies (portals and enterprise search, and now, semantic layers, knowledge graphs, and AI) exposed these poor assets. The answer to this issue is to ensure that you have properly addressed the security and entitlements on the knowledge assets that will be included in the semantic layer framework. A unified entitlements approach to security uses security policies to replicate security rules to these knowledge asset sources. This approach ensures that proper entitlements are automatically applied in a consistent fashion across all knowledge assets.

While assessing your assorted knowledge assets, you should also try to pinpoint gaps. Many organizations complain about "not knowing what they don't know," a nefarious concern that has historically been difficult to address. As we mentioned earlier in the book, however, a semantic layer can actually help to identify gaps in knowledge. With an enterprise taxonomy and ontology applied against your organizational knowledge assets, you'll be able to see topics or other semantic terms that are not being leveraged to the degree that they should. This can be a clear indicator that the organization does not have the necessary knowledge assets for those specific business areas.

We created the acronym ROCK (Relevant, Organizationally Contextualized, Complete, and Knowledge-Centric) to express what you should be looking for as you assess your knowledge assets:

- **Relevant**—In short, do you have the right knowledge assets in place and accessible?

- **Organizationally Contextualized**—Are the knowledge assets specific to your organization and do they include the semantic components necessary to ensure they can be connected?
- **Complete**—Have you identified and filled any potential gaps?
- **Knowledge-Centric**—Have you gone beyond the traditional knowledge assets of content and data, including other types to round out your organizational knowledge and semantic layer capabilities?

Rather than dealing with "garbage in, garbage out," readying your knowledge assets for the semantic layer and advanced use cases like AI is a critical step in the design and implementation process. Well-prepared knowledge assets will help to deliver results that are:

- **Correct**—Results are factually accurate and logically sound. They reflect verified data and align with the known truth or accepted standards in the domain. Misinformation and hallucinations do not occur.
- **Complete**—Outputs are comprehensive, addressing all relevant aspects of the query or task.
- **Consistent**—Results provide stable and repeatable outputs when given the same inputs in the same context. Predictability builds trust and ensures smooth integration with workflows and systems.
- **Contextual**—Outputs are aware of and responsive to the organization's unique knowledge and processes. They reflect domain-specific language, priorities, and current operational states and landscape.
- **Compliant**—Results align with organizational and external policies around security, privacy, access controls, ethical use, regulatory standards, bias mitigation, and brand integrity.

Implementation and Roadmap Planning Considerations

Now that we have discussed the necessary discovery, assessment, and validation methods that should take place before the actual development of the semantic layer, the next step is to consider the overall roadmap of your design within the context of your business. While we've already outlined a phased approach, starting small with one or two business units and expanding semantic capabilities through iterative use cases, there are other strategies your organization may want to consider (Tesfaye 2024). The point we wish to make here is that the semantic layer cannot be built all at once. In fact, it is a multi-year endeavor. Whether your organization wishes to pursue the semantic layer through iterative use case realization, as we outlined, or through one of the other options detailed next, is up to you, your leadership, your semantic layer task force, your organization, and its needs:

- **Semantic Layer Use Cases**—Iterating based on use cases is typically the best approach, as it delivers a complete solution that has been continuously aligned and re-aligned with business needs. The key to this iterative approach is to identify and choose use cases that are neither too large nor too small. Use cases that incorporate two to three knowledge asset sources and don't require a complete enterprise taxonomy and ontology design tend to fit into the "just right" category. At this scope, they are often achievable within a matter of months and are also encompassing enough to prove the value of the semantic layer and demonstrate its ability to integrate assets of different types and from different source locations. It should be noted that to iterate use cases, the components of the semantic layer will need to be developed use case by use case. Recall that the realization of a single use case may not require all six components of the semantic layer, but your next use case may require those components that weren't developed in the first iteration. In this way, the resulting semantic layer will inevitably have all of the components, but it is important to understand that components will be developed in this way, and not all at once. We will outline how to go about developing each component in the coming sections of this chapter.

- **Components**—If, based on your technical assessment, you have discerned that your organization does not contain any of the core semantic components you may wish to build the semantic layer framework component-by-component. Instead of brainstorming semantic layer use cases that will motivate the incremental development of components as necessary, your semantic layer task force can instead compile incremental use cases for each individual component. The challenge with this approach is that the components of the semantic layer often complement each other or work in tandem, and it can become challenging to realize use cases without relying on undeveloped semantic functions, even when the use cases are geared to a single component.

- **Asset Sources**—Most organizations possess a myriad of potential knowledge asset repositories or sources. Regardless of the number of repositories that exist within an organization, we have found that the most valuable assets are loosely arrayed on a Zipf curve. Zipf's law states that when a list of measured values is sorted in decreasing order, the value of the n-th entry is often approximately inversely proportional to n (Hosch 2025). Put a lot more simply, even the most complex organizations likely have no more than 20 repositories that hold the vast majority (up to 90% in most cases) of valuable knowledge assets. The number of repositories within an organization may be easily intimidating, but by focusing on those that hold the greatest potential value and feeding those to the semantic layer framework, you may be able to realize results with less complexity and effort. Once you have identified these few sources, you can integrate additional sources over time. You will likely find that you have executed nowhere near an exhaustive integration of all of your organization's sources in order to have met the business needs of your organization. For the purposes of this book, this logic is worth keeping in mind once you have begun to implement your semantic layer use cases and are thinking about which data sources are necessary to integrate into the semantic technologies you have developed to realize a given use case (Fig. 3.11).

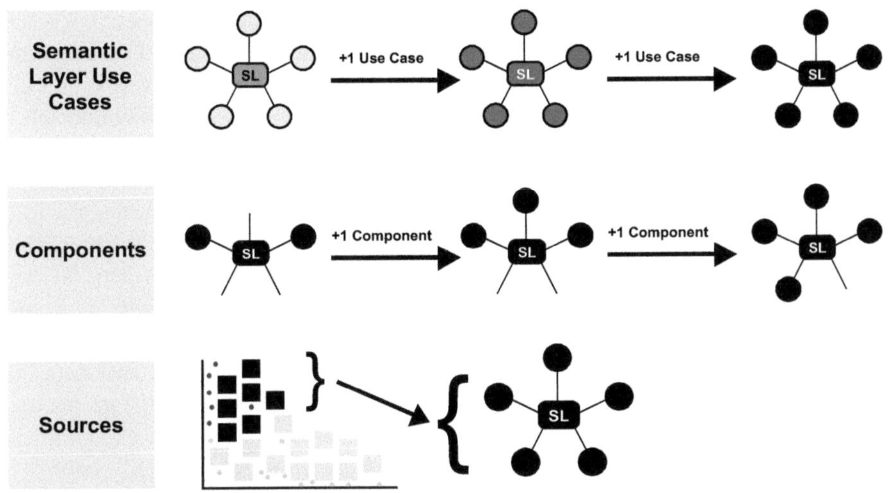

Fig. 3.11 Three considerations for developing a semantic layer

Consider these three options as three decision-making models and three ways of explaining the scope of your semantic layer initiative. Ultimately, these three ways of thinking about iterative design are intertwined but are worth discussing in this discovery and design stage. The key thing to consider in this stage is that your design will strike an appropriate balance between timeliness and achievability, while also expressing some business value along the way. If your initial iteration is too simple, you risk an underwhelmed response from investors and leadership. This will be especially true if you fail to integrate discrete knowledge assets in a way that is new for your organization. And, of course, if your initial iteration is too lofty, your design is imbued with risk and may take too long to realize. At a minimum, we recommend that your design, optimally based on your semantic layer use cases, combines at least two different types of knowledge assets, from at least two different sources and delivers at least one new capability, previously impossible, difficult, or time consuming for your business users.

Prototypes and Pilots

The iterative approach to the delivering semantic layer typically begins with a prototype or pilot. Though commonly confused as synonyms, prototypes and pilots are different, and it's important to be deliberate about which you choose to get started with:

- **Prototypes** are not put into production and are not used for actual operational purposes. Though they are functional, the primary purpose of a prototype is to prove and validate that the semantic layer will serve its purpose. Specifically, they are used to test the proposed semantic layer solution, elicit feedback, and ultimately demonstrate the function of the semantic layer to stakeholders so that they are willing to invest in a real initiative. Prototypes can be built with open-source solutions, trial licenses of software, on third-party networks, and using "dummy" knowledge assets. If you're seeking quick proof of the semantic layer, a prototype can be designed and built using these tools fairly quickly. However, prototypes often lack that "wow" factor, as they are not connected to any real knowledge assets to deliver real results.

- **Pilots**, on the other hand, are real-world systems that are simply limited in scope. In the case of a semantic layer pilot, real users would actually leverage the pilot in their work, seeking and seeing real results. Pilots are harder to progress than prototypes, as they require sign-off from your organization's security, IT, and procurement teams, but they also serve as a first real step toward realizing a comprehensive semantic layer within your organization. Pilots give you the flexibility to iteratively validate your proposed ontology model against real data and content, fine tune the tagging of internal sources for your knowledge graph, and, like the prototype, demonstrate the value of the semantic layer to stakeholders. Testing your semantic model and technologies within a confined scope will enable your organization to gain perspective on value and complexity before making a big investment. Therefore, the pilot goes beyond simply demonstrating the functionality of the semantic layer and can serve as a much more compelling tool to gather support, feedback, and interest from real users. We recommend the pilot because it positions you to be able to immediately build on the pilot as the foundation and begin iterating use cases and scaling the semantic layer solution once buy-in is earned.

It is important to note that both prototypes and pilots are functional, as opposed to wireframes or mockups, which will help the design process and help users provide feedback, but lack the back-end "wiring" to deliver actual functionality. Though these can nonetheless be a valuable step in the design process, we find it takes at least a working prototype, if not an actual pilot, to really make the value of the semantic layer click.

You should remember that there are multiple reasons to begin with a prototype or pilot, but it is all for naught if you don't get approval to proceed beyond this initial step. In other words, ensure that you're showing enough, or delivering enough, for the stakeholders, executives, and your end users to give you the commitment, funding, and approval to continue the expansion of the framework.

Iterative Roadmaps

One of the challenges with the iterative approach that we recommend is the "so what" factor, or the initial release being somewhat underwhelming, not demonstrating sufficiently new or exciting features. One of the best ways to combat this effect is to build a roadmap that shows when subsequent iterations are planned to go live and what these iterations will entail. Of course, this roadmap could quickly become overly technical or detailed in nature, so the intent should be to aim for the appropriate audience. Executives and senior stakeholders will be primarily focused on business value and outcomes, whereas your day-to-day end users will want to know more detail about how each iteration will affect them and their work. Finally, your organization's information technology and engineering groups will want even more detail. Thus, when we discuss iterative roadmaps, we're really speaking in the plural, as you will probably want to create several roadmaps, each for a different audience. These roadmaps, collectively, will be a powerful tool of communication to keep various stakeholders engaged while also setting reasonable expectations for what will come. Roadmaps should be considered living artifacts and be consistently updated as schedules change, priorities shift, and you learn what matters most to your organization (Fig. 3.12).

Next, we will discuss key performance indicators for the semantic layer. To the greatest extent possible, ensure that you know exactly what it will take, for example, what you must prove, who you must impress, in order to receive this approval. Delivering a working system is not enough if it does not also inspire organizational commitment. With this in mind, you can design and scope features and functionality into your proposed semantic layer strategically. Remember that, with each iteration, the semantic layer will grow more capable, meaning that it will be able to garner more support. The early phases are the most delicate, so design use case implementation strategically so that you maintain the support necessary to proceed.

Defining Key Performance Indicators and Measures of Success

The point of iteration is to ultimately create a mature semantic layer. Like many AI and semantic initiatives, understanding the "definition of done" is critical. As you move through this planning stage of your semantic layer initiative, you must clearly define what the target state of your semantic layer will be and what level of semantic layer maturity you are seeking.

Persona	Their Priorities	Your Goals for Them	Roadmap View
Executives and Senior Stakeholders	• Costs and benefits, in concrete terms. • Measurable business benefits. • Time to benefits and returns.	• Approve project funding on an ongoing basis. • Free up time and resources to provide guidance, oversight, and functional/technical support for the semantic layer initiative.	• High-level, executive summary view that focuses on milestones and ROI. • A supporting business case that details costs and anticipated financial benefits.
End Users	• Tools that improve their work or make their jobs easier. • As little change as possible.	• Openness to change and willingness to adopt the semantic layer. • Willingness to participate in discovery activities like interviews, focus groups, or workshops, and to provide feedback. • Patience throughout the iterative process.	• Detailed roadmap view that shows tasks, timelines, and milestones. • Specific roadmap details for tasks that involve their business area. • Supporting documentation regarding any pilots, specifically detailing the time required from them.
Technical Stakeholders	• The cost, compatibility, and risk of new technology. • Avoiding unnecessary work/responsibility. • Having a view of what sources will be connected to what, when. • Clarity around security and entitlements risks.	• Support for the technical aspects of the implementation. • Willingness to participate in technical aspects of the framework, including software selection and procurement, software implementation and operations, and integration with existing systems.	• Technology-focused view of the workstream that details technical tasks. • Supporting documents regarding IT costs and timelines for procurement of new technologies. • Specific plans for security and entitlements.

Fig. 3.12 Business-centric roadmap table

Completeness can be highly subjective if you're not careful. When you consider the components of the semantic layer, you may ask, "Is a taxonomy ever really complete? Does a business glossary ever contain every business term?" The answer is, of course, no. Completeness, therefore, does not mean that the semantic layer is connecting every knowledge asset or being able to solve every business problem within your organization. Rather, completeness will vary depending on the use cases you have defined in this design stage. This is why defining these use cases and carefully organizing them is so important. With this definition in mind, we can assess the completeness of the semantic layer in these terms:

- The components of the semantic layer and their underlying technologies are implemented and robust.
- The components are connected to necessary knowledge asset sources, with assets enhanced with metadata and governance.
- Applications powered by the resulting semantic layer function well for end users.

You should plan to define the definition of done for your semantic layer not based on what's in it and how many nodes, terms, or assets it encompasses, but rather what your organization can do with it and what answers it is capable of supplying. Thus, the key consideration for your definition of done is one of accuracy. While your goal should be 100% accuracy, this cannot also be the expectation, as this is unrealistic and nowhere near close to what existing information systems are delivering today. To set a reasonable measure of success, you will also want to consider the current state of your organization, recalling the journey maps created by your users. If the current state is rife with errors and produces acceptable and accurate results only one in five times, you'll be willing to accept less accuracy than if the current state is 99% flawless. At what point then can your task force move from testing to production? What percentage is good enough? This threshold of accuracy will also vary based on the nature of your industry (i.e., how heavily it is regulated, how critical it is), the culture of your organization (i.e., how open to risk, how patient, how experimental, how wrong are you willing to be), and your chosen semantic layer use cases (i.e., how business critical are they, how many levels of review will follow, how much human oversight will there be, etc.).

When setting your initial targets for accuracy, also recognize that some level of fine-tuning is to be expected once it moves into production and is working in "real-world" scenarios. You will want to ensure the resources are in place for this fine-tuning period and that you've also communicated the expectation for tuning to any potential users. This clearly set expectation will make them more patient with initial errors and will also encourage them to report errors and issues in order for you to incorporate that feedback into the tuning process. Treat this as part of a change management and adoption plan to get your early users communicating with you. As long as you respond to their feedback and they see incremental improvements, they will continue to be open to the process and be inclined to work with you to make it better.

Key Performance Indicators

To best understand this "definition of done," we recommend that you also set **key performance indicators (KPIs)** as part of your initial semantic design and strategy. A KPI is a quantifiable value that measures how effectively an organization has realized some goal, or in this case, the semantic layer. Because we propose an iterative approach to use case implementation and semantic layer design, you will want to consider at what stage is appropriate to assess which KPIs. For example, if your semantic layer only encompasses one business unit, it would not be helpful to assess KPIs related to business domain coverage. The purpose of these KPIs is to gauge the success of your current, realized design and should be agreed upon by the project team as well as other key stakeholders as you continue to implement use cases. There are four main categories of KPIs, and you may wish to choose to measure and report on a combination in order to justify the continued interest and investment in the semantic layer framework:

- **Business KPIs**—Business KPIs measure the performance of a business process (CFI Team n.d.). They can be used to track the business impact of the semantic layer and its alignment with strategic objectives and long-term business goals. These KPIs are measured through usage and activity.
- **Design KPIs**—Design KPIs measure the consistency, coverage, and completeness of the components of the semantic layer. They measure how well the design aligns with and addresses larger corporate goals.
- **Operational KPIs**—Operational KPIs measure the performance, reliability, and scalability of the semantic layer (Understanding KPIs 2021).
- **Organizational KPIs**—Organizational KPIs measure alignment with regards to security, governance, and other institutional policies and procedures (Guide for Setting Up and Improving Organizational KPIs 2023).

These four categories, collectively, can quantify and measure the degree to which the semantic layer "works" and it is trending toward desired completeness.

Business KPIs

Of the four categories, business KPIs are both the most important and most challenging to get right. Business KPIs tie together use cases, transformational goals, and marketing communications to express the actual business use of the semantic layer framework and its front-end applications.

It is easy to confuse adoption and use with success, and your organization should not mistake the total number of users, the total knowledge assets ingested, or the total actions performed within the framework as some mark of success. Just because someone is logged into a system does not mean that the system is valuable. Moreover, activity could alternatively be a sign of failure: a user who doesn't trust their query results, or a user who is confused about how to operate the system may spend more time logged on than a user who finds exactly what they are seeking and moves on to complete their task. Or, the organization has integrated all of their knowledge assets into the semantic layer regardless of the quality or relevance of these assets. This would not result in ease of use or accurate results.

The moral of the story here is that KPIs and other success metrics should consider quality over quantity. Business KPIs should instead measure trends over time to ensure that the semantic layer solution is consistently becoming more and more central to the business and its users. To this end, several relevant business KPIs are:

- **Number of Use Cases Realized**—This metric is useful in that it suggests that the more use cases realized over time, the more business areas are willing to adopt the semantic layer, seeing value in it and seeking to leverage it for more solutions. Use cases directly correspond with real business problems, so the more use cases that are realized, the more business problems are being solved.
- **Number of Integrated Applications**—The amount of semantic layer-powered applications, similar to realized use cases, indicated the success of the semantic layer in that the more applications are integrated, the more likely the framework is driving the speed and functionality of more solutions over time, directly correlating to its value for the organization as a whole. This correlation assumes that the integration of an application means that business users see the value in involving the semantic layer in some business process.
- **User Adoption**—While simply looking at the number of active users on a semantic layer-powered application at a given time may be misleading, tracking the trend of user activity over time indicates the frequency at which users are returning to the semantic layer to assist in their work. A user that returns to the system on a consistent basis is one that has adopted the system into their daily work life because of the value that they have found in previous interactions.
- **Number of Connected Knowledge Asset Repositories**—The sources and repositories of knowledge assets are often not owned by the group designing, developing, and maintaining the semantic layer framework. Continuously governing the semantic layer requires coordination and cooperation with the owners of these systems. The more source owners that are willing to collaborate on the semantic layer initiative within your organization may be a positive indicator of the organizational status or reputation of the framework.
- **Query to Action Ratio**—Though difficult to capture accurately, one of the greatest business KPI for a semantic layer measures the relationship between queries made and completed actions. If a user, for example, runs multiple queries without taking any actions, this is a strong indicator that the results were "wrong," or at least confusing. If a user takes many actions as a result of a single query, the user may have found relevant information. It is also possible that the results were improperly tagged and require interaction to understand. One of the most troubling ratios is zero, meaning a user ran a query and took no action, other than perhaps leaving the system. Dead ends like this typically indicate some frustration with the system. Overall, a balanced ratio that shows users taking action as a result of running a query is the goal of a healthy, functioning semantic layer.

Design KPIs

Design KPIs track the three Cs of the semantic layer: consistency, coverage, and completeness. These design KPIs evaluate the semantic layer's components:

business glossary, metadata, taxonomy, ontology, and knowledge graph. If not properly defined, the measures of consistency, coverage, and completeness can be subjective, so it is important to establish measures of success for each of these design areas.

Consistency tracks whether the definitions, relationships, and classifications of data are standardized and applied uniformly across all systems and for all users. This involves maintaining consistent terminology and data models to prevent ambiguity and to ensure that connected systems and applications deliver the same definitions and logic, regardless of the tool or team using it. Specific design KPIs that measure consistency are:

- **Adherence to Standards**—This KPI measures how well the semantic models follow Semantic Web standards and enterprise data modeling conventions (naming, data types, modeling patterns, description presence, Unified Resource Identifier (URI)/Internationalized Resource Identifier (IRI) specifications, etc.). This KPI is typically measured by regular audits or automated checks for model integrity and compliance.
- **Standardized Terminology**—This KPI assesses how often business terms are defined consistently across the tools and domains represented within the semantic layer by tracking the frequency of duplicate terms or terms with multiple definitions within the model. If a term has multiple definitions, we know that this definition has not been adequately standardized across the system.
- **Incidents of Semantic Drift**—Semantic drift is the process by which the definition of a term or the relationships between business concepts and processes changes over time. Left un-updated, these terms and relationships become unaligned from current business use. This KPI tracks the number of times changes are made without proper version-controlled model change compliance, including communication, documentation, or versioning, which impacts the consistency and synchronization of connected systems and applications. This measure, conducted through regular checks for the number of untracked/unchecked (without a changelog or version control) changes to the model, ensures that the semantic model is consistent and correct across the system.

Coverage measures the breadth of business domains, subject areas, and data sources represented in the semantic layer. Without broad coverage, the semantic layer fails to serve the whole enterprise, resulting in the same disconnectedness the semantic layer attempts to eliminate. Specific design KPIs that measure coverage include:

- **Domain Coverage**—This KPI measures that the amount of business areas (e.g., sales, finance, and marketing) are modeled and represented by the semantic layer. This representation is manifested in the prevalence of business concepts in the semantic layer's data model: its taxonomies, ontologies, and business glossary. This can be measured, too, by tracking the number of entities actively queried by users in addition to surveying how connected and modeled each domain and its corresponding knowledge asset sources are.

- **Connectedness**—This KPI measures the amount of ontology and taxonomy connections or relationships between concepts within a business process or domain. Those concepts that lack rich context in the form of well-constructed conceptual modeling may function poorly and fragment data that would otherwise be considered connected.

Completeness measures the depth and granularity of the content/data and metadata available for each business concept within the semantic layer. This depth is what minimizes user reliance on raw data or spreadsheets to find the answers to their questions. Completeness ensures that the semantic layer provides a full, rich, and usable representation of business knowledge, and is measured by:

- **Metadata Completeness**—This KPI tracks the amount of data with full or complete metadata descriptions, lineage, tags, and relationships. This measure includes tracking whether or not each entity, data product, or content/data concept has a traceable data lineage, showing its movement from source system to final semantic representation.
- **Model Completeness and Granularity**—This KPI measures the functionality of each component of the semantic layer, each of its comprising data models, and whether or not queries related to implemented use cases within a business domain use the necessary components. Additionally, granularity can be measured by the number of terms, entities, relationships, and dimensions that are captured in each of the semantic data models for a given business unit.

Operational KPIs

Operational KPIs measure the performance, reliability, and scalability of the semantic layer framework. This type of KPI can be complex within the context of the semantic layer framework because of the ways in which the framework can be broken down. The semantic layer can be some combination of integrated systems (i.e., a taxonomy and ontology management system, a graph database, and a data warehouse), a single end-use application (chatbot, semantic search), or as the "layer" powering said application. For example, a business or end user may query a semantic layer-powered search application. Even if the semantic layer and all of its components are operating perfectly, there are several other potential loci of failure: the search application itself may be experiencing some error, or perhaps the knowledge asset repository ingested by the semantic layer may be experiencing **downtime**, time when the system is not available for use. In other words, isolating the performance of the semantic layer rather than front-facing applications or knowledge asset sources is difficult. As semantic layers grow more complex, this task becomes even more challenging. To define operational KPIs, you must define, too, what exactly is, and is not, operating.

You may choose to track operational KPIs on (1) each semantic layer-powered applications; (2) each technical component of the semantic layer; or (3) the whole semantic layer framework, including data sources and applications. Here, we'll only detail those operational KPIs related to the semantic layer as a whole, which is most appropriate given this book's subject matter.

- **Response Time**—This KPI measures the amount of time it takes the semantic layer framework to return the results for a query. Acceptable timeframes are highly dependent on the type of application involved in the query or input.
- **Uptime Availability**—Measuring the uptime availability of the semantic layer framework will allow you to get a sense of the stability of the system. **Uptime** is the amount of time a system is functional and available for use. As the framework becomes more and more business critical, availability will be an important measure. In the most business critical systems, the uptime expectation should be near 100%.
- **Scalability**—Scalability is a measurement of how many additional semantic layer-powered applications and additional knowledge asset sources the semantic layer is capable of supporting without re-engineering the framework or causing performance degradation. A year-one scalability KPI may be, for example: "ability to connect with five source systems and power three applications."

These operational KPIs should all be established during the planning phases of the semantic layer initiative, as they will help to determine the scope of the design as well as the type of architecture necessary to support these goals. For instance, a system with the requirement to support dozens of applications and use cases with 99.9% uptime will require a much more rigorous governance plan and complex architecture than a simple pilot that will power a single application. How these KPIs are set will have a major impact on budget and resource requirements.

Organizational KPIs

A complete and well-designed semantic layer should reinforce the existing practices and policies of your organization. To this end, the fourth and final type of KPI focuses on organizational alignment: is the semantic layer aligned with and, in fact, reinforcing core standards of organizational security, governance, and interoperability? These standards will vary from organization to organization, but many of them will be owned by an organization's IT department. Cataloging these requirements at the outset of a semantic layer effort, then tracking them as a binary, as in, compliance or noncompliance, can help to ensure that the semantic layer framework is regarded as a collaborative initiative that supports existing organizational infrastructure and practices. This standardization may also help to minimize the increased administrative burden that comes with implementing this framework. Here are the top two organizational KPIs that we recommend are tracked by your organization:

- **Data Governance**—This KPI measures the semantic layer's ability to detect and report data quality issues such as missing or inconsistent values, reflecting the semantic layer's alignment with organizational data policies and quality standards.
- **Cost of Maintenance**—This KPI measures the overall cost associated with deploying, operating, and maintaining the semantic layer. Other relevant metrics include the cost and amount of time it takes to integrate data from different sources and the number of successful integrations. Reductions in data integration

costs may indicate that the semantic layer's transformation process is running efficiently.

Setting a Transformational Goal

While we began this chapter discussing the importance of use cases to the design and implementation of the semantic layer, sometimes, from a business standpoint, they are not enough to captivate the collective attention of an organization. Use cases, by their definition, are detailed and specific. They outline a single way in which a technology can be used by a particular user to achieve a specific goal. The value of this is that these outcomes are measurable, and projects as complex as the semantic layer can be broken down into individual, specific iterations.

The challenge, however, is that a good use case is typically too limited in its impact to inspire the type of budget and attention necessary for this initiative. Even in choosing to build your semantic layer incrementally, thereby negating the need for a multi-year budget upfront, this strategy runs the risk of potential stop and start that may disrupt the momentum and sidetrack the overall goal. If you're seeking long-term funding and upfront commitment of resources, you will likely need to go beyond a use case proposal. Instead, you will want to situate the semantic layer initiative within a broader, organization-wide goal. This transformational goal is one that would have a massive impact on the organization, usually affecting the bottom line or at least driving the organization's ability to deliver on its core mission. A few examples of transformational goals are to:

- Decrease the amount of time that it takes to fully upskill new employees from 4 years to 2 years.
- Decrease "on the job" injuries by 90%.
- Decrease time to market for new treatments and increase first-time approval rates.
- Double overall staff retention rates and job satisfaction numbers.
- Double online sales within 2 years.

Each of these is "wow" goals that could inspire any organization and are examples from real-world organizational outcomes that the semantic layer has delivered. However, these are also statements that can't be realized without real initiative. What we find most effective is to incorporate a single transformational goal into an existing use case plan, maintaining the practicality and measurable outcomes of the use case plan while also inspiring business interest among executives and stakeholders.

Why Semantic Layer Initiatives Fail

Before we move on to the next section, we would like to leave you with a succinct summary of the main reasons why we have seen semantic layer initiatives fail, hopefully safeguarding you from making these same mistakes. These concepts are just as integral to the success of your semantic layer initiative as those many recommendations we have just detailed.

- **Undefined Goals**—Without a clear understanding of what the semantic layer is supposed to achieve, it is difficult to design and implement a successful framework, and moreover, impossible to agree on a definition of done.
- **Insufficient Resources**—Semantic layer projects can be complex and enterprise-scale, so it is important to have the necessary resources in place, including budget, staff, and expertise to meet initial milestones, as well as have a longer-term view of the resources needed to extend and support the framework.
- **Limited Understanding of the Cost-Benefit Equation**—The initial cost of discovering and implementing semantic solutions to support early use cases can appear high due to the upfront work required—such as to the preliminary setup, content/data wrangling, aggregation, and fine-tuning required to contextualize and connect what is otherwise siloed and disparate data. Additionally, executives may not understand the shift from application-focused to data-driven approaches, leading to premature abandonment of semantic layer projects and missed opportunities.
- **Poor Planning and Execution**—Semantic layer projects require careful planning and execution, including identifying stakeholders, gathering requirements, and developing a detailed implementation plan. These are strategic, resource-intensive needs that require support and interest from a broad array of stakeholders and executives.
- **Lack of Buy-In from Stakeholders**—It is important to get buy-in from relevant stakeholders, including users, business leaders, and IT staff, in order to ensure that the semantic layer project is successful. This is a marked risk when these various groups may be competing for budget and other resources.
- **Technical Challenges**—Semantic layer projects can be technically complex, and it is important to have the necessary expertise in place to address potential challenges.
- **Knowledge Asset Quality Issues**—Semantic layer projects rely on high-quality knowledge assets, so it is important to address any quality issues before implementing the semantic layer.
- **Skillset Misalignment and Resistance to Change**—The success of any advanced solution heavily depends on the skills and training of the teams that will be asked to implement and operationalize it. Many data and IT professionals today continue to be trained on transactional databases and applications and lack semantic technology experience and effective training. This creates a steep learning curve, as most programming languages don't support semantic solution integration into traditional workflows.
- **Lack of Ongoing Maintenance**—Semantic layer projects require ongoing maintenance and updates, so it is important to have a plan in place to ensure that the semantic layer remains up to date and effective.

To summarize, we recommend that you use a combination of top-down and bottom-up activities to assess your organization's needs, goals, and current state and brainstorm potential use cases for the semantic layer through user personas and journey maps, creating an iterative plan for their deployment. In this initial planning phase, you will also need to prove the value of this initiative to those leaders within your organization who would be responsible for funding the realization of your plan, while also inspiring everyday business users and technical SMEs whose help you will need to workshop and actually develop the semantic layer. These business-centric considerations include creating timelines and roadmaps, choosing how you will model the first version of the semantic layer, setting a transformational goal, and embedding key performance indicators into your use case plan.

Once you have set your overarching goals and articulated your core use cases and implementation approach, it's time to dive into the modeling and design methodologies that will allow you to bring your semantic layer components to fruition. In the next section, titled "Developing Semantic Data Models," we will add on to discussion in Chap. 2 of the unique design requirements of each component of the semantic layer by providing methodologies specific to modeling but that apply to *all* of the components and how they connect to one another. By the end of this section, you should have a comprehensive understanding of how to design a semantic layer tailored to your organization's needs, ensuring it aligns with both your data architecture and business objectives.

Developing Semantic Data Models

After identifying your initial semantic layer use cases, the next step is to model the components of the semantic layer. Recall that the purpose of the use case is to outline the interaction between the user and proposed solution. Using this outline, the conceptual model, and the technology inventory, which were all realized in the discovery phase, the semantic layer task force will identify which components of the semantic layer are required to model the use case and begin its design. The purpose of the first model is to introduce semantic components required to connect and standardize existing knowledge assets and enterprise technology. Thus, the first model, and consequently the first use case, should be small and limited to no more than one to two business units: small, incremental use case deployment will ultimately give the semantic model flexibility even as it becomes more complex.

The goal of the initial model is to minimize the burden of data-related tasks on business users, eliminate duplicate data, connect disparate data sources with business users, enable scalability for evolving business needs, and support the continued generation of new information and metadata. It is important to note that not all components of the semantic layer (business glossary, metadata, taxonomy, ontology, and knowledge graph) will need to be modeled at this time; the use case solution may only involve two or three of the components.

To accomplish this initial modeling, refer back to Chap. 2 and the individual sections detailing design considerations for each component. There, we dive into each component and its unique design requirements and technological, governance, and storage needs.

Semantic Layer Component Interactions and Best Practices for Semantic Modeling

Once you have an understanding of how each component can be modeled, there are a few design principles that are worth discussing, as they apply across the board and will expedite this modeling process. To begin, the general steps to developing all of the semantic data models are the same. Once you have selected a use case, the next steps are to:

- Identify and define the relevant semantic layer components needed (business glossary, metadata, taxonomy, ontology, and knowledge graph).
- Evaluate and identify gaps in source data and knowledge assets.
- Assess and implement accompanying technology.
- Connect and integrate data and technology.
- Govern the integrated data model (Fig. 3.13).

These same steps will be repeated for each data model and are not all-encompassing. For example, if your use case would benefit from the use of ontology, metadata, and a business glossary, you will need to spend time conceptualizing the relevant business concepts and terms for each of these components, as the terms

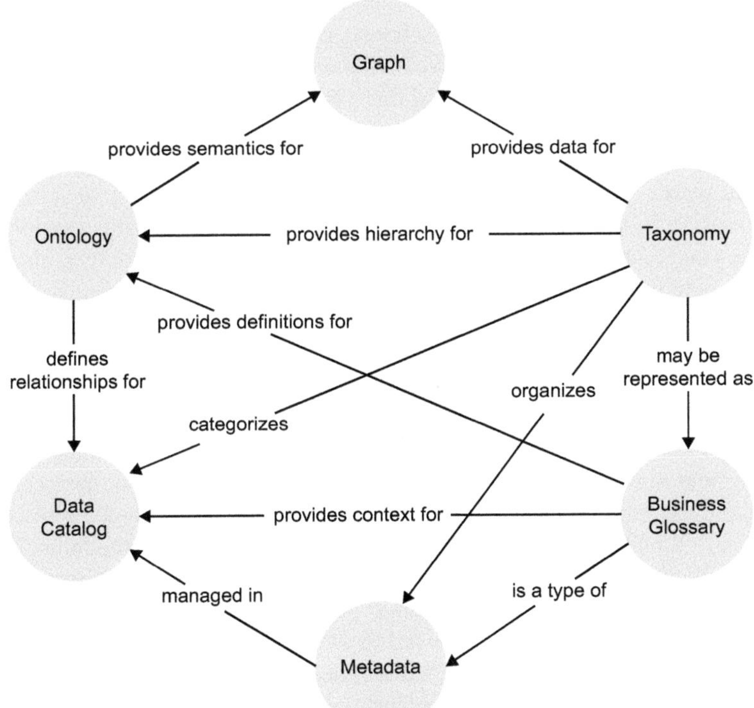

Fig. 3.13 Semantic layer components and interactions

required of the business glossary may be more extensive than those captured in the metadata, for example. Similarly, metadata may require unique terminology to describe the *type* of data being pulled for the use case, while the ontology may capture the business processes and focus less on the type of data and more so on how this data maps onto those actions and relationships. The point of this is to emphasize that, while the steps are the same for each component, the steps should be adjusted based on the component being modeled; one list of terms will not encompass each individual model because each model has a different function within the semantic layer.

Next, the identification and assessment stages of semantic data model development can and should use the same discovery methods detailed in our discussion of the top-down, bottom-up hybrid approach. A group of business users and stakeholders should spend time discussing the shared business concepts relevant to the chosen use case, creating a conceptual model of the business process that uses real business language. This conceptual model will infuse the data modeling process with the insights and language of non-technical business users. For example, to model a taxonomy for a given use case, technical SME's or your organization's taxonomist will need to understand the hierarchical nature of a business process, one that they themselves do not necessarily perform. This is why it is so crucial to enlist business users in addition to the technical stakeholders responsible for modeling the semantic layer.

In addition to leveraging your organization's people, there exist a plethora of public, industry, or domain-specific schemas available. These schemas capture the relationships between well-known business concepts within an industry or domain and are a great place to start when building your own organization's ontologies and taxonomies. Additionally, your organization may even have existing ERDs or other enterprise schemas that relate business concepts. Therefore, our first best practice is to consult public, reputable resources as well as any other enterprise schemas that already exist within your organization. Public resources will provide a strong framework for your own organization's business concepts. These resources also ensure that your organization's semantics are aligned with industry standards. We detail and recommend specific resources related to ontology modeling in the "Ontology" section of Chap. 2.

As a general rule of thumb, we also recommend that your semantic layer task force automate processes when and where possible. Extracting and mapping ontology entities using NLP, NER, LLMs, and AI-driven auto-tagging can augment data modeling and alleviate some of the time and energy spent on the process. While tools, like data catalogs and ontology editors, are not required, we recommend their use, as they allow for easy manipulation and management of the model and make it so that your task force does not need to model an ontology, for example, from scratch. The use of open-source semantic modeling tools such as Protégé, which supports Semantic Web standards, speeds up the modeling process by allowing for simple drop-and-drag editing. At the same time, it's important that NER, data labeling, and classification processes draw from a consistent set of labels and controlled vocabularies defined in the semantic layer. Doing so ensures alignment with domain-specific context and reduces the risk of inconsistencies. Addressing this proactively, as part of the semantic layer's design, prevents downstream technical debt and avoids the need for costly rework once AI systems or data pipelines are already in production.

Lastly, change management is a critical aspect of successfully implementing a semantic layer. Given the complexity of enterprise systems and the potential for resistance from business users, it's essential to approach this transformation with a clear strategy for communication and support. We recommend using Agile iterations as a best practice for designing and developing semantic models. This iterative approach allows you to build, test, and refine the models incrementally, incorporating feedback from users and stakeholders at every stage. Such iterative design and delivery ensures that the semantic layer evolves with the organization's needs, fostering adaptability and reducing push back. Additionally, ensuring strong collaboration between technical teams and business units through regular checkpoints will help mitigate friction and encourage widespread adoption across the organization.

With these design principles and best practices in mind, you can now integrate and implement these components to create a semantic layer framework.

Integrating and Implementing the Semantic Layer

To reiterate the purpose of the semantic layer, let's look to research conducted by Gartner, published in 2019. This research suggests that by 2026, "active metadata" will power over 50% of business intelligence and analytics tools (Finance Research Team 2019). This is significant in that it points to a shift in data and knowledge management, one that disregards the strategy of *consolidating* physical data as old and outdated. Instead, this research argues that *connecting* meaning and data about the data is the future. And this connection is facilitated by context-driven, business-informed, semantic technologies such as metadata, business glossaries, taxonomies, ontologies, and knowledge graphs, all of those components that we have discussed and that make up the semantic layer. Adhering to the "zero-copy" principle, there is a growing tendency among organizations to build a data architecture that greatly reduces or eliminates the need to copy data from one system to another, thus allowing business users to access and analyze data from multiple sources in real time without duplicating it. With the semantic layer, it is no longer a problem if your organization's information is siloed and unstructured, and this is a primary motivation for the implementation of semantic architecture (Tesfaye 2024).

In this section, we will provide a general overview of semantic layer architecture, which contains source systems, the semantic layer, and end-user applications, culminating in what we have referred to as the semantic layer framework throughout this book. We will detail the three possible semantic architectures that we have seen to be commonly adopted, along with their pros, cons, and best uses.

Architecture Overview

There are three key parts that make up the enterprise architecture surrounding the semantic layer framework. The first is your organization's source systems. These systems, which we have referred to as both data sources and knowledge asset repositories throughout this book, are exactly that: they are the systems that store your data, content, and other knowledge assets. In developing the semantic models necessary to realize your use case, you also would have, per our recommendation, done some preliminary assessment of the state of your data and the knowledge assets repositories that will need to be integrated into your semantic layer iteration. These source systems may range from enterprise resource planning (ERP) and customer relationship management (CRM) platforms to file, database, content management systems (CMS), and cloud applications. By tapping into your data through business applications, you can better understand the context of your raw data. This context will allow for more accurate enrichment of metadata, which will ultimately ease semantic integration. Additionally, by mapping out source systems, you can ask and answer questions like: are all critical entities and relationships present in the data represented in my data models? are there blind spots in data lineage or ownership?

Now that you have identified the source systems that will need to be integrated into the semantic layer to realize your use case, let's discuss the next critical part making up the semantic layer framework: the semantic layer itself. At the core of the architecture lies the semantic layer, the "brain" of the semantic stack. Using components like the business glossary, metadata, taxonomy, ontology, and knowledge graph, the semantic layer transforms raw data into knowledge assets that are structured, enriched, and queryable across systems. Integrating this second part, the semantic layer, into your enterprise architecture results in:

- **Reusability**—Once mapped, concepts can be reused across departments, projects, and systems, allowing you to iterate use cases. Depending on the use case and scale, this typically requires an enterprise semantic solution stack that includes a taxonomy/ontology management system, a graph database, and/or ETL/ELT integration solutions.
- **Consistency**—The implementation of the semantic layer reduces the duplication of definitions and logic across analytics, applications, and integrations.
- **Limiting point-to-point integration**—By introducing a shared semantic layer that standardizes data access and interpretation across systems, minimizing the need for custom or direct connectors between individual source systems and each application.
- **Machine Readability**—By embedding context into data, the semantic layer supports artificial intelligence and machine learning, making the model understandable to algorithms.

Finally, a successful semantic layer doesn't live in isolation. The most practical and scalable semantic architecture powers a variety of downstream applications and end-user experiences, making up the final entity of the semantic architecture. This way, an organization can "plug" semantic components into other enterprise solutions, applications, and services. You can also think about these applications as your realized use cases. These applications include:

- **Enterprise Search**—Contextual, relationship-aware search tools that surface content and data.
- **Data Visualization and Business Intelligence**—Business intelligence tools such as Tableau, Power BI, or Qlik can be integrated with the semantic layer to present data in a business-friendly way.
- **Chatbots and Digital Assistant**s—The semantic layer allows chatbots to provide context-aware responses and recommendations.
- **Automation and AI Services**—The semantic layer enables NLP, entity recognition, machine learning, and automated classification to enhance findability and usability of knowledge assets. It can also drive the automated categorization of content to augment data and AI governance practices.

Next, we will discuss how to fit these three parts together to construct a semantic enterprise architecture. There are three ways of approaching their integration.

Three Semantic Layer Architectures

Different architectural implementations of the semantic layer range from tightly coupled, centralized models to more distributed, decoupled, "headless" architectures (Tesfaye 2024). Each approach offers a different balance of control, flexibility, and scalability. The decision of which to implement depends on an organization's specific needs for governance, speed, and business context.

Metadata-First or Decoupled Architecture

The metadata-first architecture is the most common and scalable model that we see used. It has been implemented across industries and for various use cases, delivering enterprise-wide applications. The metadata-first architecture is also a logical architecture, which means that it involves the creation of a logical layer that abstracts the underlying data sources using metadata. This approach is a **decoupled architecture** that abstracts the semantic layer from any tool, providing greater flexibility, scalability, and resilience compared to traditional, monolithic systems. A decoupled architecture is a system design approach where its components can exist and function independently, interacting with one another via clear, well-defined protocols. This approach acts to centralize the management of semantic definitions and business logic to make them accessible to various consumption tools via APIs or platforms that support this model.

As depicted in Fig. 3.14, this architecture allows business users to access and relate data without the need for the physical consolidation of that data. Data remains in its original source, while the semantic layer extracts and connects relevant information using its abstracted components (glossary, taxonomy, ontology, etc.), providing a unified view of data relying on the contextual or semantic data *about* the raw data. This approach rejects application centricity, instead leveraging the

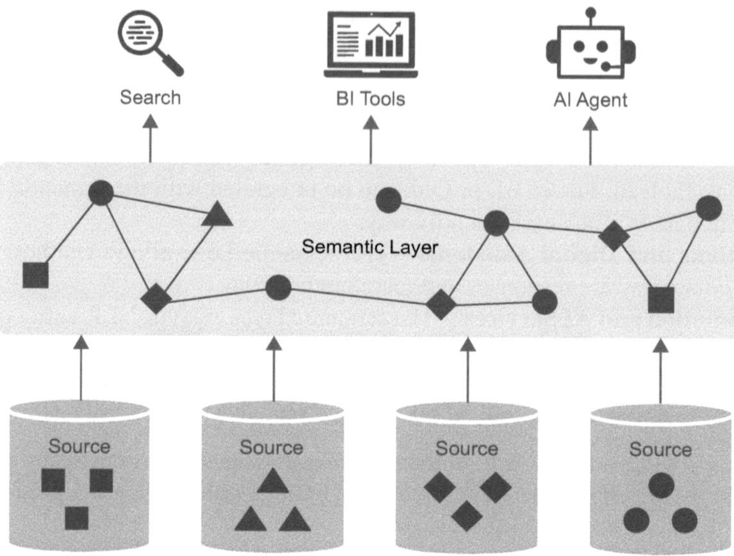

Fig. 3.14 Metadata-first architecture

capabilities of stand-alone tools to manage and store relevant components of the semantic layer. This allows various teams across the organization to define semantic components once and serve them to any tool, analytics application, content or data system, or AI model, ensuring consistency regardless of the tool. Another benefit of this approach is that it ensures consistency through shared data definitions and is managed at the enterprise level, while still providing flexibility for individual teams to manage their unique, secondary semantic data requirements.

This metadata-first approach to semantic layer implementation poses some challenges, too. This approach requires incremental development to maintain its connectivity and prevent the fragmentation of semantic layer components and systems. Additionally, depending on the selected synchronization approach of the layer with downstream and upstream applications, ETL pipelines will need to consider centralized (built on top of a central, pre-integrated asset repository) or decentralized (built on top of individual/distributed domain-specific data products) data orchestration to ensure ongoing alignment.

This is the most scalable, adaptable, and our recommended approach to architecting semantic layers implementations as it ultimately allows the organization to have centralized control of its business meaning and logic with decentralized access to semantic components, providing semantic data to users through the tools that they prefer.

Decentralized or Distributed Architecture

The decentralized architecture allows for flexibility and autonomy at the business unit level. Unlike the metadata-first architecture, which deploys a semantic layer at the enterprise level, across all data sources, the decentralized architecture, as seen in

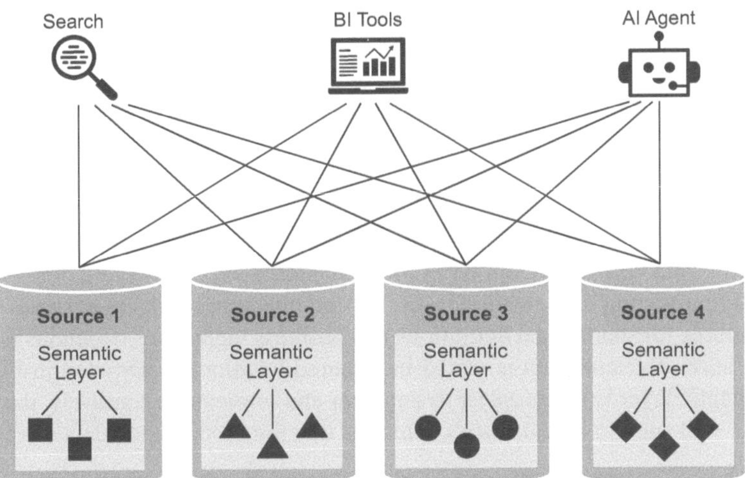

Fig. 3.15 Decentralized architecture

Fig. 3.15, applies semantic layer components within individual applications and stand-alone data systems. The implementation of this architecture is more siloed in that each individual domain or department, for example, marketing, sales, product, etc., is typically responsible for designing, executing, and managing its own semantic layer, tailoring its components to the department's specific needs and requirements. Most business function-specific systems, such as content management systems (CMS), digital asset management systems (DAMs), customer relationship management systems (CRMs), and data analytics or business intelligence dashboards inherently contain semantic components. While simplistic, and with varied maturity and flexibility, these components result in a decentralized architecture of multiple, system-level semantic layers. The decentralized architecture gets its name from these existing, department-specific systems.

The benefit of this decentralized architecture is its ability to empower business domains or departments to leverage existing, built-for-purpose platforms, not just generic content and data repositories. Department agility and an understanding of knowledge assets for the purpose of specific business functions and analysis may be attractive for some organizations. The downside, however, is that, because data is not unified under a shared enterprise semantic layer and governance strategy, the decentralized approach typically leads to data siloing, separate interfaces, semantic drift, inconsistencies in data definitions and governance, content duplication, and other data quality issues. Business units can become misaligned and potentially interpret data elements differently, leading to confusion, inaccuracies, and other risks.

Therefore, this decentralized approach is advantageous for diverse and complex organizations that have many business units that already function independently. This is because the individual semantic layers will allow for more unit-specific definitions and context, alleviating potential semantic mishaps and increasing the speed of adaptation to evolving business needs. If these business units are already used to functioning in isolation, it may be easier for them to navigate issues of governance and alignment. Individual business users will also have more control over their data and will not have to rely on a centralized team that may or may not fully understand their business needs.

Centralized Architecture

The centralized architecture structures data into an enterprise data warehouse (EDW) or data lake before applying the semantic layer, simplifying data engineering and centralizing the semantic layer. This architecture results in a single, authoritative source for shared data definitions and business logic across domains within an organization. Because data is stored in a shared location, as depicted in Fig. 3.16, the semantic layer is much easier to engineer and implement. Similarly, the semantic layer will support any analytics solutions that use cloud-based data warehousing

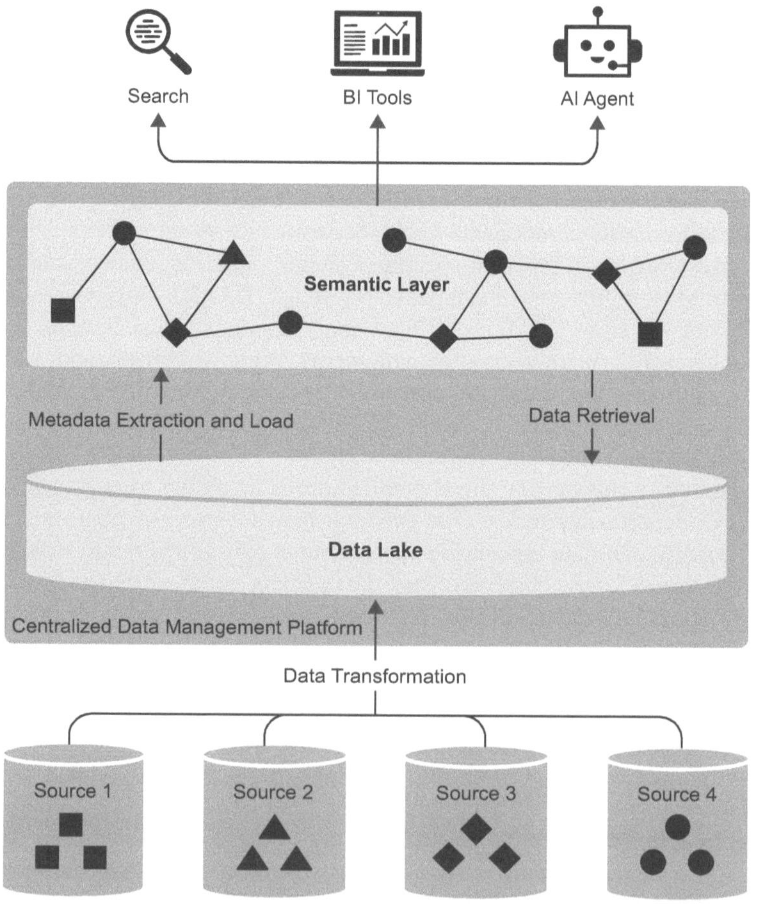

Fig. 3.16 Centralized architecture

platforms. This architecture is most commonly adopted by organizations that have already gone through transformation efforts to create a data lake with data consolidated from various sources to create a standardized interface for data access.

Because the centralized architecture requires data to be consolidated and co-located in a data lake or other repository, the implementation of this architecture requires collaboration between business and data teams to organize this data. Additionally, small, singular use cases are essential to the stability of the model. These incremental use cases will ensure that the scope of the model is valuable and focused on business outcomes. This model can then be iteratively expanded across the organization's knowledge assets, but this process takes time and requires consistent maintenance. Thus, we often support this approach for data-driven teams or data management, data analytics, and BI groups that are committed to continuous data ingestion and management can alter data structures and enforce business rules through dedicated ETL pipelines or APIs and have the regulatory mandate to ensure enterprise-wide data is consolidated and governed.

This approach is particularly beneficial for large organizations with complex but shared data requirements. These organizations typically necessitate rigid data governance and compliance already because they produce their own data products and need a reliable way to ensure the accuracy of knowledge assets that are created, analyzed, and shared externally on a regular basis. These organizations include financial institutions, healthcare organizations, bioengineering firms, and retail companies.

Ultimately, selecting a semantic layer architecture requires balancing governance and consistency with business unit autonomy, agility, existing systems, AI models, and cost considerations. Regardless of the approach, the most important anchor is the set of business use cases defined during the planning phase. At the same time, adhering to established modeling and Semantic Web standards will help you avoid vendor lock-in, ensure interoperability, and support resilience of the framework and the solutions involved as technologies evolve.

Semantic Layer Governance and Expansion

Now that you have a semantic layer framework modeled, architected, implemented, and in active use, the focus shifts to governing and expanding. **Governance** is the process of setting standards, defining rules, establishing policies, and implementing oversight to ensure the quality and maintenance of a system. Effective governance ensures consistency, compliance, and alignment across business units, while expansion allows the framework to scale with new content/data sources, AI models, and evolving business needs. Together, these practices safeguard the integrity of your semantic foundation while enabling it to deliver greater value over time (Tesfaye 2021).

So, how do you actually update, maintain, and expand an enterprise semantic layer framework? We often see organizations succeed in building pilots and prototypes that adequately demonstrate the potential of the solution, but fewer organizations are actually successful in deploying these solutions across their enterprise. By successful, we mean that the deployed semantic layer actually yields business value or ROI. Governance and the success of the semantic layer are intertwined in that, if the semantic layer is not properly governed, it will quickly become useless to its business users. In this section, we will share the key approaches to governance that we have found effective in maintaining and managing the semantic layer, once deployed, to ensure its functionality and future within your organization.

Ownership of the Semantic Layer

An effective semantic layer governance model will define a set of standards and processes to handle requests for changes to the solution and peripheral systems. Specifically, these governance processes will be allocated to individuals within the organization who will dedicate time to the fulfillment of governance duties, taking on a specific governance role and responsibility. These governance roles also touch on the question of ownership. With such a diverse and complex set of functions, where should the ownership of the semantic layer actually rest? In very few organizations will ownership of all of the components of the semantic layer and all of the systems of the framework rest within a single person. Therefore, instead of thinking about semantic layer "ownership," it is really more helpful to consider this function as stewardship or sponsorship. Nonetheless, there does need to be a shared, organizational structure to realize the promise of the semantic layer. Shared or centralized ownership is critical for several reasons:

- **Alignment**—Without a group consistently overseeing and checking for business alignment and connectivity, several competing initiatives are likely to form. The semantic layer initiative, even with its origins in a single business unit, should only be done once. Multiple initiatives should be taking place at the same time, within different units, as this will create duplication in the semantic layer's components, require duplicative resources, and cause semantic drift. A shared or centralized group for a semantic layer will ensure alignment and functionality across the whole organization, uniting business units and stakeholders, delivering a succinct marketing message, and setting transformational and attainable goals.
- **Availability of Semantic Data as a Service**—Successful, organizational shared-services facilitate the operating models and infrastructure to deliver semantic data models as a service to the rest of the organization. This ensures that all teams, from business SMEs to data scientists, can access consistent, governed, and business-ready semantic data through standardized interfaces.
- **Budget, Staffing, and Resources**—Fully realized semantic layer frameworks require organizational investment in software, staff, and experts over the course of multiple years. Centralized, permanent ownership will support and validate this budget as it evolves over the course of its development.
- **Priorities and Goals**—One of the greatest indicators of the success of the semantic layer is the number of groups within your organization interested in

using it for their needs. This can be measured in the amount of semantic layer-powered applications, the amount of realized use cases, and the amount of business users served. What this may translate to is a formidable number of requests. Taking on too much too soon can corrupt the success of the semantic layer and overwhelm the team responsible for its design. Therefore, having a single group that possesses the authority to set use case priority as well as decline proposed extensions and projects is important to the sustainability of the semantic layer.

- **Advocacy and Championship**—As with any high-profile, high-cost program, there will be those who question the value of the semantic layer. A shared or centralized team plays a key role in marketing and defending the value of the semantic layer, finding opportunities to track and broadcast its use, value, and return on investment to the organization. Therefore, this team acts as an advocate and as a layer of transparency. Combined with a demonstrated backlog of future projects, this marketing is an important strategy to ensure the long-term viability of the semantic layer.
- **Addressing Rogue Programs**—The central body should also work to address those groups or programs within your organization that are either attempting to develop a competing effort or attempting to use the semantic layer for a use case or application that is not a good fit for the enterprise. To ensure that the usability of the semantic layer remains strong, the centralized owners of the semantic layer should prevent these detrimental maneuvers.
- **Quality Assurance**—The role of this ownership team should also be to ensure the quality, accuracy, and consistency of the semantic layer. The semantic layer must be reliable, and if it is not, it is the job of this team to address constructive feedback, quality issues, and other user experiences to always keep improving the semantic layer.

With these responsibilities in mind, where should the core semantic layer staff sit within the organization? There are several potential ownership models, ranging from highly centralized to decentralized. Given the organizational reach of the semantic layer, our experience shows that hybrid models are typically the best. In practice, a hybrid ownership model often includes a smaller core team of semantic experts and decision-makers able to guide and manage the design and prioritize use cases and next steps, accompanied by a distributed grouping of business representatives to offer inputs, guidance, and approvals, ensuring the semantic layer framework operates cohesively while still garnering interest and inputs from across the business. With this in mind, the governance team should typically include a taxonomist, ontologist, data engineers, database and application administrators and managers, content owners, and business representatives or analysts.

Strategies like **RACI**, which stands for Responsible, Accountable, Consulted, and Informed, help governance teams outline who should be responsible for what work, who is ultimately accountable, who and when the team needs to consult outside guidance, and importantly, who and how changes should be communicated. Informing end users, consumers, and stakeholders before, during, and after major changes to the semantic architecture or model is one of the most important ways to keep the whole organization engaged in the semantic solution (Fig. 3.17).

RACI Table　　　　R = Responsible　A = Accountable　C = Consulted　I = Informed

Governance Level & Task	Business Owner	Semantic Model Designer	Semantic / Data Engineer	Content or Data Owner / Steward	IT / Platform
Request updates / changes or provide use cases	R	C	C	R / A	I
Approve / validate new semantic model definitions	C	R	C	A	I
Apply naming / modeling standards	C	R	A	A	I
Enforce mapping of model to content	C	A	R	A	C
Manage access controls	I	C	R	A	A
Monitor content / data quality in semantic layer	I	C	R	C	I
Maintain lineage and change log documentation	I	A	R	A	I
Monitor semantic engine health / performance	I	I	R	C	A
Deploy and scale infrastructure	I	I	C	I	R / A
Maintain SLA and uptime tracking	I	I	C	I	R / A

Fig. 3.17 RACI table

In addition to this model, we often find that these five positions most commonly play some role in the semantic layer governance/ownership team:

- **Chief Data and AI Officer (CDAO)**—The semantic layer is born of many data initiatives that came before it. These initiatives are often owned by an organization's data office. For organizations that have taken a broad definition of data to align more closely with our definition of knowledge assets, housing a semantic layer initiative under the CDAO makes sense. However, for organizations that have drawn hard lines between structured and unstructured data, with the CDAO only owning responsibilities for the former, this may be too limiting.
- **Human Resources and/or Learning and Development**—Semantic layer initiatives with mature People and Expertise components and use cases may consider housing ownership within HR and L&D departments. Use cases that support learning, access to experts, and knowledge transfer may align best with these departments, especially when we consider their outcomes and measurable KPIs. However, as the semantic layer evolves, incorporating new use cases and knowledge assets, these departments may no longer fit the needs and goals of the initiative.
- **Business Lines**—Business lines are those departments within an organization that drive its business, such as marketing, sales, or products and services. These departments differ between organizations, but whatever is considered the revenue-generating or customer-facing part of an organization may be an ideal starting point for the semantic layer. This is because it will be much easier to draw a connection between ROI and the first use case of the semantic layer. Though the core semantic layer staff can be housed in a business line during its initial stages, it is typically unwise for this to be its "final" home, as this will limit

the scope of the semantic layer initiative. In most cases, the semantic layer should be considered an enterprise framework that enables relevant business lines and shared use cases, rather than a subset.

- **Chief Operating Officer (COO)**—To truly place the semantic layer at the core of an organization, the semantic layer ownership team should consider reporting to the COO. This is because, at its core, the semantic layer enables and facilitates enterprise operations. Though this is not yet the most common placement, it is, in our opinion, the ideal placement, as it adequately encompasses the full life-cycle of the semantic layer.

Depending on the stage of a semantic layer effort, any of the above four options are viable. There are many other options, depending on the organization, but only in rare cases do we recommend a semantic layer be owned by the information technology office. The reason for this is simple: if you treat a semantic layer initiative as a technology-first effort, you will miss the human and semantic focus that actually drives business value. Getting the technology right is a core success factor, but secondary to the core semantics, knowledge assets, and user-driven design elements we've already discussed.

A Shift in Enterprise Roles and Operating Models

In a final thought on governance ownership and responsibility, one of the most subtle yet significant changes that we have seen over the past couple of years is the blending of traditionally siloed data management functions. What used to be a data governance team made up of officers and compliance specialists who guarded data quality, privacy, and security is now made up of knowledge managers. The effect is that of enablement: Data is no longer seen as something to be simply controlled, but as something to be used and accessed. In other words, knowledge managers see, make visible, and unlock the business potential of data. The industry-agnostic shift toward AI initiatives has heightened the visibility of KM and is pushing organizations to identify more optimized ways to organize governance teams and measure and convey the value of KM to organizational leaders.

Additionally, as AI fuels the democratization of knowledge and data, there is a growing recognition of the interdependence of data, information, and knowledge management teams. Therefore, the role of the knowledge management specialist is increasingly important to organizational collaboration, access, self-sufficiency, and attractive business initiatives like AI. This is not to say that these original roles and quality assurance teams are now obsolete: data officers and KM teams will continue to play a critical role in ensuring data quality, privacy, and security. But, as roles shift in function from governance to enablement, these teams will increasingly focus on established frameworks that support transparency, user independence, collaboration, and compliance across a more data-centric enterprise, availing self-service analytics tools that allow even non-technical business users to analyze data and generate insights.

Semantic Layer Expansion Roadmap Considerations

Expansion and roadmap considerations for building enterprise-scale semantic layers require a phased, iterative approach that prioritizes immediate, high-value business use cases. The strategy we have adopted throughout this book began with developing a design focused for a single, high-impact domain or use case to establish a quick win and build organizational confidence. This foundational work can then be extended to additional use cases, knowledge asset sources, and architectural components. A critical roadmap element is ensuring that this process is not confined to an isolated team but involves domain experts from the beginning to ensure that the models accurately reflect business logic and user needs across the enterprise. This iterative cycle of design, validation, and implementation is crucial for adapting to the dynamic nature of an organization's knowledge and ensures the model remains relevant and robust over time.

As your semantic model matures and gains buy-in, the expansion roadmap should focus on leveraging enterprise knowledge assets to build out the semantic components that connect previously siloed information. This involves incrementally integrating semantic components with actual enterprise content and data from multiple sources, such as CRMs, ERPs, PIMs, etc. A key consideration is the technical infrastructure, including the selection of semantic data storage and management tools and defining standardized data integration processes (ETL). Expansion and development activities should also be iterative, starting with targeted releases on small but representative use cases and data sources, validating the results against business questions, and then progressively expanding to encompass more sources and domains across the enterprise. This phased expansion allows for continuous validation, reduces the risk of large-scale failures, and provides tangible value at each stage of development (Fig. 3.18).

Finally, as we discuss in detail next, long-term roadmap considerations for enterprise-scale semantic layer development focus on automation, governance, and enterprise-wide application. A robust governance strategy is essential to manage the evolution of the semantic layer at scale, including processes for updates, conflict resolution, and ensuring ongoing content/data quality and consistency. By following this iterative roadmap, your organization can transform a limited pilot project into a scalable, enterprise-grade asset that fundamentally improves how it manages and leverages knowledge and data.

Long-Term Governance

It is imperative to recognize that a semantic layer will never reach a permanent state of completeness. Even as you work toward maturing your semantic layer use case by use case, the semantic layer will always require care and fine-tuning. As your business changes, as your needs shift, as new use cases are identified, the semantic layer framework will need to be amended and expanded.

This is why governance is so important. Governance ensures not only the consistent operation of a system but also reflects those changing needs of your organization. It allows the system to be flexible, to adapt. Governance in semantic tools like

	Pilot	MVP	Operationalize	Institutionalize
Use Case Design & Gap Analysis	**1.1.** Define pilot use case and create backlog	**1.2.** Select 1-2 use cases from backlog for MVP	**1.3.** Incorporate MVP use cases into 1-2 business processes and policies	**1.4.** Incorporate MVP use cases into 2+ business processes and policies
Knowledge Asset Preparation & Mapping	**2.1.** Conduct knowledge asset inventory and cleanup	**2.2.** Map semantic models to 1-2 knowledge assets	**2.3.** Map semantic models to 2+ knowledge assets	**2.4.** Expand mapping to enterprise knowledge assets
Semantic Layer Modeling & Validation	**3.1.** Design FIV taxonomy and ontology	**3.2.** Create MVP model (taxonomy and ontology design)	**3.3.** Expand semantic model to additional domains	**3.4.** Expand semantic model enterprise-wide
Implementation, Integration, & Instantiation	**4.1.** Develop Semantic Layer Proof of Concept (PoC)	**4.2.** Deploy PoC Semantic Layer architecture	**4.3.** Operationalize piloted use cases; move to production	**4.4.** Roll out, phase by phase, enterprise-wide
Governance & Operating Model	**5.1.** Pilot recommended operating model	**5.2.** Develop Semantic Layer governance plan	**5.3.** Conduct training for operating model members	**5.4.** Conduct enterprise-wide training

Fig. 3.18 Sample expansion roadmap

taxonomy, ontology, metadata, and their management systems is challenging because their design is highly dynamic and their terms and their definitions may need to change often to accommodate business thinking. When you think about a complete semantic layer framework as an integrated combination of discrete technologies, semantic design components, and source knowledge assets, the challenge of governance can be overwhelming.

For this reason, the long-term governance plan of your organization's semantic layer should be conceptualized well in advance of the release of the framework. Depending on budget cycles and how funding works in your organization, you may wish to make semantic layer governance its own workstream, occurring alongside the design and implementation of the semantic layer itself. To summarize, there are costs and resources that will be to be accounted for in the long-term governance plan, and these should be identified and established well in advance of the launch of the layer itself. At minimum, the long-term governance plan for the semantic layer framework should include the following components:

- **Ownership and Responsibilities**—In accordance with the previous section on ownership, your governance plan should define who has control over each of the design and technical components of the semantic layer framework, as well as the associated responsibilities for each. This should include a clear understanding of decision-making authorities for creating, editing, or deleting/archiving design components, such as taxonomy terms, synonyms, ontology relationships, and business glossary terms and rules. At a higher level, this plan should also outline who has the ability/responsibility to set priorities about which use cases to address next, which design components to expand upon, or which source asset systems to integrate with. This will be your semantic layer task force or team.

- **Processes to Address Issues and Errors**—One of the previous responsibilities (or sets of responsibilities) defined in the bullet point above will revolve around proactively and actively addressing issues with the outputs and results of the semantic layer, identifying conflicts, spotting problematic patterns, or responding to feedback. This will include the use of tools to flag inconsistencies or errors, especially during the auto-tagging or data integration stages, creating and supporting feedback loops for end users to report errors or suggest improvements, semantic data quality or metadata-driven data quality checks to validate accuracy and consistency based on meaning and relationships, and processes for handling inconsistent terminology, misaligned definitions, data integration challenges, and semantic drift. It is important to note that a successful governance plan will detail not just what decisions need to be made, but *how* these decisions will be made. This will build consistency and leave "political" factors out of the equation.
- **Collaboration and Communication**—In addition to the feedback mechanisms we mentioned above, the governance plan should cover how different groups, experts, stakeholders, and even the core project team will coordinate and communicate. You can consider this as a project or program charter if that is language familiar to your organization, but the basis of this idea is to set standard meeting times, agendas, and goals for collaboration. Outside of the core team, this can also cover how to solicit, capture, and act on feedback from an assortment of stakeholders and end users. Many programs do a fine job of soliciting feedback, but a distinguishing factor for the semantic layer program should not just be to solicit feedback, but to respond to it. We refer to this as a two-way communications plan, which is a valuable tool to drive change management and adoption. A good two-way communication strategy facilitates user feedback and requests. This feedback is often negative, not due to flaws in the system, but because users are more likely to notice things that aren't working than those that are. Instead of hiding this negative feedback, it should be publicly responded to, which can improve buy-in and demonstrate commitment to ongoing improvements. This shows users that their opinions are heard and considered, typically eliciting more feedback and greater engagement in making the program a success.
- **Monitoring and Analytics**—One of the means by which ongoing decisions should be made, and specifically how potential issues should be proactively identified, is through the use of system analytics. The use and distribution of terms within semantic components and the frequency of edits to definitions and synonyms can be analyzed, while the connections between the components, the data sources, and end applications should be monitored. There are, in a framework like this, many points of potential disconnect. Establishing service level agreements (SLAs) or targets for uptime and connectivity could also be an element of this, though highly dependent on the use cases and applications selected and markedly more important for business-critical systems with real-time implications and requirements.
- **Training and Enablement**—Associated with the roles and responsibilities defined within the governance program, necessary training, competencies, and

experience required should be outlined. Pairing with the communications discussed above, some governance plans may also include end-user training on the value of the semantic layer, how its components function, and how to make change requests. Again, this is use case-specific but can further drive adoption.

To summarize, the governance plan should also include processes for monitoring and correcting unclean data being fed from the semantic layer's data sources; processes for adding new data sources to the semantic layer; processes for changing the underlying semantic data model (i.e., adding, modifying, or depreciating ontological classes, attributes, synonyms, and relationships); processes for updating text analytics and extraction tools that automate the organization of content and apply tags or relationships to data; some standard operating procedure (SOP) outlining communication and messaging best practices for stakeholders and end users; and finally, metrics of success and a meeting cadence for the review of the knowledge graph by governance leadership.

In addition to these factors, there are several potential governance models and organizational models that can support the semantic layer framework, ranging from highly centralized to largely decentralized. However, given the distributed nature of the semantic layer and its requirement to stretch across an organization, our experience shows that hybrid models are typically the best. In practice, a hybrid model often includes a smaller core team of semantic experts and decision-makers able to guide and manage the design and prioritize use cases and next steps, accompanied by a distributed grouping of business representatives to offer inputs, guidance, and approvals, ensuring the semantic layer framework operates cohesively while still garnering interest and inputs from across the business.

We have found that the most successful governance strategies have three distinct but interconnected levels:

Model-Level Governance

The first is governance of the semantic layer model itself. This governance is focused on ongoing semantic clarity and usability, ensuring that the definitions, relationships, and hierarchies business concepts are programmatically standardized, versioned, documented, and approved before being exposed to business users. The key purposes of governance at this level are to enforce naming conventions and modeling standards; approve new terms, relationships, and definitions; maintain lineage and change history; and prevent semantic drift.

Versioning

Iterative changes to the semantic model are necessary for use case scalability and business value (Kass 2023). Thus, the governance plan will need a mechanism to ensure that updates to the semantic model are transparent, interoperable, and scalable. This mechanism is most likely some sort of **versioning**, which is the process of tracking and communicating changes that have been made as a system is updated, usually through version numbers. Versioning allows users to track and view changes made to the system. Additionally, this mechanism ensures the alignment of newly integrated terms and relationships across the semantic model and that changes made to the model are backward compatible, meaning that the new version can still use and access data from the older one. Tracking changes via a versioning plan provides longevity to the semantic model over time and in the face of change.

There are a few ways to execute versioning. First, versions of semantic models can actually be stored within the model itself. For example, ontologies can record the version numbers through the OWL annotation property owl:versionInfo or, if the ontology is not built with OWL, the RDF property rdfs:comment. Another way to execute versioning is using the semantic versioning standard SemVer, which constructs version numbers as MAJOR.MINOR.PATCH (Semantic Versioning 2.0.0 n.d.). MAJOR, MINOR, and PATCH are numbers that are increased numerically, or incremented, based on specific versioning actions (i.e., 2.0.0, 2.0.1, 2.1.1). MAJOR is incremented when a change has been made that is API incompatible; MINOR is incremented when a function is added that is backward compatible; and PATCH is incremented when a backward-compatible bug fix is made. The purpose of this version number format is to communicate more specific information about an update to software developers.

It is also important to capture changes made in between versions. Typical semantic model editing solutions do not write entities in a specific order, so changes to this order will be incorrectly flagged as updates. Version control systems like git or GitHub allow for the logging and tracking of changes between versions. The record of these changes can also be tracked manually by the semantic model designer. Finally, outdated entities within models should first be deprecated before being deleted. **Deprecation** is the act of marking versions as outdated, which signals to users that the entity will soon be removed. Unlike deletion, which is the immediate removal of an entity, deprecation allows users of the ontology, taxonomy, or other semantic model to understand why the entity is being deleted and to prepare for its removal.

Automation

Using technology to automate your governance activities can simplify the process and ultimately support the future growth of your semantic data model (EK Team 2020). For instance, even though it is rather challenging to train a knowledge graph to automatically know the right way to organize new information, the ability to track and check why certain attributes and values were applied to existing knowledge assets should be part of the design and applied to all data that is aggregated into the solution (Tesfaye 2019). One technique that we have used is to segment inferred or predictive data into a separate graph reserved for new and uncertain information. In this way, uncertain data can be isolated from observed or confirmed information, making it easier to trace the origins of inferred information or to recompute inferences and predictions as your underlying data or artificial intelligence models change (Tesfaye 2021).

Confidence scores or ratings in both entities and relationships can also be used to indicate graph accuracy. Additional effective practices that provide checks and processes for creating and updating a knowledge graph include instituting consistent naming conventions throughout the design and implementation (e.g., URIs) and establishing guidelines for version control and workflows, including a log of all changes and edits to the graph. Many semantic models also support the SHACL Semantic Web standard, which can be used to validate your model when adding new data and check for logical inconsistencies.

Knowledge Asset-Level Governance

Content and data level governance ensures data quality, access controls, business glossary and taxonomy alignment, and proper data classification (e.g., sensitive, regulated, PII) (Tesfaye 2021). The specific governance activities include validating and reporting on data quality, mapping data elements to business terms, enforcing access policies and role-based permissions, and ensuring regulatory compliance (e.g., GDPR, HIPAA). The most effective practice is to consistently handle this governance at the source system or data ownership level prior to injecting or connecting data with the semantic layer. To be successful, a primary consideration for the purview of this governance is the type and frequency of change and volume of the data. A viable semantic layer solution is closely linked to the business model and content/data generated by the organization, which means that this data should always be kept up to date. In the context ofa semantic layer, changes to organizational content and data include:

- Adding new content/information or processing new data
- Updating your entities, definitions or metadata
- Adding or removing relationships between entities/content/data
- Updating the query that maps your semantic models (due to a change in your content), etc.

These types of changes should be anticipated and not require the rebuilding or restructuring of your entire solution. As such, depending on your industry and use cases, determining the frequency and update intervals as well as your governance model is a good way to effectively govern the solution. For organizations in the accounting and tax domain, for example, the industry and organizational vocabulary and metadata remain relatively unchanging. This means that real-time updates or edits to their semantic models may not be a primary focus for their governance team.

For organizations in the digital marketing and analytics industry, however, their business is dependent on obtaining a 360 view of consumers in real time. They need to know when, for example, a "marketable consumer" changes their address or contact information so that they can continue to reach them through their marketing initiatives. It is imperative in this case that such rapidly changing business domains have the capabilities and automation necessary to update and govern their semantic models at scale. These examples manifest the reality that organizations can realize savings by shifting away from enterprise level metadata management tools or large-scale data engineering solutions and toward effectively and uniquely defining their data model and governance.

System-Level Governance

System-level governance manages the technical infrastructure that supports the semantic layer, including its deployment, scalability, reliability, and integration with enterprise systems. Key responsibilities include ensuring system availability and performance, managing ETL/ELT or API integration and tool compatibility, tracking system usage and capacity planning, and monitoring SLAs and the uptime of the semantic engines (Tesfaye 2021).

As detailed in the section, "Integrating and Implementing the Semantic Layer," developing programmatic access points to connect organizational applications is a foundational building block for effective solution governance. Enterprise semantic solutions are often constructed through data transformation pipelines. This renders a repeatable process for the mapping of structured sources and the extraction, disambiguation, classification, and tagging of unstructured sources. This also means that the main way to affect data in the knowledge graph is to govern the input data (e.g., exports from taxonomy management systems, content management platforms, database systems, etc.). Otherwise, ad hoc changes to the layer will be lost or erased every time new data is loaded from a connected application. Therefore, designing and implementing a repeatable data extraction and application model that is guided by source system governance is one of the fundamental architectures necessary to the semantic layer framework.

References

CFI Team. (n.d.). "What are Business Metrics?" *Corporate Finance Institute.* https://corporatefinanceinstitute.com/resources/valuation/business-metrics/.

EK Team. "Best Practices for Successful Metadata Governance," *Enterprise Knowledge.* June 29, 2020. https://enterprise-knowledge.com/best-practices-for-successful-metadata-governance/.

EK Team. "Extracting Knowledge from Documents: Enabling Semantic Search for Pharmaceutical Research and Development," *Enterprise Knowledge.* March 3, 2025. https://enterprise-knowledge.com/extracting-knowledge-from-documents-enabling-semantic-search/.

Finance Research Team. "Data Management: A Single Version of the Truth No Longer Works," *Gartner.* December 5, 2019. https://www.gartner.com/en/documents/3975965.

Gartner. "Gartner Predicts 80% of D&A Governance Initiatives Will Fail by 2027, Due to a Lack of a Real or Manufactured Crisis," February 29, 2024. Stamford, CT. https://www.gartner.com/en/newsroom/press-releases/2024-02-28-gartner-predicts-80-percent-of-data-and-analytics-governance-initiatives-will-fail-by-2027-due-to-a-lack-of-a-real-or-manufactured-crisis.

"Guide for Setting Up and Improving Organizational KPIs," *American Society of Administrative Professionals.* July 3, 2023. https://www.asaporg.com/guide-for-setting-up-and-improving-organizational-kpis.

Hilger, Joseph and Zachary Wahl. *Making Knowledge Management Clickable: Knowledge Management Systems Strategy, Design, and Implementation.* Springer, 2022: 16–32.

Hillenbrand, Philipp, Dieter Kiewell, Rory Miller-Cheevers, Ivan Ostojic, and Gisa Springer. "Traditional company, new businesses: The pairing that can ensure an incumbent's survival," McKinsey & Company. June 2019. https://www.mckinsey.com/~/media/McKinsey/Industries/Electric%20Power%20and%20Natural%20Gas/Our%20Insights/Traditional%20company%20new%20businesses%20The%20pairing%20that%20can%20ensure%20an%20incumbents%20survival/Traditional-company-new-businesses-VF.pdf

Hosch, William L. "Zipf's Law," *Encyclopædia Britannica*. August 8, 2025. https://www.britannica.com/topic/Zipfs-law.

Kass, Ben. "Top 5 Tips for Managing and Versioning an Ontology," *Enterprise Knowledge*. January 10, 2023. https://enterprise-knowledge.com/top-5-tips-for-managing-and-versioning-an-ontology/

Tesfaye, Lulit. "How to Build a Knowledge Graph in Four Steps: The Roadmap From Metadata to AI," *Enterprise Knowledge*. September 9, 2019. https://enterprise-knowledge.com/how-to-build-a-knowledge-graph-in-four-steps-the-roadmap-from-metadata-to-ai/.

Tesfaye, Lulit. "How Do I Update and Scale My Knowledge Graph?" *Enterprise Knowledge*. January 12, 2021. https://enterprise-knowledge.com/how-do-i-update-and-scale-my-knowledge-graph/.

Tesfaye, Lulit. "The Top 3 Ways to Implement a Semantic Layer," *Enterprise Knowledge*. March 12, 2024. https://enterprise-knowledge.com/the-top-3-ways-to-implement-a-semantic-layer/.

"Understanding KPIs: 12 Types of Key Performance Indicators," *MasterClass*. November 2, 2021. https://www.masterclass.com/articles/key-performance-indicators-explained.

Valle, Isadora, Tiago Prince Sales, Eduardo Guerra, et al. "Unraveling the Pain Points of Domain Modeling." *Information and Software Technology* 183 (July 2025): 107736. https://doi.org/10.1016/j.infsof.2025.107736.

"What is a Use Case? How to Write One, Examples, + Template," (n.d.). *Figma*. https://www.figma.com/resource-library/what-is-a-use-case/.

Zhang, Xin, Ravi Mangal, Mayur Naik, and Hongseok Yang. "Hybrid Top-down and Bottom-up Interprocedural Analysis." Proceedings of the 35th ACM SIGPLAN Conference on Programming Language Design and Implementation, ACM, June 9, 2014, 249–58. https://doi.org/10.1145/2594291.2594328

Real-World Success Stories

4

Throughout the book, we have told several real-world stories about semantic layer implementation. In this chapter, we will build on these case studies by detailing a series of semantic layer success stories and lessons learned from each. These stories are important because they each illustrate, in both qualitative and quantitative ways, the value of the semantic layer framework, and this value cannot be understated, especially if you are interested in pitching a semantic layer initiative to your own organization. Though these stories have been anonymized, they are all real examples of the successful implementation of a semantic layer, each with individual use cases, approaches, and outcomes.

Each of the following sections details a specific industry example, discussing the challenge or challenges the semantic layer was designed to address, identifying the semantic layer components that were realized to meet these challenges, and finally, specifying the order in which these components were implemented. Furthermore, each section covers the outcomes the organization obtained from the effort. The reader should note that, because many of these efforts are still new, these outcomes may be anticipatory and not yet realized or captured to a reportable extent.

By the end of this part, the reader should understand how the semantic layer can be implemented in real-world scenarios and should feel comfortable walking through these examples at a level of detail that will elicit interest and support from colleagues and executives.

Global Financial Services Firm

Explaining the Challenge

One of the largest financial services organizations in the world was struggling with risk management for their non-financial and operational risks. As a heavily regulated financial services firm, their leadership understood that they required a more

J. Hilger et al., *Bridging Knowledge, Data, and AI*, https://doi.org/10.1007/978-3-032-17178-8_4

comprehensive and complex risk management structure. This new structure needed employees to thoroughly account for risk and report it in detail to regulators. It also necessitated accurate, timely, and detailed data and information to inform risk assessment. The firm sought to create a holistic and connected risk assessment and control capability to increase transparency for the firm and regulators, reduce the burden on employees, and enable real-time reports and insights into firm risk levels.

As the firm looked at solving this problem, they identified several challenges in managing risks across the organization. First, data originated from various bespoke/legacy sources with different terminology and classifications, making it difficult to connect related information. This resulted in weeks-long efforts to aggregate information for regulators and gaps in key information required to maintain risk levels that fit the firm's appetite. Second, the risk data needed to be centralized for easy access and consumption by various stakeholders and applications across the firm but was siloed in process-specific applications. Finally, the complexity of the data created a need for a more intuitive and efficient way for employees to interact with and understand this information. These challenges required a solution that could align terminology and classification, centralize data, enhance usability, and make the information easily accessible for various purposes across the organization.

Components Used

The firm identified a semantic layer and corresponding solutions as a key enabler to address their risk management issues. As part of this new initiative, they developed a strategy to implement the structures and technology required to create a data-centric risk assessment (beyond current process applications). As part of this semantic layer solution, the firm implemented the following components (Figs. 4.1 and 4.2):

- Standard forms were created to capture risk information as **metadata** that is captured in the knowledge graph and used to drive risk management processes.
- **Taxonomies** were defined for the types of risks, business units, products, and legal entities to ensure interoperability across different systems and use cases and to enforce consistency across all of the different business units managing non-financial risks.
- To enhance data connectivity, the project team developed a domain-specific **ontology** that re-used existing data structures where possible and met semantic standards, allowing for reuse as needed.
- A **knowledge graph** now serves as a central repository for all risk-related data, capturing the complex relationships between data points and providing a holistic view of the risk landscape. It allows users to explore and understand key data relationships via a graphical user interface and acts as a central repository for risk data that can be published and consumed from an authoritative source of truth.

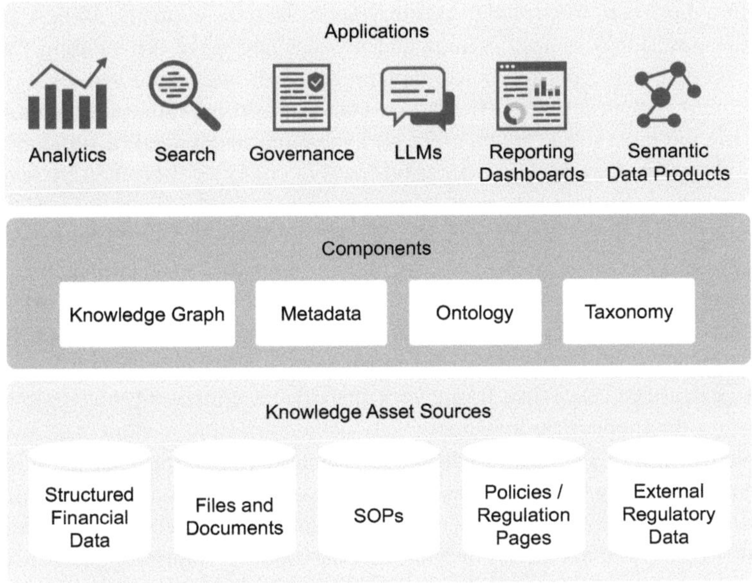

Fig. 4.1 Global financial services firm semantic layer components

Component	Benefits
Metadata	• Metadata is captured in forms so that it can be reported on in a risk dashboard and standardized across business units.
Taxonomies	• Taxonomies for types of risks, business units, products, and legal entities allow the business to report on non-financial risk faster and in a more consistent manner. • These same taxonomies allow risk teams to review risks across business units to identify trends or anomalies in the risks being reported.
Ontologies	• Domain specific ontologies were developed to map how risk information is integrated across systems.
Knowledge Graph	• The knowledge graph ties together risk information from across as many as nine different applications so that users can see a holistic view of risk related information across the firm.

Fig. 4.2 Benefits of each component for a global financial services firm

Implementation Order and Approach

Once the team had agreement on the problems that the risk-based semantic layer needed to address, they were able to start work on implementing the semantic layer.

The initial step on the process was to develop a conceptual model of the firm's risk landscape to help both business and technical stakeholders understand the connection between risk-related entities (such as risk, controls, issues, policies, regulations, etc.) across applications and process and drive the scoping for incremental development, iterations, and planning. This was followed by taxonomy enhancement and structuring efforts that standardized operational terminology by identifying the most used topical areas and vocabularies in need of standardization. Examples include free-text risk descriptions that could be shortened by leveraging an AI pipeline with humans in the loop to create standardized data items, mismatched organizational constructs that were extrapolated to common levels and groupings, and a proliferation of product taxonomies that were concatenated into a cohesive, central "Product" taxonomy. As a result of these efforts, the team was able to achieve common categorization across representations of risk types, business units, products, and legal entities, among others.

This centralized, evolving framework provides a consistent way to categorize and classify data, ensuring interoperability across different systems and use cases. By implementing this structure within the risk assessment application and encouraging its adoption by other data providers, the project team ensured that all parties were using the same terminology when handling related datasets. This improved data consistency and accuracy, facilitating data sharing, analysis, and actions. The framework has been designed using semantic standards, so that it can be expanded with additional use cases and implemented in additional systems, as it is an extensible source for descriptive metadata that applies across the firm.

Once the **minimum viable product (MVP)** of the standard terminology was in place, the team was able to build the domain ontologies and the graph that ties all of this information together in a coherent fashion. An MVP is a basic version of a product that meets the minimum necessary requirements for initial use and testing, intended to gather user feedback before investment in further development. To enhance data connectivity, a domain-specific ontology and knowledge graph were developed through net-new design, reuse of existing structures, and uplifts to meet semantic standards. This knowledge graph serves as a central repository for all risk-related data, capturing the complex relationships between data points and providing a holistic view of the risk landscape. The knowledge graph enables users to easily explore and understand key data relationships via a graphical user interface layer and acts as a central repository for risk data that can be published to and consumed from as an authoritative source of truth. This solution provides a foundation for advanced analytics, reporting, and decision-making while also accommodating future growth and evolving data needs.

Use Cases Implemented

The semantic layer allowed the firm to resolve a number of the issues they were seeing in their non-financial risk processes and operations. The three big issues they were trying to address were the siloed risk reporting processes and the confusion around risk terminology that resulted in contradictory actions, and most importantly, in inconsistent and untimely reporting of risks to regulators and senior management.

Each business unit had their own terminology and methods for reporting and acting on risks. They created risk reports that lacked structure and consistency. One group would provide a short, bulleted summary of their risks, while others would compile 15–20-page reports. Each unit's view of the potential impact of the risk and how it would be addressed was frequently inconsistent. This opened the firm up to substantial risk.

The new semantic approach ensured that risks were all reported in a consistent manner. Risk forms were created to capture risk information using the taxonomies of business units, products, legal entities, and risk types. The taxonomies were put in drop-down metadata fields so that business units had to select from a standard set of choices. As a result, the reports from the business units were standardized and delivered with much less effort.

While the metadata-enriched forms provided a structured framework for reporting risks, they didn't guarantee that users fully understood what they were reporting or that the risks were being accurately evaluated. The knowledge graph addressed this challenge by connecting risk information across the organization. It allowed users to explore related terms or topics and view a complete, contextual picture of each risk (its definition, commonly associated products, and real-world examples of how it is reported). The graph powered an intuitive user interface with consumer-grade capabilities, designed to make interacting with data more intuitive by mirroring the experiences end users have online every day. Consumer-grade capabilities include an advanced search function that allows users to quickly find the information they need, as well as recommendation engines that proactively suggest relevant data and insights for a given risk. As the graph matured, the system began alerting users to critical changes or potential risks. All of these capabilities empower users to interact with risk data more effectively, improving productivity and decision-making.

Lastly, when it comes to the use case for streamlining the reporting of risks to regulators and senior management, a central risk team was typically tasked with compiling the risk reports for senior management and the auditors. This process originally took weeks to complete and often had errors or inconsistencies. The new, semantically based risk reporting process provides structured reports that are automatically integrated and presented through dashboards. Reporting of non-financial risk has now become consistent, more accurate, and available on demand, allowing the firm to manage and investigate non-financial risks in real time, trusting in the information that they see and proactively addressing the most critical issues. Senior management now has immediate access to non-financial risk reporting, and the risk team can focus on validation of the reports and investigation into potential data anomalies.

Outcomes

The firm has established a robust foundation for enhanced risk management. By shifting risk operations from application-centric to data-centric views, the standardized terminology structure fosters consistency, accuracy, and connected data usage across the organization. The addition of consumer-grade capabilities enhances user experience and streamlines access to critical insights through embedded dynamic knowledge panels, search capabilities, reporting dashboards and downloads, and a flexible knowledge graph visualization layer. Furthermore, the development of a robust semantic layer architecture ensures seamless integration and interoperability across the organization's knowledge management infrastructure.

To date, the semantic layer has collapsed the Risk dataset from over 30,000 free-text risk descriptions into a streamlined process with 1100 standardized taxonomies for risks. Additionally, eight core taxonomies are being leveraged in five key applications. The knowledge graph connects information across 11 different applications. The ontology and knowledge graph provide a centralized, interconnected view of risk information (without the need for data migration), facilitating better analysis and decision-making. These advancements are empowering the firm to proactively identify, assess, and mitigate risks, improve regulatory reporting, and foster a more data-driven culture across the firm.

Additionally, the firm is now in the process of expanding this semantic model and ecosystem to additional business units and use cases to support data analytics and operational use cases such as criminal infestations, fraud detection, and vendor management, respectively.

Investment Management Agency

Explaining the Challenge

A large sovereign wealth fund was struggling to make informed decisions about their potential deals and their existing investments. Information about their most strategic assets were divided across as many as 12 different systems, and there was no single place to see all of the information an asset manager or senior leader would need to know. When we first began our engagement, the organization shared a number of stories about problems they faced as a result of these information silos.

A member of a deal team shared an anecdote about a time that they had pursued a new deal against a number of other investment banks. The details of the deal were similar to those of another deal that the organization had pursued in the past. Unfortunately, the team had no members who had been on the prior, related deal, so they did not have access to the financial information and documentation created at that time. This information was critical, as the team was hoping to compare the financials of the two organizations to help better cement their decision and create a more compelling proposal, and quickly, for this new deal. The team requested access to the financial systems and the SharePoint sites that housed the research documents, but it took over 2 weeks to obtain all of the information that they needed. Because this had been a competitive opportunity and the team was unable to respond quickly enough, they subsequently lost the deal.

Similarly, a deal team manager shared a time when they were trying to work out a complicated financing arrangement with a bank but were receiving pushback. This was a bank that the organization had worked with in the past and had previously felt comfortable with. The bank ultimately denied the arrangement, and the entire investment process was delayed while a new bank was identified. A month later, the deal leader found out that another group at the sovereign wealth fund had successfully executed a similar deal with a different individual at that bank. Had the deal team manager been aware of this, the team would maybe not have been rejected and would not have had to start the process over with a new bank, which exposed the fund to risk and slowed the investment process significantly.

Finally, a sector manager shared that the fund was wasting money by buying the same research over and over from their consulting partners. Deal teams would identify a need for research on a specific topic or sector and contact an on-call consulting firm that would develop a research report and deliver it to the deal team. The problem arose when different deal teams requested the same research from the same consulting firm. Each research report was tens of thousands of dollars, which meant, according to the manager, that the fund was wasting hundreds of thousands of dollars on what they believed to be duplicate research reports or reports containing much of the same information. More importantly, the consulting firms took time to craft each report, slowing the research process for each deal that requested a new report, potentially leading to lost opportunity.

These stories are just three examples of the organization's challenge, and this challenge can most simply be summarized as one of siloed knowledge. If the deal teams could have easily searched for existing research and documentation related to deals, the frustration of losing a deal or wasting time and money could have been avoided. Once the organization identified this core business problem and understood how a semantic layer could tie all of these disparate knowledge assets together, they were anxious to start implementing a solution that would provide their decision-makers with the assets that they need.

Components Used

The organization needed a single application (in this case, a knowledge portal) that could serve as a lens into all of their deals and investments. We developed this knowledge portal using four components of the semantic layer: metadata, taxonomy, ontology, and a knowledge graph.

- **Metadata** was added to all of the unstructured documents in SharePoint. This metadata enabled these documents to be integrated into the knowledge graph-powered, front-end application, allowing users with permission to view each deal and investment the ability to do so. Metadata was also used to limit the visibility of sensitive documents.

- Our team created **taxonomies** to define the structure of the organization, relevant industries, document types, and investment types. These taxonomies were applied as tags to documents in SharePoint Online and used to categorize the people, investments, and deals that were captured in the knowledge graph.
- The organization wanted to be able to view information about their business from different perspectives, so we developed an **ontology** that supported these perspectives. We also ensured through the ontology that the knowledge graph closely aligned with how the organization views and does their business and therefore how they wanted their knowledge portal to function.
- The **knowledge graph**, built using the ontology, captured the relationships between investments, deals, companies, deal team members, banks, and the industries that the companies worked in, all of the important knowledge assets related to the fund's business. The knowledge graph either stored this information itself or connected users to the systems that did.

Using these components, we developed a semantic layer-powered application that allowed decision-makers throughout the organization to view information captured in the knowledge graph. The initial function or view of the graph was a consolidated picture of all of the fund's deals and investments, including financial information as well as pitch decks and contractual agreements related to these entities. Once this view was realized and deemed successful, we added a view of the people within the fund's organization, illustrating the projects they had worked on and the documents they had authored. Similar views were created for the banks and industries that the organization worked with and in so that users could see the people with whom they had worked in the past and might wish to work in the future (Figs. 4.3 and 4.4).

Implementation Order and Approach

The implementation of the organization's semantic layer framework followed the process of many transformational projects. Leadership began by selecting a simple, starting use case that was low risk and would act to test the value of the semantic layer. This first task involved the development of relevant business taxonomies. We defined a core set of taxonomies and added them as metadata tags to deal and investment documents in SharePoint. These taxonomies quickly improved the findability of these documents, as decision-makers could search for key documents quickly and were much more confident that the document they found was the one they were looking for. For example, the final pitch deck for each deal was tagged as such using the document type taxonomy. This allowed decision-makers to find these pitch decks from prior investments and compare them with ones they were currently putting together. Many deals had a number of decks that looked like pitch decks, but the taxonomy weeded these out. These same tags also allowed analysts to identify

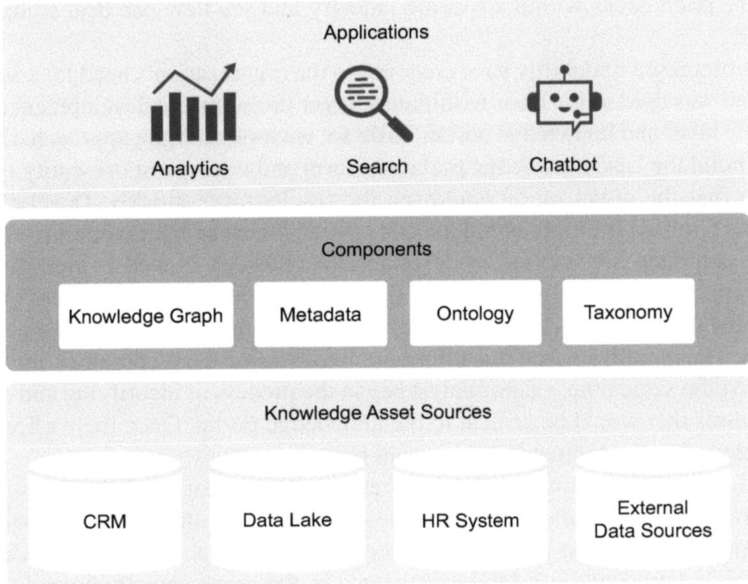

Fig. 4.3 Investment organization semantic layer components

Component	Benefits
Metadata	• Document metadata allows for faceted search of research documents. • Document metadata is used to surface key documents that memorialize the decision-making behind deals.
Taxonomies	• Geography and Industry taxonomies allow researchers to analyze their investments across common fields. • Industry taxonomies allow deals teams to confirm other investments in the same industry for guidance on deals. • Geography and Industry taxonomies allow the portfolio teams to make sure that they have balanced portfolios.
Ontologies	• Ontologies define the structure of the most important entities, including: deals, investments, companies, funds, employees, and banks.
Knowledge Graph	• The knowledge graph serves as a map that automatically pulls structured and unstructured data from multiple sources into a consolidated picture of deals, investments, companies, funds, employees, and banks. • The knowledge graph provides the security layer as to what information each person can see. • The knowledge graph provides context that will be used by the planned Generative AI implementation.

Fig. 4.4 Benefits of each component for an investment organization

all of the pitch decks within a specific industry and see how one deal compared to another.

This increased findability gave credence to the organization's need for a semantic layer and was used as the basis to initiate a larger program, the development of a full semantic layer and knowledge portal. To do so, we took an Agile approach. Our goal was to build the base knowledge portal platform and implement one entity type at a time so that the organization could see the results more quickly. Developing the platform required multiple simultaneous efforts. Because the taxonomy work was already complete, we focused on designing the ontology as well as identifying relevant data. An ontologist worked with the organization's business leaders to understand how their business functions and what knowledge assets are more important to them. The ontologist used this information to develop a base ontology for the new portal. At the same time, a data analyst began the process of identifying and cataloging datasets that would be critical to the knowledge portal. Once these efforts were completed, the development efforts could begin.

Next, the organization procured a graph database that we helped install. The structure of the database was based on the initial ontology that was developed by the ontologist. Our architect assessed the ontology and available data and made a plan as to which data would need to be replicated in the graph and which could instead be pointed to. We developed ETL processes to do so, enabling the knowledge graph to pull data or links to data into itself. Our goal was to release the knowledge portal embedded with data related to investments and deals first and then integrate more knowledge assets over time.

Once this first batch of data was populated into the knowledge graph, our developers were able to create a front-end application that allowed business users to search for investments and deals and then view an aggregated picture of each entity on a single page. This application used the graph database to retrieve data from wherever it was stored. The initial solution was launched and well-received, allowing us to move forward with additional enhancements to the semantic layer.

The next step in building out the knowledge portal involved two areas. The first area was security: the solution had to support a complicated security model. The security model required that certain information and documentation remained inaccessible to some users and accessible to others. To do this, we updated the ETL process to tag knowledge assets with information about who is entitled to access that asset. The application was updated to look at the entitlements of each information element and display only the ones that the user had the rights to see. Once this security model was in place, we were able to add data elements to both deals and investments that were initially excluded from the application because of these security concerns.

The second area was additional views. Recall that the knowledge graph allows us to look at information from different lenses. The first two views or lenses were that of the organization's deals and investments. Now that these views had been realized in the application, we were able to focus our attention on those additional views, which included people, banks, and company executives.

Use Cases Implemented

The knowledge portal addressed a number of key, organizational needs. At a high level, the application provided decision-makers with a single access point to the information that they need on a daily basis to run their business, but additionally, the semantic layer resolved a number of specific use cases. These use cases came out of the initial conversations that we had with the organization. For example, the organization could now see all of the investment research reports that the organization had already purchased from their consultants. As a result, deal teams could identify whether or not the research that they needed already existed, reusing those existing reports and saving the organization money and time (Fig. 4.5).

Deal teams had also shared their desire to see who in their organization had knowledge about specific industries or companies. The portal now allowed them to search by industry or company and see who had worked on those relevant deals. They could even click on a person listed on a specific deal and see what other deals they had worked on. This gave deal teams a way to quickly find experts within their organization that could help them make faster, more informed decisions.

Additionally, the "bank" view allowed deal teams to view the banks that they had worked with in the past as well as the deals that the banks had supported and rejected. Now, when the deal teams are selecting banks to work with, they can prioritize those that have supported similar deals.

Finally, the knowledge portal helped to speed up the pitch deck preparation process. Deal team members were able to traverse the knowledge portal to find existing pitch decks related to the current deal. The information in these existing decks can now be used to quickly develop key parts of the new deck, resulting in the creation of new, high-quality decks in less time than it took before the knowledge portal existed.

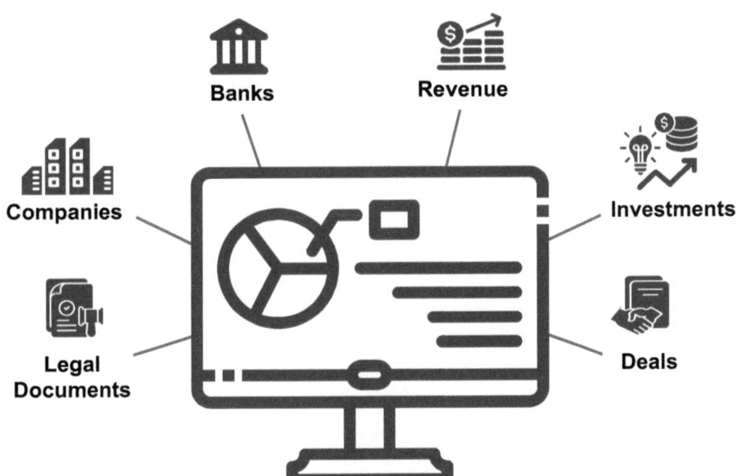

Fig. 4.5 Knowledge portal

Outcomes

The knowledge portal is now used by every key decision-maker in the organization on a daily basis. It is considered the primary window into the business activities of the organization. For the first time, employees across the organization are able to see a complete picture of all of the knowledge assets related to their work. Based on interviews with the organization's leadership, we found that they feel more confident in their business decisions and have noticed that cross-team collaboration has increased considerably.

The realization of this solution has also led to some more easily quantifiable benefits as well. The improved access to research and reports has saved the organization both time and money. Research papers are now accessible to teams, and, as a result, the organization has been able to cut spending on reports. In addition, the people who need these reports are able to access existing research instead of waiting for the firm to create duplicate research. Of course, reports are still requested when necessary, but the knowledge portal has decreased the number of requests for duplicate or redundant research.

The negotiation process with banks is also much stronger. Prior to the rollout of the knowledge portal, individual teams knew about the work that they did with specific banks, but not the work that other teams did with each bank. Teams are now able to see a complete picture of all of the banks the organization has worked with, giving them more leverage in new deals with familiar banks.

Access to information has increased tremendously as well. Prior to the knowledge portal, an individual would have to request access to information about a deal or investment across as many as eight different systems, and getting permission to access all of these systems could take 2–3 weeks. Once access was granted, it was never removed, resulting in a completely different problem. As deals move through their natural lifecycle, permissions need to be able to change. The knowledge portal was able to centralize these access permissions so that rights could be applied automatically and according to organizational policies.

The knowledge portal backed by a semantic layer is now one of the most important and impactful systems within the organization in that it has provided a way for employees to see information in a way that aligns with their business, increasing productivity and decision-making confidence.

Service Organization

Explaining the Challenge

An international services firm with offices around the world needed a better way to understand the work that they were doing across all of their different lines of business. As with most services firms, the information about their people, projects, contracts, and clients was spread across a fragmented set of systems. Sales and client information was captured in Microsoft Dynamics; staffing information was stored in a custom time and billing system; contractual information was in a contract database; deliverables were in SharePoint Online. The organization also had a data warehouse that was used for financial reporting (Fig. 4.6).

As you can imagine, the organization had a great deal of information, but no easy way to see or interact with it all in context. Specifically, the organization wanted to be able to answer business-necessary questions like the following:

- I have an important position I need to fill for a client. Who in our firm has experience with change management in U.S. auto manufacturing?
- I am doing a digitization project with a content management system that my team does not know very well. Have we ever done work with this system before?
- I am responding to a proposal from a potential client in the biotech space. Have we done similar work with anyone else? If so, can I use them as a reference?
- I am an executive trying to decide which industries to focus on. In which industries have we done the most work? In which industries has this work been most profitable?

Prior to implementing a semantic layer, the organization was only able to answer half of these questions, none in real time. Getting answers depended on finding the right person, which could take weeks. The inability for the organization to answer these business questions meant that some opportunities were lost, all because experts could not be found and previous work could not be surfaced.

Components Used

The key components of this semantic layer implementation were a knowledge graph and ontology, which associated information relevant to multiple different repositories; metadata to identify these asset repositories; and a taxonomy to categorize information about staff, clients, projects, and deliverables (Figs. 4.7 and 4.8).

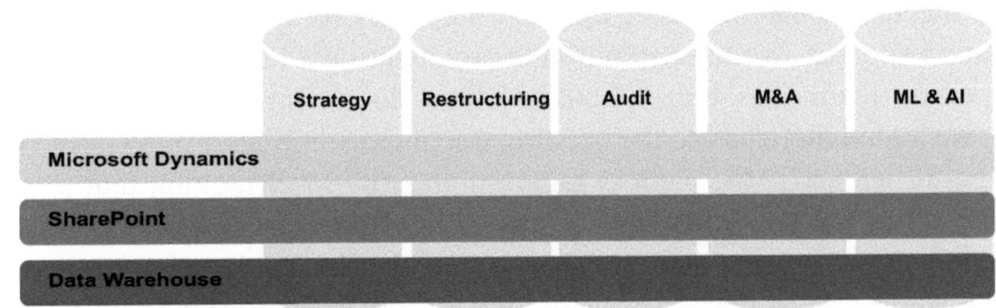

Fig. 4.6 Fragmented lines of business

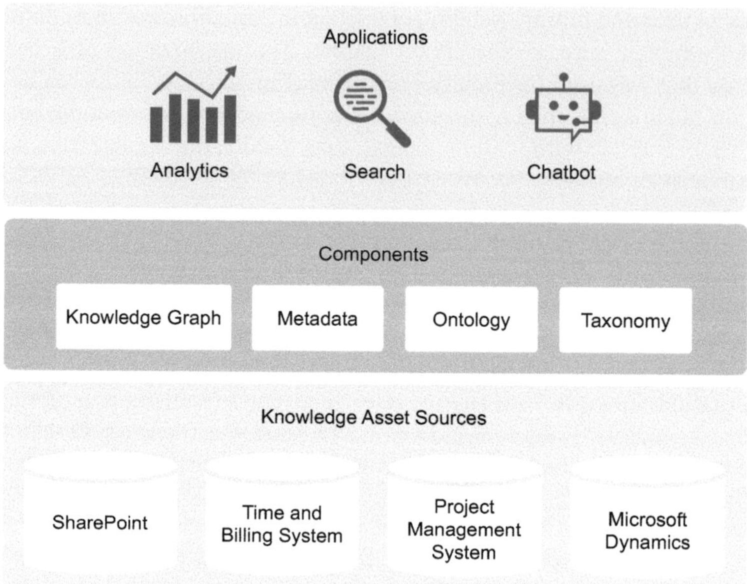

Fig. 4.7 Service organization semantic layer components

Implementation Order and Approach

The work began with the creation of a taxonomy and the application of metadata in both SharePoint Online and the organization's data warehouse. Taxonomies were developed for people, clients, and projects. The "people" taxonomies included concepts like skills, region, level, and role, while the "client" taxonomies included concepts such as industry, sub-industry, revenue category, and office (primary to the partnership). Project taxonomies related to project type, industry, department, and staffing model. These facets all provided the organization with a consistent way of searching for information on people, clients, and projects.

With the taxonomy in place, the next step was to apply metadata to relevant information sources. We worked with the organization's IT team to implement content types on team sites that contained client documents. Before launching this update, we added metadata to the existing documents in SharePoint Online through auto-tagging with a TMS, manual tagging, and site-level tagging that propagated tags onto all of the content within a site. This allowed us to provide information about clients and projects that could be assumed from the location of the content. Once metadata was in place, we were able to add facets to the SharePoint search function so that users could filter their search results based on concepts like clients, industries, type of project, and region. A similar approach was taken to the datasets in the data warehouse. Many of the same metadata fields that were applied to the content in SharePoint were also applied in the data warehouse's data catalog.

Component	Benefits
Metadata	• Metadata stored in SharePoint and the Data warehouse enables the faceting of search results. • Metadata allows the knowledge graph to systematically recognize the projects documents were associated with.
Taxonomies	• Taxonomies allow staffing managers to find people with related industry experience based on the projects they have worked on. • Taxonomies allow partners to understand the performance of their projects across service lines, industries, and geographic regions.
Ontologies	• The ontology ties together people, projects, clients, deliverables, services, and industries across the applications the firm uses.
Knowledge Graph	• The knowledge graph serves as a map that automatically pulls structured and unstructured data from multiple sources into a consolidated picture of people, projects, clients, deliverables, services, and industries. • Staffing managers traverse the graph to understand who has worked on similar projects and then what other projects they have worked on in the past. • Directors use the graph to find out who has knowledge of projects related to the work they are selling to new clients. • Partners use the graph to understand what projects they have done with large clients, project performance across specific industries, and the success of specific service offerings.

Fig. 4.8 Benefits of each component for a service organization

We then began working on the ontology and knowledge graph. The ontology model, based heavily on the taxonomy work already done, showed basic relationships between staff, projects, and clients, and was later expanded. The ontology was then transformed into a knowledge graph, and ETL processes were developed to load the information about staff, clients, projects, and deliverables into the graph. This information was loaded from a wide range of systems, including Microsoft Dynamics, the time and billing system, the contracts database, the data warehouse, and SharePoint Online. These ETL processes run each night so that the graph has the organization's latest information.

Once the knowledge graph was populated with the organization's data, we were able to use a graph analytics tool to answer the core business questions posed by the organization at the start of their semantic layer journey.

Use Cases Implemented

The project delivered on a number of use cases over time. The first three that drove most of the semantic layer development were based on the following user stories:

- As a director, I need a way to find people who have done similar work to the work I am bidding on so that I can provide resumes of experienced people to increase my chances of winning the bid.
- As a staffing manager, I need to find people who have the right experience to support my client's needs. I would prefer to hire from within the firm first to save money and protect the livelihoods of our existing consultants.
- As a partner, I would like to understand which services are responsible for the most revenue and which ones result in the most profitable projects.

The answer to each of these posed questions was solved differently. The director, for example, can now use the graph-powered analytics tool to find the people and resumes that they needed to help with a bid. This is because the graph contains information on each of the organization's past projects, including who was staffed and what the project actually entailed. Users can now search the application for similar projects and view the people staffed. They can even view whether or not those people are currently staffed on other projects or if they have availability to be staffed on the new project, if the bid is won.

Staffing managers can use the same graph analytics tool to search for people whose resumes included relevant skills. Once they found the right people, the manager could then use the tool to see the projects each person had worked on in the past, projects they are currently staffed on, and when they might be next available.

Finally, partners seeking to understand which services are responsible for the most revenue or most profitable projects can easily access this information through the data warehouse. This easy access is facilitated by the taxonomies that established a list of the organization's services and the knowledge graph which tagged data related to a project with its associated service. This information was then collected in the data warehouse so that partners can receive reports ranking services by revenue.

Outcomes

The semantic layer helped connect a wide range of systems, from sales, staffing, and project delivery that had historically been siloed within the organization. The services firm potentially saved millions of dollars by reallocating existing consultants to new projects as opposed to hiring new people. They also enhanced their proposal work by giving proposal leaders and coordinators better access to experts and previous project information. Finally, leaders in the highly decentralized organization were finally able to see compiled information about their staffing and project performance, allowing them to make better decisions in the future.

The implementation was so successful that the organization boasted it as a differentiator when bidding against competitors, using it to show that they had a better way to staff experts on their clients' projects and that they had tools to ensure that knowledge gained in one project could be re-used in others.

Product and Retail Organization

Explaining the Challenge

The next story is about a very large retail organization with a wide range of products and thousands of stores around the world. The organization had grown rapidly for over 20 years, and their data environment showed those challenges inherent to this type of growth: their data was incredibly complicated, there were only a few people who truly understood the data architecture, and there was often disagreement within the organization about simple concepts. The organization had made many of the right decisions as they grew, but their data simply lacked a semantic layer that could ensure that their data could grow and change without creating confusion and cost.

As we engaged the organization, we discerned four challenges that elucidated how complex and costly its data environment had become. The first challenge was the answer to a simple question: "What is our average transaction?" Because the organization had 12 different point of sale (POS) applications, each capturing the sales information differently, there was little agreement across the organization as to what exactly a "transaction" was. If a person ordered three or more products, were they buying for multiple people? or was this one transaction? Also, how is sales tax handled? Should it be included in the transaction? Some systems included sales tax while others excluded it. This one simple question would, in this current state, take months to answer, and there would still be little confidence in whatever the data team came up with.

The second problem was the effort required to create dashboards, or visual displays of KPIs and other metrics and data. Creating a single dashboard could take as long as 6 months and would cost over three quarters of a million dollars. The reason behind this complexity was the same reason for the difficulty in answering the "transaction" question: every area of the business and every system were plagued with inconsistency. In addition, many products were seasonal or regional in nature, which made time-based comparisons nearly impossible to calculate.

The third challenge was the complexity of the organization's data infrastructure. The organization had over 1500 ETL processes manipulating their data. Any changes in the structure of their data, like the introduction of a new data source, for example, would require a complicated project to figure out which ETL processes of the 1500 would be affected and how they should be updated. This research process was time consuming, crushing value and often leading to data quality issues when an ETL process was missed. This issue was so pervasive, and the organization had jokingly coined it "death by 1,500 ETL pipelines."

An outcome of these three challenges was a whole new challenge: the challenge of finding and keeping experts. There were very few people within the organization that actually understood the data in each domain. Requests, therefore, were piled onto these one or two individuals per domain, resulting in their constantly being spread too thin. When we spoke to one of these individuals, they told us that they wanted help, but felt it was impossible to get someone up to speed with the level of understanding that was required. In fact, it took no <6 months for someone new to become acquainted with the system. On the other hand, executives relied heavily on these experts and were constantly worried that they would leave. This created an unusual power dynamic within the organization.

Given these challenges, the organization was in desperate need of a standard way to define the structure and language of its business to the messy data that had spiraled out of control over time. The organization needed a semantic layer.

Components Used

This large, complex data ecosystem needed every component of the semantic layer in order to solve their data challenges.

- We used a **business glossary** to provide definitions of terms (like "revenue") that were used commonly within the organization to describe business functions. We employed **metadata** to describe the purpose, quality, and timeframe of datasets so that these details could be easily accessible to people tasked with handling this information. Finally, we housed these components in a **data catalog**.
- We developed **taxonomies** to catalog transactions. For example, a "Product" taxonomy delineated seasonal products ultimately support reporting functions like comparing product sales over time. Regions and stores could also be categorized for quicker reporting.
- We modeled the business through an **ontology**, which formed the basis of the **knowledge graph**. This knowledge graph mapped datasets onto this business model, and as new datasets are created, these too can be mapped in both a human- and machine-readable format.

Together, these semantic layer components gave the organization a centralized translation layer that simplified all of their most complex problems (Figs. 4.9 and 4.10).

Implementation Order and Approach

The organization had recently purchased a new data catalog, so we used this initiative as a starting point for the development of the semantic layer. This initiative supported three semantic layer activities: the development of the business glossary; the creation of core taxonomies; and the design of a metadata model for the new catalog.

The first completed task was the development of the business glossary. We held a number of workshops with key stakeholders to establish agreement on those key terms that would be necessary to define. In later workshops, we facilitated discussions as to the meanings of the glossary's most contentious terms. The glossary was to be managed within the new data catalog and would then be integrated into tools used to manage/query data by the catalog.

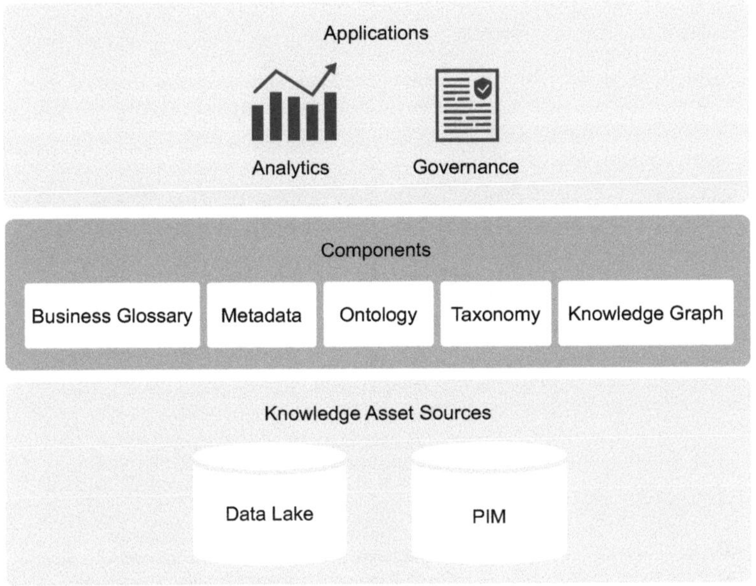

Fig. 4.9 Product organization semantic layer components

The creation of taxonomies was begun at the same time but took longer to complete. We took a top-down, bottom-up approach to their creation, using a series of workshops to brainstorm a list of candidate taxonomies and researching existing data to surface relevant concepts. Once we developed these initial taxonomies, we loaded them into the metadata catalog and used this to update key datasets based on taxonomy values. The organization chose not to invest in a taxonomy management tool, so these taxonomies were implemented and maintained manually (Fig. 4.11).

Concurrently, we also designed a metadata model for the datasets within the catalog. We started by specifying a core set of metadata fields to support operations and additional topical fields to improve findability. We also created metadata fields that supported the taxonomies that were being implemented. To establish these fields, we conducted interviews with data stakeholders across the organization to understand their data processes and user needs. This implementation process took over a year, as we allowed the organization's users to interact with the model and provide feedback on what was and was not working. By the end of this iterative process, we had come up with an agreeable model that was populated with a complete list of metadata fields.

As people within the organization began to see the value of these first few tasks, and as we gained a better understanding of the organization's data ecosystem, we started our work on the ontology. The goal of the ontology development was twofold. First, we wanted to model the organization in a way that aligned with how business users would think to interact with their data in the resulting knowledge graph. Second, we wanted to define relationships between datasets that allowed us

Component	Benefits
Business Glossary	• The business glossary provides agreed upon definitions of key analytics terms such as average transaction, store revenue, and product line to ensure that analytics are reported on in a consistent fashion.
Metadata	• Metadata is maintained in the data catalog to make it easier to find data tables for the creation of dashboards and new data products. • Metadata is maintained in the data catalog to automate governance processes such as automated searches for missing data and initiating regular data audits.
Taxonomies	• Taxonomies help define consistent product groups so that directors can measure performance across related products. • Taxonomies define regions and store types so that executives can see performance by type of stores in specific regions to make decisions on stores to open and close. • Taxonomies define the types of data sets that the organization manages to drive governance activities such as audits of data and ensuring that data refreshes are happening on a consistent basis.
Ontologies	• The ontology provides a model for how the over 100,000 data sets should be related to one another in order to align with how business executives think about the business.
Knowledge Graph	• The knowledge graph provides a machine-readable map of data tables to run ETL processes that used to be driven by custom SQL procedures. • Dashboards are populated with information pulled either directly from the knowledge graph or from data that is pointed to by the knowledge graph. • The knowledge graph associates structured data with documents about products to provide executives with a complete picture of the products they are reviewing.

Fig. 4.10 Benefits of each component for a product organization

to replace the logic within the ETL processes with the logic of the graph. Because knowledge graphs are people and machine-readable, our goal was to simplify the ETL process by rewriting them so that they could read and rely on the structure of the graph rather than code to manipulate data assets.

Once the ontology was defined, we were able to begin developing the knowledge graph. This knowledge graph required integrations on two levels: we needed ETL processes to load instances of key business entities as well as a way to keep ETL pointers to datasets current. In other words, we needed an ingestion and update routine. Additionally, the organization's data engineers had begun to update existing ETL processes from code to graph. These updated ETL routines used graph queries to retrieve the graph structure and then process data according to this structure. The greatest value in this approach was that, now, a single person could update the graph

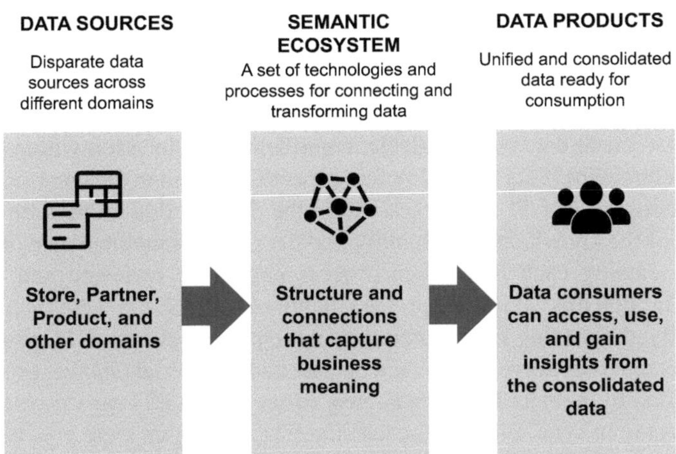

Fig. 4.11 Integration between the company ontology and taxonomies

with new logic as necessary, and this update would immediately affect the necessary ETL processes.

To conclude, this was a large and complex organization, and making changes took time. As part of our approach, we implemented solutions incrementally based on prioritized use cases. This allowed the organization to see change and value more quickly, which allowed us to keep the ball rolling.

Use Cases Implemented

As with many of these case studies, we used the three challenges presented at the start of our engagement with the organization as inspiration for the organization's semantic layer use cases. The organization, as you may recall, had a great deal of disagreement over terms and how key metrics should be reported on. Because of this, we took on 20 of the most divisive metrics within the organization and made sure that all of the relevant terms behind these metrics were documented in the glossary. After the glossary was updated, we used these definitions to establish how ETLs calculate these metrics. Each reporting tool was also updated to include an explanation of the calculation behind each metric with the purpose of reinforcing business alignment. This effort improved the confidence the organization had in reporting metrics and shortened the amount of time it took to create these common reports by months. Simple dashboards now took only a week to curate. The result was that executives could get data faster, and the cost of producing these dashboards would be in the thousands and not hundreds of thousands.

Prior to the semantic layer, developing a new dashboard could take 6 months and could cost over three quarters of a million dollars. The data was messy, often unusually named, and generally misunderstood. Any dashboard that relied on data from an ETL process or required a new ETL process required an undue amount of time and effort on the part of a data engineer to determine which of the 1500 ETL processes needed to be updated. The semantic layer addressed each of these issues. Now, metadata tagged each dataset and ETL process with its purpose, making these searchable to data engineers through the data catalog. In addition to metadata, taxonomies also made data more findable, regardless of its location within the organization's architecture. This findability was especially useful in the creation of reports.

The cataloging of ETL processes within the data catalog along with the implementation of the knowledge graph mitigated the stressful maintenance of these processes. To catalog each ETL, each process had to be reviewed and assigned a purpose. Through this cataloging process, hundreds of ETL processes were archived. Additionally, the catalog illuminated the relationships between ETL processes and the datasets that they served. Now, if a dataset had a material change, or a new dataset was added to the data lake, it was easy to see which ETL process needed to be updated to stay in sync. Finally, because the ETL processes were now based on the business relationships defined in the knowledge graph, changes to the data lake could be added to the graph, which would, in turn, automatically update the processes. These semantic efforts turned the once-chaotic management of ETLs into a structured and controlled process.

Outcomes

To conclude, the organization had a very large and complex data ecosystem that they had completely lost control of. The semantic layer helped those people who interact with data have more control, confidence, and understanding of the data that they worked with. Additionally, the new, semantic-driven environment saved the organization millions of dollars and months of time on the delivery of dashboards. Because data was now controlled by a knowledge graph and fully documented in the data catalog, data quality improved. Finally, the maintenance requirements of the data environment, specifically those ETL processes, were cut in half. As a result, the CDO was able to cut the size of their team by 25%, and yet they were still more productive and responsive than ever.

Health/Education Organization

Explaining the Challenge

A healthcare workforce solutions provider wanted to increase engagement and learning outcomes across their platforms as part of an initiative to expand interactive and adaptive learning capabilities using cutting-edge knowledge management and NLP techniques. The organization was looking to develop and improve personalized content offerings (specifically, tailored course recommendations) to connect users with the exact courses that would help them better master key competencies.

Although custom course recommendations drive better learning outcomes, augment the value of courseware, and provide demonstrable evidence to customers of the effectiveness of their learning offerings, the organization's existing course recommendation approach failed to consistently deliver relevant tailored content to the user. The content was difficult to maintain and didn't meet the learning needs of users.

The organization quickly understood the power of the semantic layer and how it could increase control, make information more findable, and provide a foundation for a cutting-edge recommendation engine for content. The organization decided to begin a semantic layer initiative with the goal of creating an improved recommendation engine.

Components Used

The semantic layer for this healthcare workforce solutions provider used four components: metadata, taxonomy, ontology, and knowledge graph (Figs. 4.12 and 4.13).

- The organization had already invested heavily in **metadata**. All of their content was managed in either a CMS or an LMS, and both systems were designed to have metadata associated with all of their content. This metadata was used to improve findability through a faceted search on the site and to provide a recommendation engine for courses.

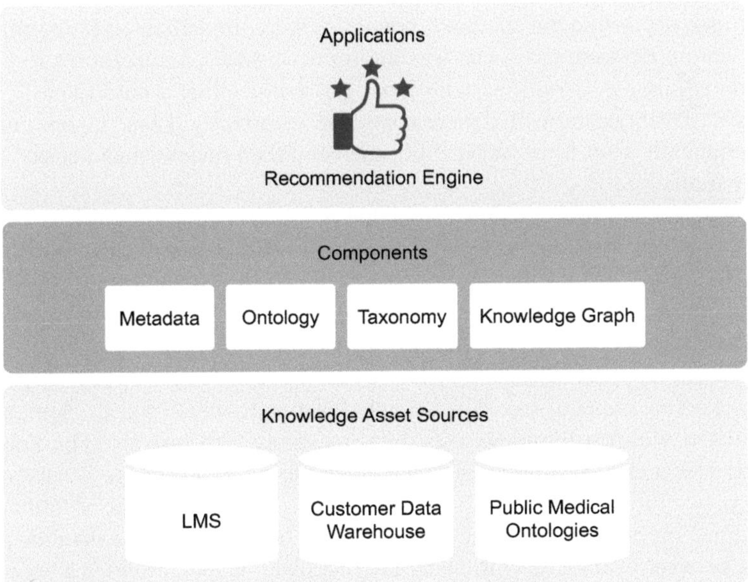

Fig. 4.12 Health/education organization semantic layer components

Component	Benefits
Metadata	• Metadata is added to the courses in the LMS and the questions in the exams to support the mapping of how they relate to one another in the graph.
Taxonomies	• The topical taxonomies identify the key medical information in each test. • Taxonomies around symptoms, diseases, drugs, and treatments ensure that these topics are addressed in a consistent way.
Ontologies	• The ontology defines how the different taxonomy terms relate to one another so that the AI system can make intelligent recommendations. • The ontology defines the structure for how the recommendation engine determines which courses most closely relate to which questions or types of questions on the exams.
Knowledge Graph	• The logic for how the content in questions is related to course topics is stored in the graph. • The recommendation engine traverses the graph to recommend courses when one or more questions are answered incorrectly.

Fig. 4.13 Benefits of each component for a health/education organization

- The organization had both industry-standard **taxonomies** and custom taxonomies to better organize their website. The industry-standard taxonomies ensured that content was organized in a way that could be understood by others within their industry, while the custom taxonomies were implemented to improve website search. Because our focus was on improving the organization's recommendation engine, we identified additional taxonomies that would identify lessons related to test questions that were answered incorrectly. These taxonomies were automatically built through NLP libraries and then reviewed and edited by content experts.

- We required an **ontology** that associated medical terminology (diseases, conditions, injuries, medical, surgical, diagnostic services, and drug vocabularies) with the test questions and the lessons in the LMS. The ontology was designed based on the results of the custom taxonomy work. The goal of the ontology was to define a structure as to how this information could best associate the test questions to the relevant lessons.

- This structure then informed the **knowledge graph**, which was implemented and populated with taxonomies, tests, test questions, and lessons. The knowledge graph was a critical component of the semantic layer because it served as the backbone of the recommendation engine. The graph enabled the identification of relationships between metadata that were much more advanced than the associations between two items with matching metadata. It also provided a way to trace how recommendations were made and to improve the recommendation engine when results were not accurate.

Implementation Order and Approach

The implementation of the semantic layer began with an analysis of the current-state recommendation engine. The purpose of this analysis was to understand to what extent components of the semantic layer were already in place. Based on this initial evaluation, we determined that it was critical to develop taxonomies, an ontology, and a knowledge graph. It was also clear that management would not invest in the entire project without some proof that this new approach would show meaningful improvement to the existing engine.

In order to address these concerns, we built an end-to-end **proof of concept (PoC)** recommender to assess the current functionality of the existing taxonomies and current-state data quality. A PoC is a small-scale demonstration or experiment, typically focused on one or two priority use cases. The purpose of PoC is to prove the value and technical feasibility of a new idea, product, or technology before an organization decides to commit significant resources to its long-term development. This PoC allowed us to quickly demonstrate the value of a graph-based recommendation, while spotlighting the areas of the taxonomy that needed to be improved. Once the PoC was completed and the second phase was approved, we began work on an MVP. As part of the MVP, we developed the recommendation engine into a production-ready microservice API using data science libraries and the organization's cloud infrastructure. We used custom named entity recognition (NER) models to extract key terms and topics from the content in order to rapidly build relationships among and between this content. The use of NER models to automatically pull out terms from the content was critical: there was far too much content to rely on a manual process to identify these terms. This process also set the groundwork for the ontology and knowledge graph model.

Once the graph was in place, the recommendation microservice could be fully developed. Our client created a set of data to test the recommendation microservice, and we iterated throughout this process, both training and tuning the engine. Once this work was complete, the recommendation microservice was integrated with the organization's learning platform, successfully delivering courses and learning paths relevant to each user's exam performance.

Use Cases Implemented

Our work on the semantic layer enabled two important use cases: a course recommendation engine and improved findability for courses on the organization's website.

The organization had needed a better course recommendation engine in order to improve the learning outcomes for its members and to continue to differentiate its offerings from its competitors. The new course recommendation engine worked at the question level. As members took exams, the recommendation engine would review their answers. Those questions answered incorrectly would result in the recommendation of courses that address the learner's weaknesses. The members noticed this improvement in course recommendations, and feedback showed that members thought the system demonstrated a real understanding of their strengths and weaknesses. This led to an increase in the number of courses taken, and, as a result, better trained healthcare professionals (Fig. 4.14).

In addition, to the improvements in course recommendations, the new metadata and taxonomies were applied to the website to make it easier for people to find the courses they needed. The site search was enhanced with the additional facets to allow people to more quickly find the course that they were looking for among a large library of course offerings.

Outcomes

This healthcare workforce solution provider saw both expected and unexpected benefits from this new semantic layer. The expected benefits included:

- A greatly improved recommendations engine that provided better course recommendations for people preparing for certification exams.
- Increased engagement with courses because of their increased visibility.
- A differentiated product offering that could separate the organization from its competitors.

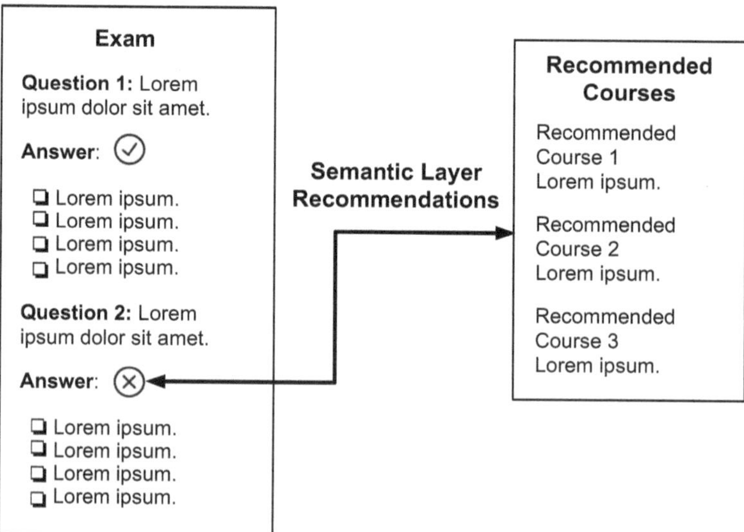

Fig. 4.14 Semantic layer recommendation engine

The unexpected outcomes were of greater value than the planned ones. As the organization started working with the semantic layer and, in particular, the knowledge graph, it quickly saw a number of other ways that this semantic layer could be used to enhance its course offerings. This led to a number of planned initiatives, including:

- Repurposing the recommendation engine to email recommend courses to the organization's members based on their historical training plan.
- Using the knowledge graph to identify topics that were consistently incorrectly answered in testing in order to determine which courses needed improvement.
- Enhancing the knowledge graph to incorporate members to better personalize their experiences and to identify and invest in their future training needs.

Powering Artificial Intelligence and Beyond 5

When we are asked to visualize artificial intelligence, the first image that often comes to mind is that of a robot or humanoid figure, perhaps something straight out of *The Terminator* movies. But our focus here is not on robots, droids, or physical machines. Instead, we turn our attention to what truly powers artificial intelligence, the underlying data and logic that make it possible. A key theme throughout this Chapter is the role of the semantic layer in artificial intelligence, and the essential function it continues to serve as a bridge between data, humans, and machines. Looking ahead, the semantic layer will be a critical component of effective organizational intelligence, providing shared language, context, consistency, and structure across increasingly complex data ecosystems. As AI solutions become more autonomous and decision-driven, the semantic layer will ensure that data remains interpretable, traceable, and aligned with business intent.

In this final chapter, we will focus on how the semantic layer framework actually enables AI models to access, understand, and reason over information in ways that align with human understanding, intent, and organizational context. We will examine the core types of functions of artificial intelligence within the enterprise, explore the two-way relationship between AI and the semantic layer, and discuss practical approaches to either embedding AI into your semantic layer architecture or infusing semantic context into your existing AI initiatives.

Finally, in the closing section, we look to the horizon, examining how mature organizations are evolving their semantic ecosystems and offering informed predictions on how the semantic layer will continue to generate value, drive responsible AI adoption, and become a defining competitive advantage in the years to come.

© The Author(s), under exclusive license to Springer Nature
Switzerland AG 2026
J. Hilger et al., *Bridging Knowledge, Data, and AI*,
https://doi.org/10.1007/978-3-032-17178-8_5

AI and the Semantic Layer

The concept of artificial intelligence has been around for more than 70 years, evolving from a theoretical pursuit into a transformative force reshaping nearly every industry. What sets today apart from just two decades ago is the unprecedented convergence of computing power, data availability, and sustained investment from governments, enterprises, research institutions, and more.

When we talk about AI, it's not just about algorithms or the vast amounts of data these systems process. At the core of any effective AI strategy is the ability to organize, structure, and connect data in a meaningful way. This is where the semantic layer plays a role. The relationship between AI and the semantic layer is inherently symbiotic: the semantic layer structures human knowledge and data, making it understandable and actionable for AI systems, while AI, in turn, helps refine, enrich, and extend the semantic layer. Together, they form a continuous feedback loop, one that strengthens the accuracy, transparency, and adaptability of both (Tesfaye 2025).

What the Semantic Layer Does for AI

AI needs access to a shared, consistent view of enterprise data to avoid conflicting actions, poor decision-making, or the reinforcement of data silos. Increasingly, autonomous AI, specifically AI agents, will need to interact with external data and coordinate with other agents, which compounds the risk of misalignment, duplication, or even contradictory outcomes. This is where a semantic layer becomes critical. By standardizing definitions, relationships, and business context across knowledge and data sources, the semantic layer provides AI with a common language for interpreting and acting on information. One way to think about the role of the semantic layer is as the map for information, where data is labeled and grouped according to meaning and relationships. As such, the purpose of the semantic layer is to structure data in a way that allows both machines and humans to better understand and interpret it.

It is also important to note that generative AI and large language models (LLMs) are currently limited in fully making inferences across different domains due to lack of contextual reasoning, domain-specific logic, or ambiguity in cross-domain contexts as multiple studies and applications have shown (Thibaud 2025). This is why the semantic layer incorporates more symbolic components and acts as a bridge to address some of these issues by structuring and organizing knowledge in a way that allows AI systems to better understand and process domain-specific contexts. By integrating symbolic reasoning and more explicit representations of knowledge, the semantic layer helps AI systems "understand" complex concepts across domains, making inferences more accurate and contextually appropriate.

Each of the semantic components discussed throughout this book work together to create this cohesive understanding of data across different contexts, departments, and systems:

- **Metadata and Taxonomies: Organizing Data Hierarchically**—A taxonomy acts as a "language" for AI systems, enabling them to understand nuances like synonyms, hierarchies, and contextual meanings. Taxonomies are less flexible than ontologies, as they rely on a hierarchical structure (parent–child relationships) that classify entities according to predefined categories. However, taxonomies are incredibly useful in organizing data in a way that allows AI systems to quickly retrieve relevant information. For example, in a content management system, it is best to use taxonomies to classify content and documents based on their subject matter, such as "Technology," "Engineering," or "Finance." This hierarchy makes it easier for AI systems to filter and understand the information, offering users more relevant results when searching for topics related to those categories.
- **Ontologies: Structuring Knowledge**—In the world of AI, ontologies allow systems to reason about concepts and make inferences. For instance, in healthcare, ontologies define the relationships between diseases, symptoms, treatments, and patients. This allows an AI solution to not just process individual data points but to understand how those points connect to broader concepts, real-world entities, and patterns.
- **Knowledge Graphs: Visualizing Relationships**—Graphs are powerful in representing the interconnectedness of data, and they are especially useful in AI systems designed for recommendation engines, fraud detection, and social network analysis. For instance, intelligence analysis applications use knowledge graphs to represent people (usually persons of interest) as nodes, with edges connecting them to the object they own or have been otherwise linked to. This allows AI solutions to track patterns and make intelligence action recommendations based on a user's behavior and relationships to other users. Graphs are also essential for NLP, as they help AI systems understand the connections between words and concepts. By using graph-based models, an AI solution can distinguish that "Giants" might mean towering figures from legend in one context and an American football team that occasionally remembers how to score points in another, depending on the surrounding words and relationships.

In totality, the semantic layer ensures that AI is working from the same trusted source of truth and enables it to exchange information coherently, aligned with organizational policies, and deliver reliable, explainable results at scale. It's important to note that, in a multi-AI system with multiple domains, different AI capabilities may not work off the same semantic layer and may require multiple, domain-specific semantic layers. Each capability will then have the organizational context to interpret messages from each other.

Without this reasoning layer, the "black box" nature of AI's decision-making processes erodes trust, making it difficult for organizations to adopt and rely on these source systems. Whereas, across several of our recent projects, implementing a semantic layer has improved the accuracy and precision of initial AI results from around 50% to between 80% and 95%, depending on the use case (Tesfaye 2025). By giving the AI access to trusted business knowledge instead of relying solely on general training data, semantic layers make the AI's results much more relevant and reliable.

What AI Can Do for the Semantic Layer

On the flip side, AI does not just consume structured, contextual data from the semantic layer; it actively contributes to its development, refinement, optimization, and governance. Specifically, AI supports the semantic layer through:

- **Semantic Model Generation**—While traditional taxonomies and ontologies are manually curated (requiring domain experts to define the relationships, classes, and properties that exist within a specific knowledge domain), AI plays a key role in automatically generating and refining these semantic models by analyzing large datasets. Using techniques like NLP and unsupervised learning, AI is able to extract and identify new relationships, entities, and concepts that aid in semantic model development. Over time, this allows the semantic layer to evolve and adapt, keeping it up to date with new data and changes in the domain.
- **Knowledge Asset Enrichment**—AI algorithms, especially those using machine learning or graph-based models, are applied to "enrich" unstructured data by tagging it with relevant entities, relationships, or concepts from the semantic layer. In many scenarios, for example, an AI-powered tool is able to analyze a document and automatically assign it to the correct category in a taxonomy or identify the relevant concepts from an ontology. This semantic annotation or enrichment process expedites and improves the quality of the semantic layer and ensures that AI can continue to extract meaningful insights from changing organizational content and data.
- **Governance and Real-Time Updates**—In many fast-moving industries, the data landscape is constantly evolving, and so too must the structures within the semantic layer. Organizations are leveraging AI to address this problem by continuously monitoring the model and underlying data and recommending updates to the semantic layer based on new patterns. For example, AI helps identify areas where taxonomies may be outdated or incomplete. By analyzing data patterns and applying machine learning algorithms, AI can suggest new categories, help refine existing categories, and make the taxonomy more dynamic and responsive to emerging trends. This AI-augmented governance and adaptability ensure that the semantic layer remains relevant and useful in a constantly changing environment.

While AI already plays a key role in enhancing the semantic layer (improving discoverability, enriching metadata, and accelerating semantic model generation), its impact does not stop there. As we move from isolated AI capabilities toward more autonomous systems, the rise of AI agents marks the next frontier. These agents do not just support content and data organization; they perform it autonomously. Empowered by the context and consistency that a semantic layer provides, AI agents are now poised to take on increasingly complex, goal-oriented tasks, extending their influence beyond the semantic layer and into the broader knowledge and data management lifecycle.

The New KM, Data, and Enterprise AI Ecosystem

When discussing the topic of enterprise AI architecture, the real challenge is not the models, it's the underlying organizational data and the cost–benefit of AI application and adoption. Without proper context, raw data or text is often messy, outdated, redundant, and unstructured, making it difficult for AI algorithms to extract meaning or deliver real and reliable results. The key step to addressing this AI problem involves having the right architecture in place to organize and connect all types of organizational knowledge assets. The semantic layer should therefore sit at the center of any enterprise AI architecture, as it provides a programmatic framework to make organizational context, content, and knowledge machine-readable.

Techniques such as data labeling, taxonomy and business glossary development, ontology modeling, and knowledge graph creation form the backbone of this layer, enabling AI to not only access information but also understand and reason with it. Within this context, a well-architected enterprise AI stack should be anchored in the following principles:

- **Planning For Non-Human Consumers**—The modern enterprise AI, KM, and data ecosystem must plan for more than just humans as consumers of information. Increasingly, machines, AI models, and automated agents will also consume, interpret, and act on enterprise data. This means data and knowledge assets must be machine-readable, semantically rich, and interoperable across systems.
- **From Application-Centric to Data Focus**—Applications create information silos specific to the purpose of the application. The semantic layer associates data across applications in a model that better aligns with how an organization operates. This broader picture makes AI more accurate and effective in interpreting the data it uses to generate answers.
- **Design for Meaning, Not Just Storage and Access**—Traditional data architectures emphasize pipelines and storage. In contrast, the semantic layer emphasizes relationships, ensuring that data reflects real-world business concepts. This alignment allows AI to reason across domains, beyond operational silos and artificial system boundaries.
- **Separate Knowledge from Infrastructure**—By abstracting business logic and meaning away from specific systems, the semantic layer becomes durable even as technology stacks evolve. This allows AI models to scale without constant reengineering.
- **Governance and Operating Models**—AI adoption brings new challenges around compliance, ethics, and lineage. A governed semantic layer ensures transparency as to where data originated, what it represents, and how it should be used, which is crucial for trustworthy AI. Architecture and governance should

extend beyond technical security policies to include operating models that embed human-in-the-loop review, subject-matter expertise, and the right skillsets to continuously steward and evolve semantic assets.

Enterprise AI Architecture Layers

There are five pillars to the AI semantic layer architectural patterns we see across implementations (Fig. 5.1):

1. Compute and Infrastructure Layer

This foundational layer provides the raw processing power, networking, and storage required to run AI models and applications end-to-end. It is typically part of enterprise shared services and supports resource-intensive tasks such as model training and expansion. Considerations for this architectural component involve assessing the specific requirements of the anticipated AI workloads for the organization, storage capacity, and network bandwidth for real-time inference. Based on this assessment, infrastructure can be provisioned either on-premises, in a hybrid cloud environment, or fully in the cloud, depending on scalability, security, and cost considerations. Once the infrastructure is chosen, it's pragmatic to understand the requirements and extend existing networking configurations to ensure that models can access the data and compute resources they need for both training and inference reliably.

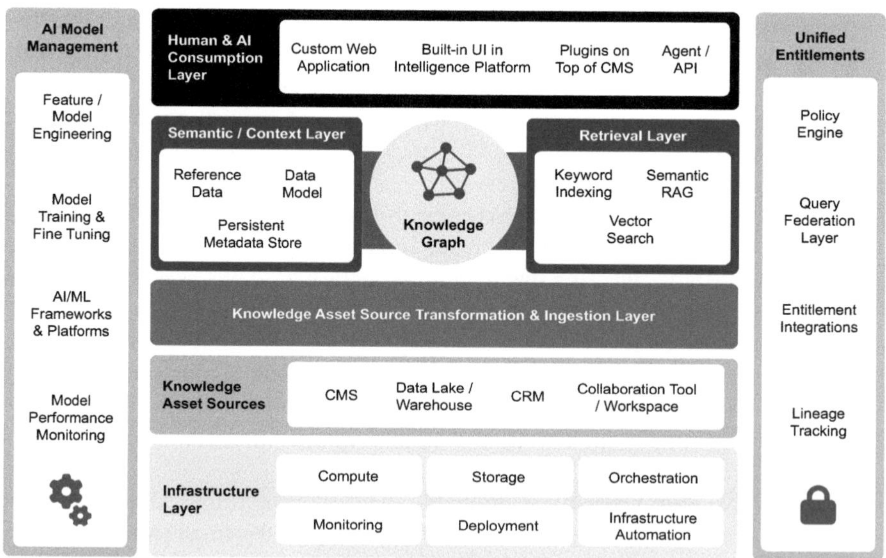

Fig. 5.1 Emerging enterprise AI, KM, and data architecture layers

Finally, monitoring and automation at this layer are critical. In contrast to the predictable expenses of standard software, AI project costs are highly dynamic and often underestimated during initial planning. Many organizations are grappling with unexpected AI cost overruns due to hidden expenses in data management, infrastructure, and maintenance, which can severely impact budgets. Tracking system utilization, scaling resources dynamically, and implementing automated provisioning allow organizations to maintain consistent performance and optimization for AI workloads, even under variable demand.

2. AI Model Management Layer

This is the architectural layer where AI algorithms and machine learning models are built, trained, validated, and optimized. The first step is to select the right AI approach for the task, whether it be NLP, structured data modeling, computer vision, or RAG. Once the model is in place, curated knowledge assets are fed into pipelines for training, with attention paid to preprocessing, normalization, and feature engineering.

Because training models involve iterative experimentation, tuning, and distributed computation, it is paramount to have benchmarks and business objectives defined from the onset to optimize model performance. AI model and lifecycle management solutions help with the management of this process at enterprise scale by tracking model versions, automating retraining schedules, and managing deployments across environments. Finally, the validated models should be ready to be connected with the semantic layer resources.

3. The Semantic Layer

As discussed in detail throughout this book, the semantic layer provides domain-specific context and alignment of AI initiatives with clear business objectives, rules, and meaning. Its role within enterprise AI architecture is to mine both structured and unstructured data and convert them into business-aware semantic assets.

Architecting AI with a semantic layer starts with knowledge mapping. Start by identifying organizational knowledge assets to model for. These can be both explicit (documents, databases, reports) and tacit (expertise, processes, best practices). Then, map the relationships, corresponding to how concepts relate across departments and systems.

The next step is to ingest and apply the semantic models to structured and unstructured data from internal systems and external sources, specifically applying tags, categories, and classifications to make the data discoverable and searchable by AI. This information can be pushed into the source system or pulled within the semantic layer as a knowledge graph. For more detail about the semantic layer development process, refer to Chap. 3.

Specific semantic models such as the business glossary, taxonomy, and ontology can also serve as stand-alone schemas or reference data, providing standardized vocabularies and terms for AI to leverage during extraction, classification, and interpretation tasks. When integrated into AI pipelines, these semantic models enhance the model's ability to perform complex cognitive tasks such as entity recognition, intent detection, and relationship extraction.

At each of these architecture and development stages, it is paramount to have SMEs review outputs, correct errors, and refine models, and use the features in the solutions discussed above to track and update taxonomies, ontologies, and AI models as business knowledge evolves.

4. The Knowledge Asset Layer

The knowledge and data source layer ensures that AI models receive high-quality, relevant data. This includes planning for architectural solutions and components that support:

- Data ingested from internal systems, third-party datasets, and user-generated content.
- Feature engineering that transforms raw inputs into structured representations suitable for AI model consumption.
- Automated data quality and governance checks to ensure compliance, minimize bias, and track lineage for transparency.

By maintaining rigorous knowledge asset management practices at this layer, your organization can ensure that downstream AI applications operate on trustworthy, contextualized, and enterprise-aligned information, increasing both accuracy and impact. Integrating these datasets with the semantic layer also ensures that extracted knowledge is tagged with meaningful metadata and aligned with taxonomies, serving as grounding for AI reasoning.

5. Deployment and Consumption Layer

Once models and semantic knowledge are prepared, the deployment layer ensures that AI capabilities are accessible across enterprise applications. This architectural layer requires a mature AI or data operations (AI/MLOps) deployment environment and pipelines to expose AI model functionality, not only to human consumers but also AI models. This includes smooth integration between frontend interfaces and backend services where end users can easily interact with AI features and insights, while tracking model performance, detecting drift, and identifying opportunities for improvement. Human-in-the-loop feedback mechanisms should be established from the onset, enabling SMEs to review AI outputs, refine semantic models, and provide ongoing guidance to ensure relevance and accuracy. Continuous monitoring further ensures that AI models remain reliable, performant, and aligned with evolving business objectives.

Ultimately, this layer completes the architectural lifecycle. By capturing, processing, and contextualizing knowledge through the semantic layer, organizations can maintain governance, drive continuous improvement, and become truly "AI-ready." Once an organization is AI-ready, AI can be embedded into everyday enterprise workflows, delivering measurable business value.

While architecting enterprise AI with a semantic layer at its core lays the foundation for scalable and trustworthy organizational knowledge intelligence, architecture in most cases is only the beginning. As technologies evolve and organizations mature in their use of AI, the question shifts from *how* we build to *what's coming next*. In the following section, we look ahead to emerging trends, challenges, and opportunities shaping the future of AI-powered enterprises.

Looking Ahead...

As we come near the conclusion of the book, you should have a clear sense of the value a semantic layer can bring, but also a crystalline understanding of the effort it takes to successfully design, implement, and sustain one. Throughout the book we have provided myriad examples of what a semantic layer framework can do for your organization, with real-world case studies pulled from our client's successes and the field writ large. We'll conclude by sharing what organizations that have invested in semantics are achieving, how it has driven change in these organizations, and what broad impacts it has had. Though we titled this section "Looking Ahead..." the reality is that the moment is *now* for organizations that have already laid the proper foundations and made the right investments.

These semantically mature organizations have avoided the easy route of just dropping a monolithic AI application into their environment and instead are leading with design of their semantic components, enhancement of their knowledge assets, and establishment of organizational structures necessary to support and iteratively improve these components.

Because these organizations have invested in the semantic layer and other foundations, they are starting to unlock the following strategic and long-term capabilities and applications for their business, employees, customers, operating models, and their industries. Over time, these organizations will also realize softer returns, including improved employee satisfaction and increased collaboration and innovation, with tedious and redundant tasks that currently consume the time of highly skilled workers automated or drastically improved.

All of these capabilities have rippled through the organizations, incrementally changing the structure, operations, and even the culture to reflect the future way of working. The following subsections detail these changes and will give you a sense of what to expect in your own organization.

Open and Interoperable Ecosystems

As technology stacks and data ecosystems become more complex, the future of data-driven organizations depends on seamless collaboration across systems, business partners, regulators, and even competitors. The semantic layer that is built on open standards is now evolving into a kind of universal translator that allows data to move intelligently between platforms and institutions. It is enabling organizations to link, exchange, and reuse data without losing context or control. This shift is marking a transition from silos toward connected ecosystems where knowledge, not just data, flows freely across industries and boundaries.

Rather than being tied to a single application, tool, or proprietary vendor platform, forward-thinking enterprises and sectors are embracing open standards and linked data principles to ensure this interoperability. Initiatives such as the Open Data, FAIR Data, and Linked Data movements are driving the creation of vendor-neutral semantic frameworks that preserve context and meaning across systems. These standards and supporting technical solutions are allowing organizations to exchange data securely and consistently while minimizing legacy process and system challenges. This is resulting in a more dynamic and collaborative digital economy, one where shared semantics enable diverse systems and partners to work together programmatically, regardless of technology stack or geography.

We are already seeing tangible examples of these semantic layer-powered ecosystems take shape across industries. In life sciences, the OpenFold3 consortium, which includes Bristol Myers Squibb, Takeda, Johnson & Johnson, and many more, is using a federated semantic data-sharing model to train AI on protein–small molecule interactions accelerating biomedical discovery, without exposing proprietary data (OpenFold Team 2025). In finance, the XBRL (eXtensible Business Reporting Language) standard enables regulators like the U.S. SEC to analyze corporate filings through machine-readable taxonomies and metadata, improving transparency and automation (XBRL International 2025). Meanwhile, NASA's Linked Open Data initiative has been publishing its vast scientific archives in RDF format, allowing researchers to create "semantic mashups" that combine earth observation and space data with external datasets for new insights (NASA 2025). These efforts demonstrate how the semantic layer is anchoring open, trustworthy collaboration across sectors that were once defined by data isolation.

Emerging case studies across healthcare, government, and finance further showcase the next frontier of these capabilities. Agencies in public health are starting to invest in semantic interoperability to harmonize electronic medical records, lab results, and case data, to enable faster outbreak response. On the other hand, we are currently working with government agencies that are connecting seemingly "unrelated" data (such as public records, reports, and criminal intelligence) through semantic models that reveal hidden links between people, places, and events, supporting the prevention of crimes like human trafficking, smuggling, and more. The financial institutions discussed earlier in this book are also leveraging their foundational semantic ecosystem to enhance their fraud investigation capabilities by linking internal case data with global trade and open-source datasets, using **graph analytics** solutions to detect patterns of illicit activity. Each of these examples demonstrates how the semantic layer empowers organizations not just to exchange information, but also to reason collaboratively across domains and traditional boundaries.

Looking ahead, we will see how open and interoperable ecosystems powered by the semantic layer are redefined how organizations work together. Embedding standards and context directly into their data and knowledge assets will enable them to create new forms of collaboration, multi-party analytics processes, and ultimately, cross-industry innovation.

Semantic Data Products as a Revenue Stream

As we explored earlier in this book, data products make up one of the toolkits in the modern data stack and have seen significant adoption for a reason. For organizations that have reached a level of data-centricity maturity, the semantic layer is no longer just a conceptual framework, but it has itself become a product, packaged with embedded context, meaning, and standardized definitions. This evolution is the transformation of internal knowledge assets into trusted "data products" that can be monetized or shared across ecosystems, moving organizations from passive data storage to active metadata and commerce.

Two real-world examples illustrate this shift: a global digital media company that has started expanding its semantic layer components to curate anonymized customer behavior datasets as subscription-based data products for suppliers and retailers, and is now generating new, recurring revenue; and, a global veterinary company we recently worked with that has built taxonomy and ontology-based semantic models that helps them align data across hundreds of practices. This unified framework is not only automating asset normalization and improving operational efficiency for them, it is also now serving as a marketable product, allowing them to enforce a shared industry standard, and as an add-on framework to their software solutions, equally benefiting industry partners and opening new avenues for vet businesses.

What the trends in these case studies make clear is that organizations investing in foundational semantic ecosystems are now unlocking entirely new business models and ways of creating value. The once-popular trope that "data is the new oil" is being redefined: the true value of data no longer lies merely in owning or storing it, but in how it is structured, governed, and enriched so that others can confidently trust and reuse it. The semantic layer is emerging as the foundation of this new data economy, where actual value is created through connection, collaboration, reuse, and shared intelligence.

The New Geography of Data and Data Passports

Today, AI-generated assets are introducing a new set of challenges for global organizations. The challenge is when AI meets regional data regulations, primarily data privacy compliance like EU's GDPR, California's CCPA, etc. The core issue here is the conflict between AI's need for vast asset types and sources and strict, location-based regulations that govern how personal data is collected, stored, and used as knowledge assets. To give a specific example, these data privacy regulations mandate transparency regarding how personal data is processed, including securing it, how it should be strictly used for a specified purpose, and explainability as to how automated decisions are made. However, AI-generated assets compound this complexity because they often draw from vast, distributed asset sources that may have originated across multiple jurisdictions and are typically "black boxes" even to their creators. A global organization especially cannot assume that this data was collected with the necessary consent or that it was legally permissible to be used for AI training in every location they operate in. This is making it difficult for these organizations to provide the required explanations to regulators or individual data subjects, creating legal risk and compliance issues.

Inspired by the European Union's Digital Product Passport, the emerging concept of "data passports" is both a challenge and a potential solution being explored by early industry adopters for managing AI-related asset compliance at a global scale (Publications Office of the European Union 2024). A **data passport** aims to give every asset a unique identity and compliance "story." Much akin to a human passport, it carries metadata describing origin, ownership, consent terms, and permissible transfer destinations. As you can imagine, implementing such granular traceability across billions of asset types and dynamic AI workflows is daunting without a unifying framework. This is where these global organizations and regulatory entities are turning to the semantic layer framework to help embed definitions, lineage, and governance-related attributes directly into data structures so that it enables organizations to consistently and dynamically map, label/tag, and enforce compliance rules. For example, we helped a global energy company based in the EU region pilot this capability to support the traceability of data being used by their data science teams in the US. I.e., whenever an AI model pulls customer-related knowledge assets as training data in Texas or California, teams can automatically recognize regional consent tags, restrictions for processing across borders, and flag access needs in their "passport" trail, all based on the labels provided by the semantic layer framework.

This semantic layer-backed approach is transforming data passports into operationally viable solutions. Forward-thinking enterprises as well as large product vendors are starting to embed the framework within their AI and application platforms to serve as the connective tissue between data passports, AI models, and regional compliance frameworks. Ultimately, to help scale responsible AI globally by ensuring that every piece of data, from input to newly generated output, carries its contextual "passport" metadata. In essence, we see this convergence of global data passport initiatives and semantic layers redefining the future of digital privacy and governance, allowing massive, global entities to build the most valuable currency in the AI era: trust.

Empowering AI Agents and Knowledge Intelligence

AI agents are soon going to become the new "interface" between humans, organizational knowledge, and data. Yet, their effectiveness and trustworthiness will depend entirely on how well they understand the context they are operating in. The same goes for ML, LLMs, and all other non-human consumers (and creators) of organizational knowledge and information.

As we discussed earlier in this book, organizations spend as much as 30–40% of their time searching for or recreating information. Now, imagine a dedicated analyst who does not just look for or analyze data but roams the office, listens to conversations, reads emails, and proactively sends you updates, while spotting outdated data, summarizing new information, flagging inconsistencies, and prompting follow-ups. That's what an AI agent does; it autonomously monitors content and data platforms, collaboration tools like Slack, Teams, and even email, and suggests updates or actions, all without waiting for instructions. Instead of sending you on a massive data hunt to answer, "What's the latest on this client?" an AI agent autonomously pulls CRM notes, emails, contract changes, and summarizes them in Slack or Teams or publishes them as a report. It does not just react, it takes initiative.

The potential for productivity gains within organizations is undeniable, and it's no longer a distant future. The key question today is what it takes to get there. While the idea of a fully autonomous assistant handling routine tasks is appealing, AI agents require a complex framework to succeed. This includes breaking down silos, ensuring AI-ready knowledge assets, and implementing guardrails to meet enterprise standards for accuracy, trust, performance, ethics, and security. Picture a regulatory compliance and due diligence agent that autonomously cross-references internal transactions, operations, and policies with evolving regulations, flagging potential violations before they occur and suggesting remediation steps. This is an emerging use case for organizations in the financial services sector, as they are expanding their semantic layer models and solutions to address compliance challenges. This would not have been possible without semantic alignment between internal and external data sources (or future multi-model agentic framework).

This is where a semantic layer plays a critical role. The components of the semantic layer work together to provide a unified and contextualized view of data across typically siloed systems and business units, enabling not only agents but also relevant AI models to understand and reason about information with a grasp of the larger enterprise context. We have seen how grounding LLMs with a governed set of controlled vocabularies and business definitions significantly reduces hallucinations.

This is a testament to the fact that the promise of enterprise AI is about aligned understanding and organizational knowledge intelligence. This is not about replacing humans with AI, rather, knowledge intelligence powered by a semantic layer is about better linking humans, placing them in "the loop" at the right places and time to maximize learning, knowledge sharing, and overall performance. The systems that think with context and have a programmatic way to learn responsibly will define the next era of AI, not defined by what machines can do alone, but by how seamlessly they can think and reason alongside us.

Breaking Down Organizational Silos Through New Operating Models

As organizations advance in their semantic maturity, another impact of the semantic layer is extending far beyond technology, it's reshaping how enterprises are structured, governed, and operated. We're witnessing this transformation take shape in two notable ways: (1) the dismantling of technical silos that once fragmented knowledge, content, data and systems, and (2) the reimagining of organizational structures, officers, and roles. Together, these shifts are driving the emergence of new operating models that align people, processes, and technical solutions around shared meaning and connected knowledge, rather than isolated tools or asset types.

From a technical infrastructure point of view, organizations that once focused on applications and data warehouses are now refocusing their infrastructure on context and connectedness. Data lakes have continued to grow as places to prepare data, but they are leveraging semantic capabilities that include metadata management, taxonomy management, knowledge graphs, and agents.

A related shift is from managing discrete data repositories to managing knowledge assets holistically. Organizations are consolidating content, documents, records, and structured data under unified solutions, primarily for AI-readiness but also inadvertently facilitating governance. These knowledge assets are now being secured, combined, governed, and managed in a more complete and holistic manner. The massive administrative burden organizations have historically experienced from management of many discrete information systems, each with its own associated governance and management is decreasing. As organizations continue to put more and more effort into aligning their knowledge assets, they are recognizing the unnecessary costs, complexities, and inefficiencies from how they were previously managed. Most recently, the majority of new knowledge assets are in fact being coauthored by humans and AI, with generative AI creating new assets in seconds, reducing the creation timeframe dramatically and allowing the organization's employees to add critical context, validation, and human perspective where warranted.

At the same time, as the semantic layer continues to enable a shared language for the business (creating a shared language and a source of truth across departments), this alignment is fostering organic collaboration, trust, and speed. The result is an emerging cross-functional team that dissolves traditional departmental boundaries and empowers people with the framework they need to collaborate faster.

We are starting to see this evolution also seeding organizational changes. As organizations continue to embed the semantic layer and expand their AI capabilities, we are seeing entire operating models being redesigned. Functions once divided among IT, data management, records, content, and knowledge management are merging into unified, cross-functional "product teams." These teams share responsibility for data stewardship, semantic design, and AI integration, operating with agility and shared accountability.

Governance, too, is evolving. Unlike traditional governance models, this type of governance focuses on coordination over control, acting as the aligning and enablement body to help the organization manage their semantic design and systems, as well as coordinate effectively with the many repositories of knowledge assets to which it will connect.

What we are starting to see here, in addition to the technical capabilities discussed throughout this book, is indicative of the fact that organizations that embrace the semantic layer are discovering new ways to not only connect their knowledge assets but also their technology to people, making reliable human interactions with machines. As semantic maturity deepens, organizations are discovering this new kind of operating model that is neither built on hierarchy nor silos, but on connected organizational knowledge, intelligence, and enablement, all foundations for a more agile and visionary organization.

Continuous Learning and Adaptive Leadership

In addition to the aforementioned changes to staffing and organizational structures, mature organizations are experiencing a shift in leadership structures and other roles and responsibilities of traditional corporate functions, including learning and development, engineering, Human Resources, and project support teams. With semantic linking and context powering AI capabilities, the traditional training and onboarding functions are becoming impacted by this trend and are being replaced with new solutions delivering learning and knowledge at the point of need and in a largely automated and customized manner.

As AI takes on more of the mechanical and analytical tasks once handled by entry-level staff, human roles are shifting toward oversight, ethical guidance, and strategic innovation. Meanwhile, semantic solutions are providing the essential context, understanding, and logic needed to make this relevant within a given context. This combination is transforming leadership mandates, empowering employees, and enabling highly personalized and adaptive learning experiences.

From a leadership and culture standpoint, these organizations are experiencing a pronounced "flattening" of how information is shared and consumed. At present, in most organizations, executives and senior leadership are often given the information they use to make decisions in a heavily filtered or pre-analyzed form. With semantics and AI, however, this is not longer the case. Now, they can ask their semantic layer-powered applications questions directly, choosing to obtain answers and outputs in the forms they desired, ranging from reports to raw outputs. This is already speeding up decision-making and organizational intelligence while also delivering more unfiltered but aligned information directly to decision-makers. In this sense, leadership is evolving from relying on IT or data team-mediated reports to acting more like strategic orchestrators, focusing on vision, alignment, and culture and leaning on their skills like empathy, emotional intelligence, critical thinking, and creativity.

In terms of traditional corporate functions (marketing, operations, HR, and finance), the semantic layer is enabling a shift toward more Agile, integrated service models. Instead of each department maintaining its own "content or data island"

and definitions, the semantic layer is creating a shared source of truth for business logic and relationships with other asset sources. As a result, corporate functions in these mature organizations are becoming less siloed and instead operating in a shared ecosystem where they are starting to realize the impact gained from reducing rework and promoting cross-functional alignment.

On the other hand, the recruiting challenge is simultaneously becoming more complex, as these organizations require more unique skill sets for their semantic and AI efforts, and for all staff to be able to "partner" effectively with their AI counterparts, serving as human-machine translators and knowledge engineers. These new AI-driven capabilities are a part of the enablement and delivery from the use case- or product-driven AI teams and will prove to be critical, as the traditional ways of upskilling junior employees to more senior roles will grow increasingly obscure, given the decreasing number of entry-level staff.

Finally, it is in this new model that the semantic layer is becoming an invisible facilitator powering an era of collaboration and **adaptive learning** equally for AI and humans. The consistent definitions, linkage across knowledge and data concepts, and the self-service capabilities enabled by semantic components are allowing employees across the organization to engage in more autonomous learning—exploring individual learning paths, experimenting with "what-if" scenarios, and asking natural-language questions without having to know the exact key word the organization uses, or having to wait for project SMEs. This access and democratization of institutional knowledge mean that learning is becoming embedded in work rather than confined to periodic training sessions, ultimately reducing time-to-upskilling and proficiency in an exponential manner (Fig. 5.2).

	Leadership & Culture	Knowledge Assets	Technical Infrastructure	Organizational Structure & Operating Model	Talent & Workforce
Traditional Organization	Responsibility on individual employee to perform	Siloed and redundant	Application-centric silos	Redundant offices with overlapping functions	Focus on individual development
AI-Powered Organization	Employee and AI partnerships	Merged, contextualized, reliable	Data-aware AI solutions and agents	Aligned and shared operations	Learning and knowledge delivered at the point of need

Fig. 5.2 The future organization

As these examples of transformations demonstrate, we are starting to see a shift to a future where leadership is no longer held back by technical complexity, where traditional functions are operating beyond silos, and where employees have the opportunity to become lifelong learners with organizational knowledge at their fingertips. At the core is the semantic layer, which provides the framework for these organizations to align its people, systems, and knowledge assets, supporting the future of our ways of working while shaping it.

In all, the organizations that continue to adopt semantic layer frameworks, either to power AI or other forward-thinking organizational capabilities, are proving to be faster, more efficient, and, as a result, more effective leaders of their industry. There is demonstrated competitive advantage in these investments. The transition is not merely an upgrade of tools but a fundamental shift in how work is done, how value is created, and how an organization's future potential is realized. The technologies, processes, and methodologies detailed in this book stand as a testament to what's achievable, reinforced by our proven, real-world experience.

What many organizations are lacking is not the "how," but the will to be on the leading edge. Those that choose to take the journey will quickly separate themselves from their competitors, not just by achieving semantically powered AI capabilities, but in ways we cannot yet predict. That journey, and the future capabilities they deliver, will come quickly, and the organizations that are prepared will be rewarded.

References

National Aeronautics and Space Administration. "Your Gateway to NASA Earth Observation Data," *Earthdata*. Accessed October 30, 2025. https://www.earthdata.nasa.gov/.

OpenFold Team. "OpenFold: Democratizing AI for Biology," *OpenFold*. Accessed October 30, 2025. https://openfold.io/.

Publications Office of the European Union. "EU's Digital Product Passport: Advancing Transparency and Sustainability," *European Union*. September 27, 2024. https://data.europa.eu/en/news-events/news/eus-digital-product-passport-advancing-transparency-and-sustainability.

Tesfaye, Lulit. "When Should You Use An AI Agent? Part One: Understanding the Components and Organizational Foundations for AI Readiness," *Enterprise Knowledge*. September 4, 2025. https://enterprise-knowledge.com/when-should-you-use-an-ai-agent/.

Thibaud, Anne-Laure. "Where Would Reasoning AI Leave Human Intelligence?" *World Economic Forum*. January 22, 2025. https://www.weforum.org/stories/2025/01/in-a-world-of-reasoning-ai-where-does-that-leave-human-intelligence.

XBRL International. "What is XBRL?" *XBRL*. Accessed October 30, 2025. https://www.xbrl.org/the-standard/what/what-is-xbrl/.

Glossary

Adaptive Learning—Adaptive learning is a technique that uses technology and data-driven instruction to personalize an individual's learning experience in real time.

Agentic AI—Agentic (in the context of AI) refers to autonomous, goal-oriented systems that can perceive their environment, reason, plan, and take action with minimal human oversight.

Agile—Agile is a value-based, iterative project management approach, methodology, and mindset. Common attributes include an attitude of "servant leadership," focus on iterative delivery, teams over individuals, and solutions for complex problems.

AI-Powered Organization—AI-powered organizations are those that have leveraged advanced semantic capabilities, as well as distinct types of AI, including machine learning, generative AI for content creation and ideation, and agentic AI for task execution and automation, to facilitate all aspects of the organization's work.

Analytics Graph—An analytics graph supports analytics by connecting and modeling relationships between data entities to uncover hidden insights and identify trends, patterns, and correlations, enabling users to perform sophisticated queries on large, complex datasets with interrelationships that may not be easily captured in traditional tabular models.

Application Program Interface (API)—An API is a set of rules and protocols that allows different systems to communicate with one another.

Artificial Intelligence (AI)—AI is a technology that can simulate human comprehension, creativity, problem-solving, and decision-making. In the enterprise context, it involves leveraging advanced machine and cognitive capabilities to discover and deliver organizational knowledge in a way that closely aligns with how humans look for and process information.

Attribute—An attribute is a property that defines the specific characteristics or features of a class or an individual. An attribute links an individual to a literal value, such as a string, number, or date, allowing more precise identification and understanding of these individuals.

© The Editor(s) (if applicable) and The Author(s), under exclusive license to
Springer Nature Switzerland AG 2026
J. Hilger et al., *Bridging Knowledge, Data, and AI*,
https://doi.org/10.1007/978-3-032-17178-8

Bottom-Up Approach—The bottom-up approach is a content-oriented approach. It includes activities such as document reviews, assessments of existing data models, analyses of sample data, and demonstrations of current-state systems.

Business Glossary—A business glossary is a centralized collection of agreed-upon definitions of key business terms to make sure that everyone in the organization has a consistent understanding of these terms and uses the same language when describing them.

Business Intelligence (BI)—Business intelligence is the process of collecting, analyzing, and presenting organizational data to yield insights that help organizations make informed business decisions.

Business User—Business users, also referred to as "end users" or consumers, are people who are impacted indirectly by the implementation of a system or process (i.e., semantic layer), like data analysts or HR managers.

Cardinality—In the context of an ontology, cardinality refers to the number of instances that can participate in a specific relationship between two classes. When modeling an ontology, for example, cardinality can be used to enforce precise logical constraints and ensure data integrity.

Classes—Classes are abstract categories that can be used to group individuals or objects that share similar characteristics. In the context of an ontology, a class can be used to formally define entities that exist within a specific knowledge domain.

Conceptual Domain Model—A conceptual domain model is a visual representation of an organization's entities and the relationships between them.

Content—Content is synthesized data, which can refer to data or documents. Content can be codified in a range of unstructured to highly structured formats.

Controlled Vocabulary—A controlled vocabulary is a standardized list of terms that is used to organize and index information, ensuring consistency and accuracy and facilitating better information retrieval.

Dark Data—Dark data refers to the information assets organizations collect, process, and store during regular business activities but generally fail to use for other purposes, such as analytics, business relationships, and direct monetizing.

Data—Data are collected, unsynthesized facts, values, or statistics stored in a structured format such as a table, hierarchy, or key-value pair.

Data Catalog—A data catalog is a centralized, searchable inventory that collects and organizes metadata from an organization's data assets. It also serves as an inventory of available data and provides information to evaluate fitness data for intended uses.

Data Dictionary—A data dictionary is a centralized repository of metadata, providing a standardized reference for data elements like names, definitions, types, formats, and rules. This ensures clarity, consistency, and improved understanding, facilitating better data management, governance, and collaboration by offering a single source of truth. It's a critical tool for data analysis and reproducibility.

Data Element—A data element is the smallest discrete unit of information that holds a distinct and meaningful value, like an ID or a name.

Data Fabric—A data fabric is a logical data architecture that serves as a data connection and knowledge layer. A data fabric enables data federation and virtualization of semantic labels or rules (e.g., taxonomies/business glossaries or ontologies) to capture and connect data based on business or domain meaning and value.

Data Federation—Data federation is a data management strategy where disparate data sources are accessed and combined virtually, without physically moving the data to a central location, to provide a unified view of information.

Data Lake—A data lake is a scalable, centralized repository for massive amounts of diverse data (structured, semi-structured, and unstructured) stored in its raw format without a predefined schema. It accommodates all data types from any source, maintaining fidelity. Data lakes provide core data consistency and enable flexible data ingestion and various analytics, machine learning, and visualization tasks using "schema-on-read," unlike data warehouses that require prior data structuring.

Data Management—Data management is the development, execution, and supervision of plans, policies, programs, and practices that deliver, control, protect, and enhance the value of data and information assets throughout their lifecycles. It encompasses a range of disciplines and processes that collectively enable organizations to derive meaningful insights, make informed decisions, and maintain compliance with regulatory standards.

Data Mesh—A data mesh is a distributed approach to enterprise data management focused on building business-focused data products.

Data Model—A data model is a formal, visual blueprint that defines and standardizes the structure, relationships, and rules of data within a system, serving as a conceptual representation for organizing and managing information. It outlines what data an organization collects, how it is related, and the methods for storing, accessing, and analyzing it, ensuring data consistency, quality, and efficient management.

Data Passport—A data passport is a concept where a data asset is embedded with its own unique metadata and security information in order to enable transparency and compliance.

Data Product—Data products are curated, reusable datasets or knowledge assets that are designed to answer or serve specific business needs or use cases.

Dataset—A dataset is a collection of data.

Data Warehouse—A data warehouse is a repository for highly structured business data to support business intelligence and analytics needs.

Decoupled Architecture—Decoupled architecture is a system design approach where components can exist and function independently, interacting with one another via clear, well-defined protocols.

Deprecation—The act of marking versions as outdated, which signals to users that the entity will soon be removed.

Discoverability—Discoverability is when information that has not been searched for and may be totally unknown to the end user is made visible by the system because of its relevance to the query, functioning like recommended content.

Downtime—Downtime is the time when a system is not available for use.

Emergent AI—Emergent AI includes systems that exhibit unexpected or unprogrammed behaviors or capabilities that arise from scale, complexity, or architecture, especially post Generative AI, in large language models (LLMs) or advanced neural networks.

Entity—An entity is anything that an organization interacts with.

Entity Resolution—Entity resolution is a process that determines if multiple, apparently different database records actually represent the same real-world entity.

Explicit Knowledge—Explicit knowledge is knowledge that can be captured, written down, and codified in an accessible manner. This includes documents, databases, and reports.

Extract, Transform, and Load (ETL)—Extract, transport, and load refers to a data integration process.

Faceting—Faceting describes the multi-dimensional filtering of search results.

Findability—Findability is when information that is findable has been explicitly searched for.

Front-End Solution—Front-end solutions are all the elements of a digital solution that a user interacts with, including advanced searches, chatbots, recommendation engines, content assembly tools, or a customized content delivery system.

Generative AI (GenAI)—Generative AI is a type of artificial intelligence that uses deep-learning models to create new content like text, images, and video, based on patterns learned from training data and natural language prompts.

Governance—Governance is the process of setting standards, defining rules, establishing policies, and implementing oversight to ensure the quality and usability of an organization's assets.

Graph Analytics—Graph analytics is the process of analyzing data represented as a network of interconnected objects in order to understand patterns, relationships, and insights.

Hallucination—Hallucinations (in the context of AI) are fabricated information that is presented as factual information when interacting with a generative AI model.

Inference—An inference is the process by which a system/model uses its learned knowledge to derive new knowledge based on the meaning of existing data.

Information—Information is data that has been processed, organized, and structured to impart it with meaning and context, making it useful for understanding and decision-making.

Information Management—Information management encompasses the planning, strategy, and implementation of systems and practices for collecting, organizing, storing, maintaining, securing, and distributing an organization's collective information assets, meaning both structured and unstructured data across its entire lifecycle, from creation to disposal.

Instances—Instances are the specific occurrences (individual items or real-world objects) of a class in an ontology. While the ontology is an abstract, conceptual blueprint that defines the type of objects, their properties, and their relationships, instances populate the ontology as concrete data that fit these definitions and can be manipulated and queried.

Interoperability—Interoperability is the ability of systems to exchange and use information. It is also another word for cross-functionality.

ISO/IEC 11179 (Metadata Registries and Standards)—These are international standards that provide guidelines for the definition and registration of metadata, particularly for data elements.

Journey Map—A journey map is a representation of fictional users, categorized by shared characteristics, demographics, behaviors, motivations, and goals, and a description of the steps each needs to take to complete a task, looking at the user's overall satisfaction at each step and the total amount of time it takes the user to complete the task journey.

Key Performance Indicator (KPI)—Key performance indicators are quantifiable measures of success. KPIs can be used to track progress, make data-driven decisions, and identify areas of improvement in an organization. Types include business KPIs, design KPIs, operational KPIs, and organizational KPIs.

Knowledge—Knowledge is the collection of expertise, experiences, know-how, values, beliefs, and perceptions that shape the mental models that help individuals make decisions and make sense of their environment. Knowledge can be tacit in people's heads, or it can be codified into written documents or other tangible artifacts.

Knowledge Assets—Knowledge assets include the traditional concept of information that most organizations are seeking to harness and extend it to include anything that can hold information, including an organization's people, processes, products, places, or equipment.

Knowledge Graph—A knowledge graph leverages ontologies and other business concepts to represent knowledge assets and the information they contain as interconnected entities and relationships, providing a structured and graph-based approach to knowledge representation.

Knowledge Management (KM)—Knowledge management involves the people, process, content, culture, and enabling technologies necessary to Capture, Manage, Share, and Find information. The new mission of KM is to link all of an organization's knowledge, in all its forms, making it not just findable, but understandable and actionable.

Large Language Model (LLM)—A Large Language Model is trained on large amounts of text, then is able to predict the next likely word in a sequence—which can be used to perform natural language processing tasks, including interpreting, translating, predicting, and generating or summarizing, contextually relevant text.

Legacy System—A legacy system is an outdated software application that is still in use within an organization but is no longer actively supported by its vendor (applicable to a vendor product) or enhanced by its development team (applicable to a custom product).

Linked Data—Linked data is a method of structuring and connecting datasets to create a machine-readable, interconnected knowledge graph.

Machine Learning (ML)—Machine learning is the engine behind many AI systems. It enables systems to learn patterns from data and improve over time without being explicitly programmed using algorithms and statistical methods. Examples include content recommendation systems (Netflix and Amazon), fraud detection, spam filters, predictive analytics, etc.

Master Data Management (MDM) System—Master data management systems manage critical business data entities, such as customer/client records, product details, and product information.

Metadata—Metadata is data that provides information about knowledge assets, or data about data.

Metadata Graph—A metadata graph is a graph solution that captures the structure and descriptive properties of data by tracking business, technical, and operational metadata attributes, such as process, ownership, security, and privacy information across an organization, providing a unified repository of metadata and a connected view of data assets.

Metrics Layer—Metrics layer is an evolution of the original use of the term "semantic layer" and was first coined by Business Objects in the 1990s to describe a product that enabled end users to query databases without knowing structured query language (SQL) or the underlying structure of databases.

Minimum Viable Product (MVP)—A minimum viable product is a basic version of a product that meets the minimum necessary requirements for initial use and testing, intended to gather user feedback before significant investment in further development and enhancement.

Narrow AI—Narrow AI refers to artificial intelligence systems designed and trained to perform a specific task or domain and typically perform rule-based tasks like prediction and analysis using algorithms and limited data.

Named Entity Recognition (NER)—Named entity recognition is a component of natural language processing that identifies and categorizes key entities within text, such as people, organizations, and location, based on a predefined list of entity names.

Natural Language Processing (NLP)—Natural language processing is a field of AI, focused on enabling computers to understand and generate human language.

Ontology—An ontology is a defined data model that organizes structured and unstructured information through entities, their properties, and the way they relate to one another.

Open Source—Open source refers to software that has a codebase that is freely available for anyone to view, use, modify, and distribute under a specific license.

Operating Model—An operating model is a blueprint that describes how an organization delivers value by outlining its structure, processes, technology, and people to achieve strategic objectives.

OWL—OWL or the W3C Web Ontology Language (OWL) is a Semantic Web language designed to represent rich and complex knowledge about things, groups of things, and relations between things.

Proof of Concept (PoC)—A proof of concept is a small-scale demonstration or experiment, typically focused on 1-2 priority use cases to prove out the value and technical feasibility of a new idea, product, or technology before committing significant resources to long-term development.

Query—A query is a request or command that retrieves, inserts, updates, or deletes data from a system/database. It serves as a way through which users or applications can interact with a database by specifying the required data and any conditions for filtering, sorting, or aggregating that data.

Record—A record is a piece of content or document that contains policies, decisions, or other official or legal actions taken by an organization that must be preserved to ensure its memory.

Relationships (ontology)—Relationships define how classes or instances are connected to and interact with one another.

Resource Description Framework (RDF)—The Resource Description Framework is a standard model for interoperable XML data exchange on the Web that provides a logical organization defined in terms of data structures to support the representation, access, constraints, and relationships of objects of interest in a given domain.

Retrieval-Augmented Generation (RAG)—Retrieval-augmented generation describes an organization querying their own repositories for information and then sending the most relevant documents to a large language model (LLM) for processing.

Return on Investment (ROI)—Return on investment is a financial metric used to measure the profitability or efficiency of an investment, or set of investments, relative to its cost. It is calculated by dividing the net profit or gain from the investment by the initial cost of the investment, typically expressed as a percentage.

Semantics—Semantics are linguistic context and meaning. It refers to constructing and transmitting meaning through concepts and language.

Semantic Drift—Semantic drift is the process by which the definition of a term or the relationships between business concepts and processes change over time.

Semantic Layer—The semantic layer is a standardized framework that organizes and abstracts organizational information through semantics, or linguistic context and meaning, to connect business users with their organization's knowledge assets. The semantic layer framework is more than a technology or even a collection of technologies.

Silo—Silos refer to the state of being disconnected or isolated.

Simple Knowledge Organization System (SKOS)—SKOS (Simple Knowledge Organization System) is a W3C recommended standard for representing knowledge organization systems such as thesauri, classification schemes, subject heading systems, and taxonomies in a machine-readable format that can then be exchanged between computer applications and published in a machine-readable format on the Web.

SPARQL—SPARQL (pronounced "sparkle") stands for SPARQL Protocol and RDF Query Language. It is a W3C semantic query language for retrieving and manipulating data stored in the Resource Description Framework (RDF) format.

Specifications—Specifications are documents or sets of rules that specify the practical implementation of a system in specific domains or use cases.

Standards—Standards are formalized, widely recognized frameworks or guidelines for structuring and defining terms within a domain.

Structured Content—Structured content is content that has a data model or infrastructure applied to it.

System Architecture—System architecture is a conceptual model that defines and visualizes the behavior and interaction of technologies that make up or support an application.

Tacit Knowledge—Tacit knowledge is knowledge that is not captured in a codifiable way. This includes expertise, processes, and best practices.

Taxonomy—A taxonomy is a controlled vocabulary used to describe and categorize explicit concepts of information for the purpose of capture, management, and presentation.

Taxonomy and Ontology Management Systems (TOMS)—Taxonomy and ontology management systems are platforms that store taxonomies and ontologies, allowing for their integration with knowledge assets and for governance actions such as lineage tracking and editing.

Top-Down Approach—A top-down approach is a people-focused approach. It includes activities such as interviews with executive leadership and project sponsors, focus groups, and workshops.

Uniform Resource Identifier—A unique sequence of characters used to identify a resource used by web technologies, such as a document, webpage, or image.

Unstructured Content—Unstructured content is content that does not have any data model or infrastructure applied to it (files, documents, records, emails, etc.).

Uptime—Uptime is the amount of time a system is functional and available for use.

Use Case—A use case is an outline of an interaction between a hypothetical user and a system, technology, or application. Use cases allow experts tasked with developing a technology to understand a user's goals and all of the ways in which a user might interact with the technology to achieve these goals.

Index